ÖSTERREICHISCHE AKADEMI
PHILOSOPHISCH-HIST

FORSCHUNGEN DES INSTITUTS FÜR REALIENKUNDE
DES MITTELALTERS UND DER FRÜHEN NEUZEIT
DISKUSSIONEN UND MATERIALIEN

NR. 8

THE SIGN LANGUAGES OF POVERTY

INTERNATIONAL ROUND TABLE-DISCUSSION
KREMS AN DER DONAU
OCTOBER 10 AND 11, 2005

WITH 29 ILLUSTRATIONS

Vorgelegt von k. M. Heinz Dopsch in der Sitzung
am 13. Oktober 2006

Edited by Gerhard Jaritz

Cover Illustration:
Saint Peter and Saint Paul heal a lame beggar (detail)
Panel painting of a winged altarpiece from Rangersdorf
Carinthian. 1426
Klagenfurt, Diözesanmuseum, Inv. IN 760

British Library Cataloguing in Publication data.
A Catalogue record of this book is available from the British Library.

ISBN 978-3-7001-3788-7

Druck und Bindung: Börsedruck Ges.m.b.H., A-1230 Wien

Printed and bound in Austria

http://hw.oeaw.ac.at/3788-7
http://verlag.oeaw.ac.at

Table of Contents

Preface

Medieval and early modern sources deal regularly with the problem of 'poverty'. Such 'poverty' at times referred to the members of widely different groups in society: 'Poor beggars,' 'poor priests and monks,' 'poor students' and 'poor virgins' appeared as well as 'poor queens and kings,' 'poor knights,' 'poor merchants,' 'poor officials,' and so on. In such contexts, the sign languages applied to mediate these diverse 'poverties' played an important role in their textual and visual representations. Various material objects and groups of things, gestures, behaviour, and other aspects of culture were drawn on to communicate and characterise the 'poverties' addressed. In doing so, those characteristics could, on the one hand, be identical to each other or based on similar patterns of argumentation, independent of the status of the persons or groups of people being described; on the other hand, they could also be very different.

At the *Institut für Realienkunde des Mittelalters und der frühen Neuzeit* of the Austrian Academy of Sciences, such research problems led to the idea of organising an international workshop of specialists from various fields of Medieval Studies. In autumn, 2005, scholars from nine different countries met to discuss the importance, patterns, and differences in the 'sign languages of poverty,' to investigate them comparatively, and to analyse them critically. Interdisciplinary communication from a transdisciplinary vantage point was intended to offer new results with regard to these relevant questions about medieval material life and its representation.

This publication offers the results of that workshop. The contributions of it deal with how members of medieval society communicated to make 'poverties' and paupers recognisable and understandable, with the languages and dialects used to mediate the appropriate messages, and the symbols that were applied. Moreover, the essays are also intended to serve as an impetus for further study into the general relevance, re-occurring networks, and patterns of material culture in the past.

We would like to express our thanks to all the participants in the round table discussion for their important contributions to the meeting and the proceedings. We are also particularly grateful to the Austrian Academy of Sciences for the possibility of publishing this volume in one of their series and for their continuous support of the research and activities of the *Institut für Realienkunde.*

Krems, March 2007

Gerhard Jaritz

GERHARD JARITZ

Poverty Constructions and Material Culture

As the sociologist Marvin Olasky worked on his book, *The Tragedy of American Compassion,*[1] he also did research on the condition of poverty. He stopped shaving for some days, dressed in ragged clothing and joined the throng of homeless in some of Washington's soup kitchens. In one of them, he asked a volunteer server for a Bible. It was necessary for him to pose the question twice before the person understood what was being requested; and then the answer came that no Bibles were available.[2] – Poverty without the religious touch, no spiritual significance of poverty: It has disappeared, and clearly not only in this individual case. Today, poverty most often seems to be purely an economic issue with little to excite the involvement of the non-poor.[3] In that, today's 'culture of poverty,'[4] in the broadest sense of its meaning, is clearly different from the medieval one.[5] Then, poverty was not viewed as a social pathology, even when connected or associated with economic hardship. Based on the godly origin of the social system, poor people were not held individually responsible for their fate. In a society that, in many contexts, condemned this-worldly things, the poor were able to represent a religious ideal. And, as one can also trace regularly, they could become useful for all the other members of the society.

---

[1] Marvin Olasky, *The Tragedy of American Compassion* (Washington, D. C., 1992).

[2] See also F. Allan Hanson, 'How Poverty Lost Its Meaning,' *The Cato Journal* 17/2 (1997), 9 (http://www.cato.org/pubs/journal/cj17n2-5.html), last access July 18, 2006.

[3] For this and the following, see *ibidem*, 1-2.

[4] Concerning the 'culture of poverty' ('Kultur der Armut') generally, see Valentin Groebner, 'Mobile Werte, informelle Ökonomie. Zur "Kultur" der Armut in der spätmittelalterlichen Stadt,' in *Armut im Mittelalter*, Vorträge und Forschungen 58, ed. Otto Gerhard Oexle (Sigmaringen, 2004), 164-169.

[5] For the development of poverty from the Middle Ages to the contemporary world, see, in particular, Bronislaw Geremek, *Poverty: A History* (Oxford and Cambridge MA, 1994).

While confronted with this medieval idealisation of poverty, one can also find, mainly for the fourteenth and fifteenth centuries, a stronger accent on the visibly hard and threatening realities of material poverty.[6] Beggars could be connected with idleness or rootlessness.[7] One became afraid of some poor people and started to differentiate between the good paupers to be supported and the bad ones to be excluded from one's community.[8] Badges and other signs showed who the good ones were.[9]

I do not want to go on with these general aspects and statements, but will rather concentrate on one question that has to do with the 'constructions of poverty' in the late Middle Ages and the use of material culture in these contexts.[10] Concerning the material sign language(s) of poverty, what happened when very different people estimated themselves, were described or recognised as being or having become poor? How did authors create and signify poverty important enough to be mentioned, not only of such men and women who were the well-known beggars or voluntary paupers like the Mendicants,[11] but also of other 'poor' members of society?

Ever and again, a variety of sources mention people who got into some kind of problematic situation that made it possible or even necessary to represent them as having reached (a status of) poverty.[12] This, certainly, does

---

6 For the various meanings of medieval and early modern poverty, see Robert Jütte, *Poverty and Deviance in Early Modern Europe* (Cambridge et al., 1994), 9-12. See also Martin Dinges, 'Rezente Forschungstrends zur Geschichte der Armut – Frühe Neuzeit und Spätmittelalter,' *Kwartalnik Historii Kultury Materialnej* 50 (2002), 311-313, and the contribution of Katharina Simon Muscheid in this volume.

7 Michel Mollat, *The Poor in the Middle Ages* (New Haven, 1986), 251.

8 Jütte, *Poverty and Deviance* (*op. cit. supra*, n. 6), 143: "Contemporaries ... saw in the poor not only Christ but sometimes the Devil himself." Concerning the ambiguity of the evaluation of paupers and the treatment of the 'good poor' and the 'bad poor,' see also Claude Gauvard's contribution in this volume.

9 See Helmut Bräuer, 'Bettel- und Almosenzeichen zwischen Norm und Praxis,' in *Norm und Praxis im Alltag des Mittelalters und der frühen Neuzeit*, Forschungen des Instituts für Realienkunde des Mittelalters und der frühen Neuzeit 2, ed. Gerhard Jaritz (Vienna, 1997), 75-93; Groebner, 'Zur "Kultur" der Armut' (*op. cit. supra*, n. 4), 180-184.

10 Concerning material culture in context with the discourses about poverty, see also Groebner, 'Zur "Kultur" der Armut' (*op. cit. supra*, n. 4), 173-175.

11 Concerning the latter, see Gábor Klaniczay's contribution in this volume.

12 With regard to this multiple use of the words and signifying terms 'poor' ('arm') and 'poverty' ('Armut') in medieval German, mainly ín literary sources, see, particularly, Dieter Kartschoke, 'Armut in der deutschen Dichtung des Mittelalters,' in *Armut im Mit-*

not or, at least, need not mean that they really had become poor like beggars living at the margins of society. But still, their status and life situation had obviously changed for the worse. They had become 'poor' in their individual point of view or following the authors' opinions without being 'real' paupers, showing that poverty itself or talking about poverty could represent very different things and aspects of meaning.[13] In such contexts, the means and levels of the construction of 'poverty' do not seem to have depended on class or origin. In medieval society, anyone – independent of gender,[14] actual social status or original wealth[15] – could, in specific situations, have been defined or have wanted to be characterised and recognised as being poor. In these discourses, one can trace the application of the 'rhetorics of poverty' and the use of stereotypes to create paupers.[16] When 'talking' about poverty, with the help of objects,[17] texts, images[18] or the spoken word, this poverty was supposed to be easily recognisable as such. It had to exist or be constructed in a way that one could have perceived and understood it clearly.

When acknowledging such a situation, this leads to the question of to what extent the recurring signs of poverty used in descriptions followed the same or similar (material) patterns and to what extent they may have been seen as distinct from one another. Was there one appropriate medieval 'sign language of poverty' that everybody might have understood and would have connected with the multiplicity of different kinds and types of 'poor condi-

---

telalter, Vorträge und Forschungen 58, ed. Otto Gerhard Oexle (Sigmaringen, 2004), 27-78 (with rich references to older literature).

[13] Concerning the present situation, see Sarah Bouquerel and Pierre-Alain de Malleray, *L'Europe et la pauvreté: quelles réalités?* Notes de la Fondation Robert Schuman 31 (Paris and Brussels, 2006), 10: "La pauvreté est un phénomène multiforme, difficile à cerner avec exactitude."

[14] With regard to aspects of gender and poverty, see the contribution of Patricia Skinner in this volume.

[15] Concerning, e.g., the contexts of nobility and poverty, see Joseph Morsel, 'Adel in Armut – Armut im Adel?' in *Armut im Mittelalter*, Vorträge und Forschungen 58, ed. Otto Gerhard Oexle (Sigmaringen, 2004), 126-164.

[16] Concerning the use of stereotypes in the context of poverty, see also the contribution of Claude Gauvard in this volume.

[17] In this context, the analysis of archaeological evidence may offer valuable results. See David Austin's contribution in this volume.

[18] Concerning images of poverty and paupers, see Axel Bolvig's contribution in this volume. See also Thomas Raff, 'Das Bild der Armut im Mittelalter,' in *Armut im Mittelalter*, Vorträge und Forschungen 58, ed. Otto Gerhard Oexle (Sigmaringen, 2004), 9- 25.

tion'? The examples that I will use for discussing this problem are mainly taken from late medieval Central European sources.

I want to start with an example that fits well into the research field of Nancy Black.[19] For the year 1438, the Polish chronicler Ian Długosz tells the story about Barbara of Cilli, widow of Emperor Sigismund of Luxemburg.[20] During the lifetime of her husband, as the chronicler emphasises, she had annoyed and insulted members of the Hungarian nobility. After Sigismund's death, the noblemen asked his successor, King Albrecht, to do something against her. Therefore, the latter banished her from her castles, towns, and lands in Hungary, and took away the treasures and jewels that she had collected over the years. Barbara went to Poland and asked king Władysław III to accept her in his country, as a "poor orphan" (... *et se tanquam miseram et orphanam personam a rege Wladislao recolligi petebat*). Władysław did so, gave her certain revenues, and offered her other things that she needed, so that she was again able to live according to her status, meaning that she was no longer a "poor orphan."

If one takes the wording of the source, then Barbara had become 'poor' and, even stronger but still quite general: She had become a "poor orphan." The reason for her impoverishment was that she had lost lands, castles, treasures, and jewels. Such a material argument represents one of the regular methods of the 'construction of poverty' out of the most varied of reasons for kings and queens, burghers and officials, merchants, students, and so on. It might also have been applied to any type of victim, such as of treason or exile, natural catastrophe or famine. The same Ian Długosz told, for instance, about a dreadful murrain on Poland's animals, cattle and herds, in 1298, so that "many, even the rich, were impoverished" (*plurimi etiam ex locupletibus ad inopiam redigerentur*).[21] Again they had lost material goods, although in a very different respect than Barbara of Cilli. In such contexts of famine and catastrophe, the 'construction of poverty' then occured particu-

---

[19] See her contribution in this volume and, in particular, eadem, *Medieval Narratives of Accused Queens* (Gainesville, 2003), passim.

[20] *Ioannis Dlugossii annales seu cronicae incliti regni Poloniae, liber undecimus et liber duodecimos*, ed. C. Baczkowski et al. (Warsaw, 2001), 190; *The Annals of Jan Długosz. Annales seu cronicae incliti regni Poloniae,* an English abridgement by Maurice Michael (Chichester, 1997), 475.

[21] *Ioannis Dlugossii annales seu cronicae incliti regni Poloniae, liber septimus, liber octavus*, ed. S. Budkowa et al. (Warsaw, 1975), 301; *The Annals of Jan Długosz* (*op. cit. supra*, n. 20), 243.

larly generalising: ... *ut divites cum pauperibus famis inediam angustiati sustinerent*, as was, for instance, stressed for a similar situation in Lower Austria in the year 1255.[22]

Quite regularly, one is not only confronted with general statements of being poor or having been impoverished as a result of losing a variety of different material objects, but also with very specific and ostentatious 'signs of poverty' that were applied frequently, sometimes so obvious that it was no longer necessary to speak about 'poverty' explicitly. Everyone understood and knew from the beginning what was meant.

There is the well-known story, in 1462, about the three-year-old child who later became Emperor Maximilian I. In the course of the inner-Habsburg troubles between Emperor Frederick III and his brother, Albrecht VI, it came to the siege of the castle of Vienna, where Frederick and his family lived. In his "Buch von den Wienern," Michael Beheim describes the following situation:[23] During the siege, severe deficiencies occurred for the imperial family. Frederick and his wife could be served neither deer nor fish, nor white bread. They had to be content with dry black bread and bad meat. Neither could their son Maximilian be served the meat that he loved so much, but just barley and peas. One day, again being served peas, he did not touch them but sent them back, saying that this food was not appropriate for him but should be given to the enemy:

Ains dages braht man im arwaiss,
und e daz er ir ye enpaiss,
sprach er 'er het ir ain genug,'
daz man sy wider dannen trug,
dy speiss wer im nit eben,
Man solcz den veinden geben!

---

[22] *Annales Mellicenses Continuatio*, Monumenta Germaniae Historica, Scriptores IX, ed. Georg Heinrich Pertz et al. (Hannover 1851; reprint Stuttgart, 1983), 509. See also Fritz Curschmann, *Hungersnöte im Mittelalter. Ein Beitrag zur deutschen Wirtschaftsgeschichte des 8. bis 13. Jahrhunderts* (Leipzig, 1900; reprint 1970), 178 (also containing a large number of similar examples out of chronicles from the period).

[23] *Michael Beheim's Buch von den Wienern, 1462-1465*, ed. Theodor von Karajan (Vienna, 1843), 128-129. See also Gerhard Jaritz, 'Der Einfluß der politischen Verhältnisse auf die Entwicklung der Alltagskultur im spätmittelalterlichen Österreich,' in *Bericht über den sechzehnten österreichischen Historikertag*, Veröffentlichungen des Verbandes Österreichischer Geschichtsvereine 24 (Vienna, 1985), 529-530.

The story goes on.[24] One day, a nobleman sent eggs, pap, flour, and milk to the castle, representing food that was needed for young Maximilian. But a bad man of the besiegers took these supplies and trampled on them.

In these situations, everything is clearly related with specific objects and signs that everybody knew and understood: The lack of status-proper food and having to suffer from improper nutrition was normally connected with paupers and lower-class people.[25] At the end of the story, the author, Michael Beheim, concluded with a statement that would have been evident for everyone from the very beginning of the report without necessarily having to be emphasised. He wrote that if Maximilian had not been the heir to the reigning lord he would have been recognised as a child of poor people whom one should have pity on: [26]

> *wer er nit gewest ir erpherr*
> *und her von fremden landen verr,*
> *gewesn ain kind ains armen,*
> *ain solchs solt sy erbarmen!*

In these 'constructions of poverty,' improper food was one of the most regularly applied signs of poverty, often connected with the lack of other basic necessities. Ian Długosz' chronicle tells the story of a dispute between rulers. In 1300, the elected but still uncrowned Polish King Władysław Łokietek was divested of his authority and Václav, King of Bohemia, was elected and crowned instead. Władysław now "has to endure extremes of cold and heat, to suffer rain and hunger, to sleep on the bare earth and endure every sort of hardship, as well as the poverty unworthy of a king, which forces him to spend his nights in marshes, woods and trackless wastes, seldom under a roof" (*doctus frigora et caumata, imbres ac solem iuxta pati, humi requiescere, inediam et quemlibet laborem egestatemque contra decus regium tolerare, et in paludibus, densis quoque silvis et aviis locis noctu raro sub tecto delitescere*) [27] The "poverty unworthy of a king" is explicitly connected with lack of the basic human needs that would have made it clear for everybody that Władysław Łokietek had lost.

---

[24] *Michael Beheim's Buch von den Wienern* (*op. cit. supra*, n. 23), 130.

[25] Concerning the context of poverty and food, see also the contribution of Melitta Weiss Adamson in this volume.

[26] *Michael Beheim's Buch von den Wienern* (*op. cit. supra*, n. 23), 131.

[27] *Ioannis Dlugossii annales seu cronicae incliti regni Poloniae, liber nonus*, ed. S. Budkowa et al. (Warsaw, 1978), 15; *The Annals of Jan Długosz* (*op. cit. supra*, n. 20), 245.

The discourse about poverty unworthy of one's status and its sometimes-detailed material description can be found regularly in various primary sources, particularly chronicles. Medieval literature also contains such situations in large number.[28] Again, such examples concentrate on specific material signs of poverty, especially concerning food and nutrition or dress. In Konrad of Würzburg's thirteenth-century "Partonopier and Meliur," Prince Partonopier's exile is described in the context of his poor apparel and bad food: water and miserable bread made out of barley:[29]

... er leit sô bitter ungemach,
daz ich mit tûsent münden
niht möhte gar ergründen
sîn angestlîche herzenôt.
ûz gersten jâmerlichez brôt
az er unde eht anders niht.
dar zuo tranc er, als man giht,
eins küelen kalten brunnen.
dâ von het er gewunnen
vil schiere jâmerlichen pîn.

One of the best known and evident instances from the area of 'poverty constructions' is *Der blôze keiser* (The Naked Emperor), written by the thirteenth-century author Herrand of Wildonie.[30] As the title already says, it was clothing that played the decisive role in the story of this emperor of Rome who possessed so many treasures that he had more than most, which made him forget his meters and bounds:[31]

... er was an schatze sô fürkomen,
daz er des mêr het danne vil.
nu brach daz guot der mâze ir zil
und verkêrte im den muot, ...

The story works with the material signs of apparel, in connection with the emperor's visit to the baths. There, with the help of an angel acting as a look-alike, he was to recover his virtues. The impact of the look-alike led to

---

[28] See Maria Dobozy's and Maria Bendinelli Predelli's contributions in this volume.

[29] *Konrads von Würzburg Partonopier und Meliur*, ed. Karl Bartsch, reprint of the 1871 edition with a new postscript by R. Gruenter (Berlin, 1970), 142, vv. 9710-9719.

[30] 'Der nackte Kaiser,' in *Herrand von Wildonie. Vier Erzählungen*, ed. Hanns Fischer (Tübingen, 1969), 22-43.

[31] *Ibidem*, 22-23, vv. 22-25.

a confusion of clothes and to the emperor's nakedness, bereft of honour and dress (... *der het ê vil und wart dô bar êren unde kleider*).[32] He had become a poor man (... *mich armen man* ...).[33] In gray servants' clothes he had to beg for food. At last, the story had a happy ending: The emperor recognised that he had done wrong and got back his clothes, crown, and honour. Again, food and clothes were used as material patterns for the discourse about virtues and vices, with the help of the contrast of riches and poverty.

The loss of status and honour, directly or indirectly connected with falling into poverty, may also be traced in urban contexts. Let me give one South German example, out of the well-known fifteenth-century Augsburg town chronicle of Burkhard Zink.[34] The master-builder of Augsburg, Ulrich Tendrich, had stolen from the town; after being caught in 1462, he was punished by being:

- deprived of his position and, at the same time,
- forbidden to carry knives with him any longer, except a small, blunt knife for cutting bread,[35]
- prohibited from wearing clothing made of marten fur, silk, or velvet and from having any silver or gold application on his clothes.

The loss of the right to possess or wear these material objects meant that everyone would be aware that Ulrich had lost his honour: ... *man verpot im alles das ze tragen, das aim erbern mann zů gehört.* Although not emphasised explicitly, it seems clear that by having lost his function and position; by being deprived of important objects of his material culture and life-style he had also become 'poor'.

All these aforementioned 'poverties' were clearly recognisable material ones and, in most cases, indispensably connected with other losses or lacks: of power, authority, position, function, social status, acceptance, and so on.[36]

---

[32] *Ibidem*, 42, vv. 648-649.

[33] *Ibidem*, 31, v. 280.

[34] *Chronik des Burkhard Zink 1368-1468*, ed. Carl von Hegel, Die Chroniken der schwäbischen Städte: Augsburg, vol. 2, Die Chroniken der deutschen Städte vom 14. bis ins 16. Jahrhundert 5 (Leipzig, 1866; reprint Stuttgart, 1965), 283-284. See also Gerhard Jaritz, 'Norm und Praxis in der mittelalterlichen Sachkultur. „Widerspruch" und „Entsprechung",' in *Norm und Praxis im Alltag des Mittelalters und der frühen Neuzeit*, ed. Gerhard Jaritz, Forschungen des Instituts für Realienkunde des Mittelalters und der frühen Neuzeit. Quellen und Materialien 2 (Vienna, 1997), 18.

[35] This is the usual formula used in any prohibitions of carrying arms.

[36] See also Katharina Simon-Muscheid's contribution in this volume.

Poverty as a lack of wealth and social status can also be found in sources which emphasise the situation, without stressing any loss, that someone possessed only the basic material necessities like food or clothes. Testaments contain such information, as, for instance, the last will of Peter Reschl, the servant of a Viennese burgher, from 1398.[37] He instructed that his clothes be used to pay his debts, emphasiing at the same time that he did not possess anything other than those clothes.

One finds similar methods of the use of such well-known material signs in all the texts about significant cases of voluntary poverty, as in the legend cycles of Saint Francis, Saint Dominic, Saint Clare, Saint Elisabeth of Thuringia, etc., and all their followers.[38] The main difference and contrast to the aforementioned cases, however, is that, in the examples of these saintly people such a situation did not lead to a loss but to the gain of spiritual and religious power and authority.

The concentration on well-known material objects in context with the sign language of poverty also could play a role in the discourses about various cases of, shall we say, 'replacement of poor people.' Two examples may clarify such a situation. In the *Liber oblationum et anniversariorum* of the Scots' monastery in Vienna, one finds a fifteenth-century entry about the donation of some money to the community to be used, among other things, for providing paupers with meat and bread:[39] *Iohannis Ernst anniv. Pro hoc dantur annuatim 3 floreni de domo iuxta waghaus, 1 florenus ad sacristiam pro laboribus, 1 florenus pro missis, 1 florenus pro carnibus et panibus pauperibus distribuendis*. A later sixteenth-century addition to this entry emphasised that this donation should be used for the members of the monastic community themselves because the monks were also paupers in the Lord:[40] *Sed nunc sacristanus totum recipit pro conventu, quia etiam et nos monachi pauperes sumus in domino licet sine defectu et mendicacione ex libro capitu-*

[37] *Die Wiener Stadtbücher 1395-1430*, Teil 1: *1395-1400*, ed. Wilhelm Brauneder and Gerhard Jaritz, Fontes rerum Austriacarum III/10, 1 (Vienna and Cologne, 1989), 190, n. 292: 1398 September 4.

[38] See Gábor Klaniczay's contribution in this volume.

[39] 'Necrologium monasterii Scotorum Vindobonensis,' in *Monumenta Germaniae Historica, Necrologia Germaniae* V, *Dioecesis Pataviensis (Austria inferior)*, ed. Adalbert Franz Fuchs (reprint Munich, 1983), 307, November 12.

[40] *Ibidem.* See also Gerhard Jaritz, 'The Good and the Bad Example, or: Making Use of *Le Petit Peuple* in Late Medieval Central Europe,' in *Le petit peuple dans l'Occident médiéval. Terminologie, perceptions, réalités*, ed. Pierre Boglioni, Robert Delort and Claude Gauvard (Paris, 2002), 90.

lari. This shows the construction of poverty and 'material needs' out of the proper monastic 'spiritual and material poverty.'

A similar example can be found earlier, in 1230, at the female Benedictine convent of Santa Maria in the Upper Italian town of Aquileia. Again, the context of an anniversary donation to the community led to such a 'replacement of paupers.'[41] The donation contained bread, beans, cheese (*4 starios panis et 1 starium fabarum in quibus si non fuerit ieiunium unus caseus 16 denarios monete Aquilegensis valens ponatur*), on fast days oil (*8 libre olei in eisdem fabis ponantur*), and wine (*2 urne vini*) to be given to the poor, but only, if there was enough bread and wine for the nuns themselves. If there was a shortage or even a lack of poor people, then these victuals were to be shared by the nuns. Here, the range of 'poverty' was clearly extended to improve the community's own material situation. The nuns themselves could take over the function of 'actual paupers' in the economic sense. Again, another 'construction of poverty' seems to have worked and become legitimate, using a similar range of material objects, that is, a sign language of poverty.

* * *

Let me summarise. Medieval sources regularly deal with problems of 'poverty' and 'becoming poor.' Such 'poverties' in the sources referred to various situations and to members of widely differing groups in society. These 'poverties' were regularly connected with economic or social loss. In all of these contexts, the 'sign language of poverty' played important roles: Material objects and groups of things, specific behaviour and gestures were drawn on to characterise and communicate this impoverishment. Patterns are discernible. The strong and also regular emphasis on contrasts was meant to strengthen the effect and 'success' of the descriptions.

The everyday matters of food, nutrition, and clothing seem to have been the most common identifying means in such descriptions and discourses of poverty. The same or similar phenomena or changes in these areas of material culture can also be found in texts dealing with beggars, victims of natu-

---

41 1230 January 26, Aquileia [Reinhard Härtel (ed.), *Die älteren Urkunden des Klosters S. Maria zu Aquileia (1036-1250)* (Vienna, 2005), 191-193, n. 102)]; see also Gerhard Jaritz, 'Vita materiale e spiritualità. Monachesimo e aspetti della vita quotidiana nel tardo medioevo,' in *Il monachesimo benedettino in Friuli in età patriarcale*, ed. Cesare Scalon (Udine, 2002), 145.

ral catastrophes, members of monastic communities, impoverished burghers or noblemen, rulers who had lost their power, and so on. Any economic and social loss or lack could become connected with a problematic situation in material life-style, particularly with regard to food and dress. Any 'constructions of poverty' can be seen as connected with the application or occurrence of material signs of poverty that were often not distinct from each other. One recognises that, in the late Middle Ages, there was an appropriate and easily understandable material 'sign language of poverty' that could be connected to the multiplicity of different kinds and types of 'the poor' and their treatment in any kind of media.

David Austin

The Presence of Poverty: Archaeologies of Difference and Their Meaning

I shall want to understand what we mean by poverty in a medieval sense and to understand whether or not we can in any physical way, through archaeology, make the poor visible, bring their signs to light. I will begin by making some general assertions: poverty as a term suggests a state of being, an allegoric abstraction or a mode of behaviour, and at the same time poverty can imply some kind of institutional presence; whereas the poor are individuals in need. Poverty, some would also argue, is a relative condition (Little 1978, 28), even to the extent that it is relative within classes or categories of society, and it would follow that archaeology, as the study of the material past, must make much of the comparative differences that exist in the surviving fabric of the Middle Ages. Those physical remains, however, are usually so composed that they permit us to talk more easily of the general structures of society, than about individuals and the physical and material actions with which they are directly associated. So we may identify poverty as an institutionalised presence more readily than we may find the poor virgin, the poor knight or even the economically poor. Reference to these kinds of individuals, familiar tropes in medieval art and literature as other papers in this collection show, reminds us also that the actions of individuals can be as much affective as they are environmentally or socially determined, and they can be momentary within the *longue durée*. Thus things, the matter of archaeology, can be adopted as signs of poverty, vocabulary articulated through a grammar of context we can often only derive from art and the written word. Things may also be a mask on the truth of condition, externally adopted to deceive the social audience about the circumstances of individual or family.

So archaeology must deal with two main issues in this theme: we have to make clear the nature of material difference and we must then attempt to understand what meanings such differences may have had in the contexts in which they are found. This is the practice of interpretation, which lies right at the core of our discipline. Within the practice, however, the methodologies of difference are essentially those of typology, taken as a fundamental norm of quantitative science. Thus with ceramics, for example, easily the most universal of artefact types from excavation, the visible characteristics are structured and ordered, and interpretations are induced empirically by application of often unexpressed understandings of human nature. So a Hispano-Moresque vase (fig. 1), distinguished by glaze, decoration, form and substance, and found in a Lincolnshire monastic drain is associated with wealth and high-class activity because it has travelled a long way from Spain, is rare and has its presence at the heart of a rich institution. Such judgements are made, however, on the basis of modern criteria of value and function. We actually know little about medieval senses of value whether monetary or aesthetic for artefacts which scarcely have presence in documents and whose appearance in art is often ambiguous, certainly before the more representational painting of the later fourteenth and fifteenth centuries. The problem is, therefore, that we have tended to privilege intrinsic character over context and that, as such, we have thus tended to interpret in terms of institutions and absolutes of meaning with reference to those of modernity rather than attempting to see the individual act and the relativities of place and time.

Fig. 1: Hispano-Moresque jug from excavations at Stamford, Lincolnshire (photo: author)

So, we are bound to ask, can we, and how do we, identify difference and then interpret it as the presence of poverty or indeed the presence of the poor human being? Since the economically poor, for example, formed, according to most historians, a very large proportion of the medieval population (one third to one half), this is a serious issue for archaeologists wishing to engage with the other medievalist discourses. However, I am not hopeful that we can succeed in any empirical sense. This may either be because our methods are defective, as I have intimated, or that during the Middle Ages the marks and signs of poverty had no specific kinds of materiality that could survive to us in the present. Indeed a search of the discourse of medieval archaeology reveals little study or even reference to the issue of poverty. The poor had no pottery only used by them; there were no metal objects only they would have; they could dwell in a ditch or the crevice of a castle. In terms of things, indeed, the poor had little; what they had already showed signs of decay; and this was often handed down for secondary use. Indeed this last point raises another fundamental issue about artefacts: they have life cycles and complex existences of their own and may be used or inhabited in a variety of circumstances by many people of varying conditions. Archaeological deposits are the contexts of final use: and they are fragmentary, jumbled, terminally decayed with primary use usually indistinguishable from secondary.

Even when we deal, not with artefacts, but the material remains of the person itself we are again in difficulty, if we seek to find poverty. In terms of marks about the body, much that was associated with poverty, such as sores, emaciation, old age or disfigurement was only skin deep or in the softer tissues, and others, such as madness or despondency existed only in the fabric of the mind. For the archaeologist there is nothing more malnourished or emaciated as a skeleton, the usual material survivor of the body. We cannot find hunger or idiocy; old age is a condition of most; disease may be found in the bone through pathology, but this is deeply problematic and hard to associate with any specific ailment of poverty. Indeed, disease, in the Middle Ages was viewed as a judgement of morality and Christian virtue rather than a direct result of poverty. This is a perception of modernity. A man or a woman may be made poor by disease, but rarely was disease seen as the product of poverty.

The tradition of poverty in medieval archaeology

Medieval archaeologists, especially those like me who excavate settlements and landscapes, have been influenced mainly by an empiricist economic history in Britain, especially those of us who have worked on rural sites. This is because medieval archaeology was created as a sub-discipline when this mode of explanation was in the ascendancy and because much of the motivation for digging came from the desire to identify the peasant way of life. The other and elder discourse of medieval archaeology was architectural and art history. The problem for the economic historian was that the poor in the sense that Chris Dyer uses ('those subject to life-threatening deprivation') were almost invisible as people from the most useful economic documents and had to be inferred from generic analyses (Dyer 1989). For Titow the defect in documents masked a bleak reality:

> … custumals, rentals and similar documents completely disregard the landless elements of the community and give us only the total tenant population. They thus present a picture which is rosier than the reality…. Fortunately this defect can be partly remedied…About 1248 [in the manor of Taunton] the amount of land per person was only some 3.3 acres, and this had probably dwindled by about 1311 to some 2.5 acres per head at the most. This represents a truly desperate state of affairs, and if it is remembered that there were great inequalities of distribution, the majority of the peasants must have been far worse off than these figures suggest. (Titow 1962, 3)

Hoskins was even bleaker:

> A country in which between one-third and two-thirds of the population were wage-earners, and a considerable proportion of the remainder subsistence farmers; in which about one-third of the population lived below the poverty-line and another third lived on or barely above it; in which the working-class spent fully 80 to 90 per cent of their incomes upon food and drink; in such a country the harvest was the fundamental fact of human life. (Hoskins 1953-4, 34)

Elsewhere he wrote:

> Fully two-thirds of the urban population of England in the 1520's lived at or very near the poverty line. Life was somewhat easier in the rural areas for a variety of reasons, but even here some 40 to 50 per cent of the popu-

> lation were wage-earners, and many others were small peasant farmers entirely at the mercy of Nature. (Hoskins 1963, 84)

The mantra for the economic historian of the central and later Middle Ages was that the lower orders of the peasant population were at the mercy of harvest failure, natural disaster, war and disease. This affected the cottage holder and the landless in particular. In the debate also about the origins of capitalism, this situation was seen to become worse in the later fourteenth, fifteenth and sixteenth centuries and required the intervention of the state and more sophisticated processes of discrimination within the charitable institutions. Most of what the economic historians wrote about poverty, other than the basic statistics of their presence, was about the strategies of survival and the systems of charity which gave support.

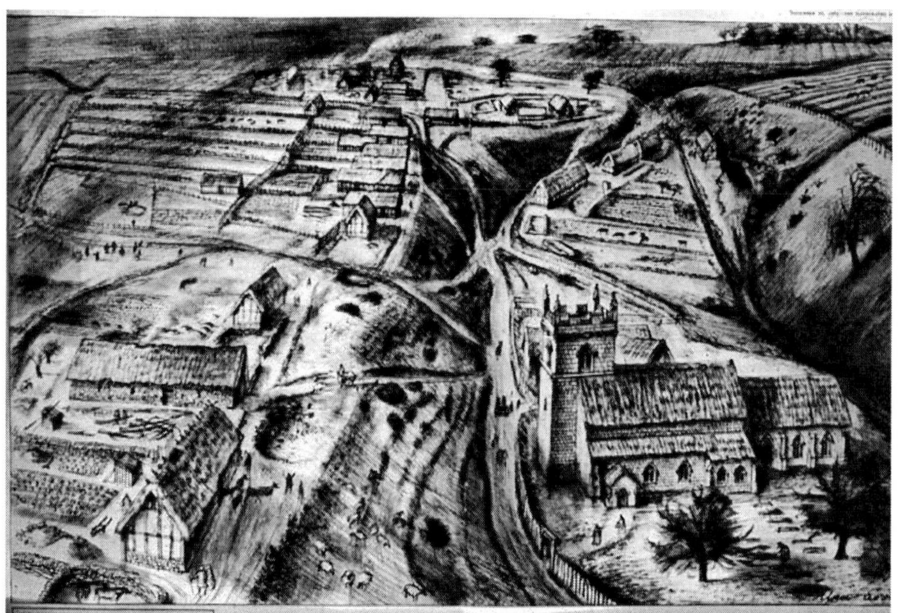

Fig. 2: Reconstruction of the Village of Wharram Percy, East Yorkshire by Alan Sorrell (Illustrated London News, no. 6485, Nov. 16th, 1963 centrefold!)

I grew up as an archaeologist, therefore, with a dark and desperate view of the life of the peasant and our reconstructions and narratives reflected this as we can see in Alan Sorrell's reconstruction of Wharram Percy (fig. 2). Our interpretations followed this Marxian vision of Apocalypse with the Four Horsemen rampant. However, the burden of more recent analysis rather suggests that the poor managed perfectly well somehow and at the end of a long chapter on poverty and charity Chris Dyer could express surprise and bewilderment, writing that: 'The survival of the medieval poor still remains something of a mystery.' (Dyer 1989, 257) But survive they did, and in droves.

The position we have arrived at, therefore, in archaeology is that poverty and the poor are hard to detect in economic documents and even harder in the material past. I should also say that the poor identified in philosophy, theology, art and literature and explored elsewhere in this volume has intruded little into our discourse.

We archaeologists have tended to accept the primacy of economic and functional explanation and have taken this as our temporal template. Given the subject of this seminar, therefore, it is ironic that poverty has been scarcely addressed in our work. We can quote, perhaps, the best general book on the archaeology of medieval towns written by John Schofield and Alan Vince. In their conclusions about future study in this field, they identified the poor as a class about which we know virtually nothing archaeologically and, drawing attention to the zonality of poverty, using a map of the poor districts of Siena created from documents, they went on to say:

> But how can archaeology identify rich and poor sites, or rich and poor households? We have not yet worked out the criteria … Normal archaeological finds, especially pottery, were not particularly good indicators of wealth, and the archaeologist must look elsewhere to study this variable. There should be more studies of the 'bottom-up' view of the medieval town. (Schofield and Vince 2003, 254-5)

Schofield and Vince, however, can offer no practical, archaeological ways in which we achieve this and I am sceptical that we can in any evidential or empirical sense.

Also, as modern historians have shown, the poor were not a single, coherent cohort of folk. There was variation from place to place, and its appearance and meaning changed through time. New forms of poverty and what some have called 'moral panic' came with the break-down of the medieval agrarian and tenurial system and the consequent failure of the traditional structures of society and their support. As criteria of access to land moved from those of customary rights to those of property the process of exclusion was accelerated. The poor of the town's market economy were also more evident than those of the countryside whence many of the urban came.

This is an argument which shows again the strong influence of twentieth century thought in which structures are privileged over agency and the plight of the underclass is romanticised and exonerated. I want to hold onto this issue of structure and agency because it is of vital concern as to how we can interpret archaeological information to achieve a perspective on poverty which may, as I have suggested already, have been, in the medieval world, more a matter of agency than structure.

In later Anglo-Saxon and medieval texts the poor were apparent, but without status and legal definition. Nor was there legal provision for them within the feudal state and this remained the case until the early sixteenth century. This means that they are not incorporated into the frameworks of medieval documents, except as the incidences of individual action whether as reality in coroner's records or as metaphor and allegory in poetry and holy texts.

There are, on the other hand, thieves, widows, the landless, poor travellers, refugees, the sick, parentless children and slaves in Anglo-Saxon and medieval manorial acta. Traditional rural society and urban institutions cared for the poor: it was the responsibility of either the kin or the powerful, both lay and clerical through charity, elemosina (alms), for which the reward was heavenly redemption. These were, however, acts in relation to the individual and not corporate actions in relation to people of a particular status or class. That was a product of modernity and the modern state.

In summary here then I would say that the archaeological relationship with medieval poverty in all its guises has been largely economic in nature and non-specific, and is structural in argument rather than having a regard for agency.

I would go further. Poverty has not actually been addressed as a social or philosophical theme by archaeologists – in other words, most of what we may term the medieval allegorised elements of the human condition of poverty have not been studied as such. In seeking the material evidence of poverty, as we shall see, there is little empirically we can use. Yet this would be true also of chastity, faith, greed, avarice, madness, vanity or any other of the states of the human condition and mind. What we can attempt to do is employ inference, but usually what we are driven to is a selection from our array of things which can represent these elements of a medieval vocabulary: in other words, archaeology as *glossarium*.

Modernity

We have also another problem when trying to form a relationship with the material we discover in our excavations or in the surviving buildings and landscapes we survey: that is, modernity. It affects our empirical interpretations, because they are still, however unconsciously, drawn from our individual and collective experience. We see a thing and we try to imagine or envisage how it worked in the medieval world. To do this we have to navigate past ourselves - not easy.

There is, at the moment, a considerable interest in poverty on the world scale by national and international governments as well as by non-governmental organisations and private individuals. This is manifested in a whole variety of ways in the European experience and constructed in the context of global capitalism, with the belief that we can do something about it and even eradicate it. Poverty reaches our television screens as images of mass starvation, of natural disaster, of war, of plague and of exploitation in faraway places. Our perceptions and judgements of these images are tempered by our own domestic histories and sense of identity – these are, in my part of Europe, predominately Protestant and capitalist in content, although now being radically tempered by multi-culturalism and class-structured ethnicity.

For us in Britain our contemporary ideas of poverty begin in the late fifteenth and sixteenth centuries, although some would argue it can be tracked back into the later fourteenth. There are many texts which make observations to Parliament that express bewilderment about how poverty appears to be on the increase despite the growing wealth brought by commerce and the changing nature of production.

Modernity, I shall argue, has a complex engagement with poverty: institutionalised to the extent of replicating it, criminalized, marginalized, patronised, and torn between thinking it is the fault of the individual and believing that it can be redeemed, even transformed or 'cured', through the intervention of the state and its proxy charities. The primary concern and discussion within the state was about vagrancy which might spawn an underclass capable of rebellion, and its early efforts were aimed at stamping this out. The Dissolution of the monasteries and the ending or transformation of their extensive networks of alms-giving also increased the impetus.

Fig. 3: William Hogarth: Two illustrations from the series illustrating the moral narrative of Idleness and Industry (Plates first published 1795-6, Hogarth 1806)

There was a rapid move through the sixteenth century toward the introduction of the Poor Law in 1601 and this changed the perception forever: the poor were the failures, marginalized, semi-criminal and indigent. Their portrayal in the Protestant work ethic, as in the moralistic engravings of Hogarth in the eighteenth century, was morally judgemental and vicious: two illustrations from his series on Idleness and Industry clearly demonstrated that idleness leads to poverty, degradation and execution at Tyburn (fig. 3). Such illustrations gave us also a powerful array of material indicators of poverty: squalor, decay, corruption, prostitution, vermin and drunkenness. By the enactment of 1601 and again in 1623, the parish became the unit of administration, entrusted to overseers who, with the church wardens, were required to assess and levy a compulsory poor rate on all householders. With these funds the aged were to be relieved and provided, if necessary, with cottages on the waste, poor children were to be apprenticed and the able poor set 'on work'. Off the back of all this a whole superstructure of state administration was put in place in the first half of the seventeenth century. The responsibility for the poor was thus delegated by the state to a middle class bureaucracy, rather than being more directly the moral and spiritual responsibility of the elite as it had been in the Middle Ages. The rural poor became physically located at the margin on land not possessed as property. This was accentuated by the move to squatting on common, usually waste, land. By this means the poor became more visible, on roadsides, upland rough pastures, fen edges, unused or derelict land. As such they were being formed into an identifiable, depersonalised cohort with new kinds of stigma and presence.

In the nineteenth century, a New Poor Law of 1834 came into existence on rationalist principles outlined by Jeremy Bentham: poor relief should only be granted to the 'deserving poor'. Those who were able-bodied together with their dependants, should be put to work in well-regulated workhouses under conditions inferior to those of the humblest labourers outside: 'every penny bestowed that tends to render the condition of the pauper more eligible than that of the independent labourer is a bounty on indolence and vice'. But with the nineteenth century too came the Romanticisation and the idealisation of the poor: William Wordsworth's *Matthew*, John Clare's own poor mad self, Henry Mayhew's *London Poor*, Charles Dickens' *Oliver Twist*, George Eliot's *Adam Bede*, and Thomas Hardy's *Jude*, all provided tragic hero figures on whom the likes of Charles Booth, Seebohm Rowntree and Thomas Barnardo built the foundations of the philanthropic institutions of the poor we still have today in Britain. Romanticisation and redefinition of the underclass and its struggle led also to socialism and a poetics of Marxism: Auguste Pugin made a graphic comparison of rationalist and scientific reactions to institutionalised poverty with those of the Middle Ages (fig. 4) and William Morris in *News from Nowhere* saw the solution to the existence of the underclass and its endemic poverty as a return to the golden age of craft, the thirteenth century in which, ironically for us medievalists, none would be poor. The black-and-white images to accompany this were those of Dorè's London (fig. 5).

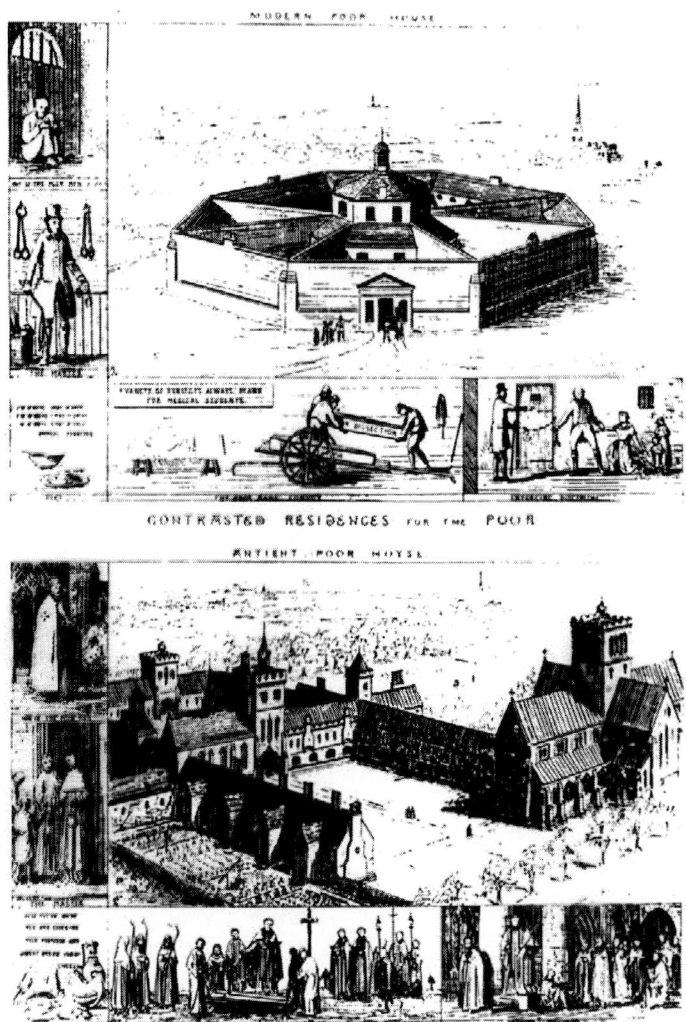

Fig 4: Auguste Pugin's comparison:
above, the (hateful) poor-house of the modern regime of the New Poor Law of 1834 with its inhuman and scientific systems; below, the (ideal) medieval hospital with its beautiful architecture and Christian Charity. (Pugin 1836; 1973)

Fig. 5: Gustave Doré: East End alley (Doré & Jerrold 1872)

Today our western images of poverty are modulated by the filters of modernity: failure, criminalisation, institutionalisation and romanticisation: in Tom Stoddart's, again black-and-white, image, taken at a feeding station in Sudan, the path of inheritance from the Poor Law to the globalised representation of poverty in the world system is clear (fig. 6). In our own modernity it is this range of images which stands in the forefront of our minds when contemplating the poverty and the poor of the Middle Ages. Our intellectual task is both to understand medieval poverty in terms of our own experience, and yet still to acknowledge and represent that it was different and coloured by other perceptions, sentiments and ideologies.

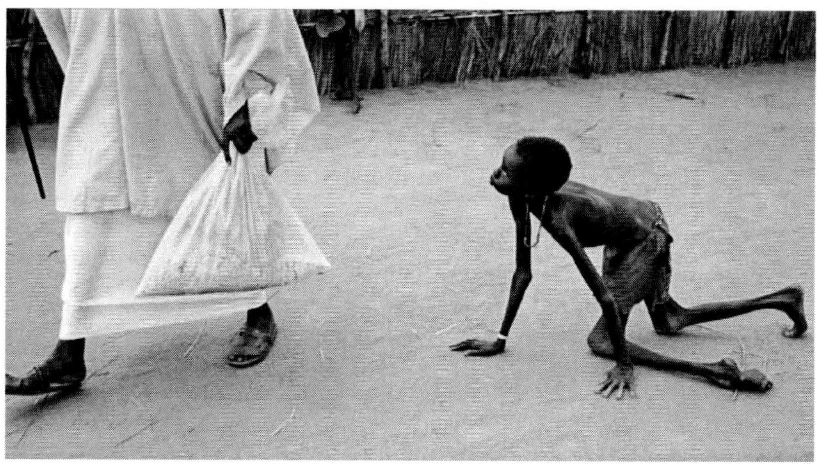

Fig. 6: Dives and Lazarus – A starving child looks on as a relatively rich man walks off with a bag of maize that he had spent hours waiting for at the emergency feeding centre, Ajiep, Sudan, August 1998 (Photograph courtesy Tom Stoddart/Getty Images)

An Archaeology of Difference

So far I have argued that the very methods of identifying and codifying difference in archaeology, the economic and structural burden of our interpretations and the filters of modernity have made any material view of the medieval poor difficult to achieve. I would further contend that we are unlikely to find a trustworthy, empirical path to identifying the presence of the poor simply in artefacts, architecture or corporeal remains. The only exceptions to this we must consider are the architectures of professed poverty and institutionalised alms: the monastery and the hospital.

That the great monasteries of Europe are institutions based on poverty is true in both an ideological and even a practical sense for many of those who took the vows. The life of prayer and work was the action of individuals and corporations, but shaped in the spaces of great richness and power. The habitus of monastic poverty, whether precinct or countryside, was designed to produce, reproduce, consume and display wealth and authority. This is not the place for a critique of monastic archaeology or indeed medieval monasticism, but the contrastive duality of the simultaneous presences of the mentalité of poverty and the materiality of wealth serves only to strengthen our interpretative dilemma.

This may also be so for medieval hospitals, many of which were established by the monasteries. The hospital was, in principle, 'a guest-house free to all-comers, where the poor travellers as well as the sick, infirm and aged could be sure of finding shelter and provision for their needs' (Godfrey 1955, 15). The act of alms was for the support of indigent individuals as they were, in theory, presented at the gate of the hospital, and, initially, this provision was conceived as personal and transitory. The traveller would pass on, the sick would be healed and the aged die. Later, however, and then only for specific groups of people, usually those privileged in some kind of way, they were seen as shelters for the pensioned: in other words for those who had paid their dues and who had made themselves worthy through Christian service and action. Thus hospitals and their architectures became places of permanent shelter and signs of opportunities for the civic display of alms, of patronal wealth and corporate authority.

These two sets of institutions are, in architectural form, the grand material signifiers of medieval poverty, and yet they are not poor: quite the opposite in any visual sense we can recognise. Yet this is what they **intended**, although this is not what they **meant**, even to the medieval observer. Poverty, therefore, can, however complexly, be made historically material, but the poor cannot. But let us remember that although poverty may be absolute and permanent, the poor are relative and transitory. This leads me to two questions:

1. How can we make physically apparent the narratives of the medieval poor – what does the material past signify? Already I have suggested that this is hard to achieve empirically, but maybe there is another question:
2. Should we, despite the empirical problems of evidence, nonetheless contribute to the assemblage of images of the medieval poor by selecting some archaeological things and material contexts to represent their undoubted presence in the past? This has dangers for archaeologists not least in justifying the criteria for selection, whether to achieve signification or representation.

To illustrate this I will finish with four pieces of archaeology taken from my own experience and leave you with some impressions and questions. I shall touch on some things that may be seen as indicators of poverty or at least of the circumstances and contexts of poverty: marginality, inequality, squalor, and damnation. The images may thus be a device to see poverty and the relics of the poor beyond the refracting lenses of Bentham, Doré or Stoddart.

1. The settlement at the margin – marginality and productive vulnerability

Okehampton Park contains the earthwork remains of medieval agriculture and settlement on the northern rim of Dartmoor in south-west England and one complete farmstead within this relic landscape was excavated (Austin 1978). The settlement was established in perhaps the later eleventh or twelfth century and abandoned in the late thirteenth or fourteenth. I have argued elsewhere that the social organisation of the spaces within the houses and yards represent a familiar and habitual structure for people occupying the economic margins of production at an optimum moment in the economic cycle of the Middle Ages (Austin and Thomas 1990). What I could also now argue with others is that the space constitutes a set of social relations familiar to a range of classes, although the material expression is located in the specific cultures of the region. What we must ask here is whether the material remains associated with the family who occupied these spaces were those which might be interpreted as signs of poverty. Whether they are or not, can they be offered here to represent the poor in medieval rural society? In terms of the absolutes of material culture, the buildings have stone walls, but they are unmortared; the roofs were thatched, but relatively low; the animals lived under the same ridge line, but the human spaces were still quite large; there was heat from the central hearth but fuel may have been uncertain; the pottery was plain or simply decorated, but was plentiful and some of the same assemblages could found in Okehampton Castle, three kilometres away. The organisation of the agriculture suggests not simply adequate arable production for subsistence, but adequate access also to the pastures of the adjacent commons and moors for their stock. Much seems potentially comfortable, but the people were at the margins of arable capacity and at the lower end of the tenurial scale. They had roofs over their heads, but life must have been precarious at the mercy of bad weather or soil infertility, and in the end the settlement failed, although this may not have been for climatic or even economic reasons. In other words, the material culture is contradictory and hard to interpret, yet here we are in some of the toughest environments in the English landscape.

There is also another issue: the buildings and their yards were occupied by a family, but as Goody pointed out many years ago, such families have life cycles of circumstance and we cannot tell from one moment to the next what lives were led by the people who occupied these spaces (Goody 1982). A stem family would at their greatest extent have had aged and corrodial grand-parents (one building had a separate space definably theirs), as well as unmarried siblings and the core family itself. In a marginal world there were also likely to be those who had a more ephemeral existence: the illegitimate and the illegal as well as the labourers of the underclasses. There were out-houses and peripheral spaces even in this marginal world which might have been occupied by an array of individuals. These are the questions archaeology can so rarely answer: who, in terms of individual people, actually lived there and how poor did they feel? Surely the family must have felt poor in comparison with many of those around them, some at least of the occupants of the castle and the town. They must also have felt inferior to the freeholders of Devon who drove their cattle by right on and off the high moors up the lanes between their fields and through their yards.

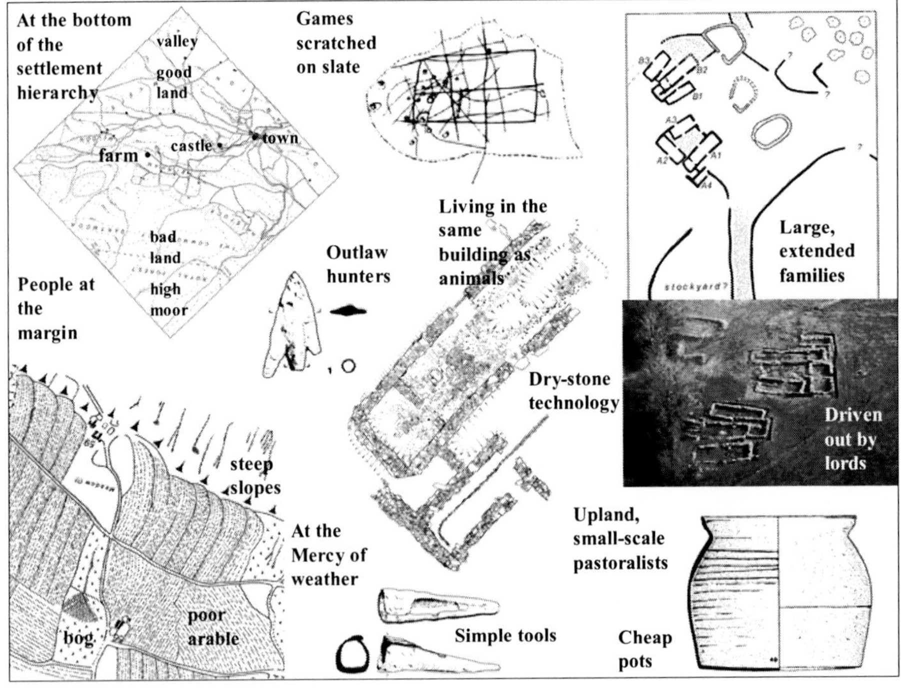

Fig. 7 *Imperatrix Fortuna*:
a representation of poverty at the margin: Okehampton Park, Devon

With all this uncertainty, however, we can be sure that, if the historians are right in asserting that between one third and one half of the population of England lived below or close to the poverty line, then these people on the edge of Dartmoor were among them. So if we assemble the array of materials we can physically associate with them and present them as an image (fig. 7), then they do at least represent medieval poverty. What they should represent is the medieval mind's own perception of their vulnerability, at the margin, to Imperatrix Fortuna, whether it is famine, climate or the will of their lords.

2. Inequality: the presence of the poor in the home of the powerful

Turning to a harder case, the excavations at Barnard Castle in Teesdale, north-eastern England, produced a huge amount of material culture and architectural fragments. In a paper in a previous publication in this series (Austin 1998), I discussed how the meaning of spaces within a great castle was contingent on viewpoint and the oscillating circumstances of habitation. So did the poor have a place even here? There was certainly the poor Queen, Devorgilla, Lady of Galloway and wife of John Balliol who spent her sad widowhood in the castle, and the poor Knight, Alan of Galloway her cousin, kept incarcerated in the same place for the whole of his adult life to prevent him being a threat to her lordship of south-western Scotland. There were also the economically poor, the peasant criminals brought before the lord's court and the agricultural labourers on the demesne farm housed within the walls of the Outer Ward. There were lesser servants, bakers' and cooks' assistants, 'gong-fermers' (boys who cleared the garderobes) and those who cleaned and prepared the rooms and courtyards. If we ask who handled the pottery in the castle, who prepared the food whose waste we discovered in the excavations, or who made the nails and hinges and pins that littered the surfaces, it is likely that many of them might be called the poor and have lived much of their lives in poverty.

In the main report on the excavations (Austin, forthcoming) I have begun to examine the deposits found to 'see the acts' of such people so that we may begin to approach the relationships of individuals to the spaces they occupied. Almost certainly the poor were there, but did their surroundings stop them being in the category of poverty during the time they inhabited these spaces? However, if we add to the images representing medieval poverty by creating an array of materiality that might have been used by the poor in the context of a castle, is that legitimate? Is it a true representation? The huge quantities of low-grade pottery, and the mountains of waste products of butchery, food preparation and consumption as well as the garderobe shafts, small chambers, kitchens, bakehouses, stables, out-houses and low overhangs of stair-cases and parapets where the poor may have worked and had their abode, may all be set alongside the assemblages of Okehampton Park, however unexpectedly, within the realms of medieval archaeology (fig. 8).

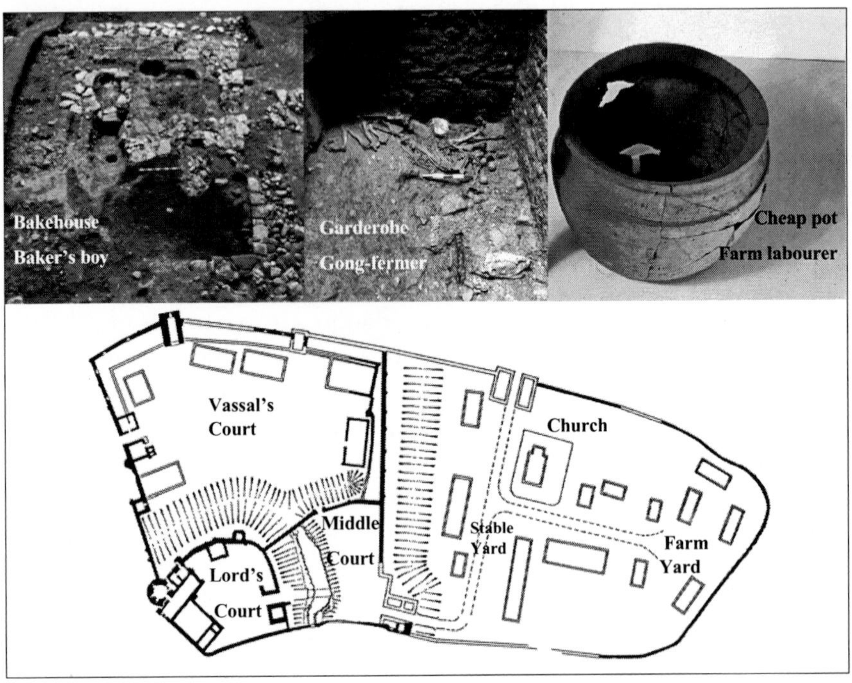

Fig. 8: *Dominus povertatis*: a representation of the poor at work in the castle: Barnard Castle, Co. Durham, caput of the Balliols, one of the richest and most powerful families in England and Scotland in the later 13th century.

3. Squalor and the environments of urban poverty

The increased visibility of the poor and of the forms of poverty, many historians have argued, came with the rush to urbanism at the end of the Middle Ages and into the modern era. Archaeology has made massive interventions into the material culture of medieval urban Europe and it is striking in one major respect: the quantity of rubbish retained and re-cycled within the urban environment was massive. Under certain conditions, particularly those of water-logging in harbour or riverside locales, towns and cities took on the characteristics of ancient tells, building themselves higher onto the decay and partial preservation of former buildings and rubbish dumps. Under other conditions rubbish was managed in systems of pits which pock-mark the excavated areas of burgage plots. At other times it was simply dumped in vacant lots and common ground. The need to dispose of waste in these 'private' and 'personal' or even 'anti-social' ways was driven in part by the lack of strong corporate management of towns and cities and in part by the often restrictive nature of access to even the nearest pieces of countryside. With urban areas also centres of production some of these deposits were also noxious if not completely toxic: the by-products of metal-working, tanning, lime-burning, pottery firing, dyeing and many others left many places hard to inhabit. In short, the overall impression gained by archaeologists is that towns and cities lived always on the brink of squalor. For an archaeologist this is wonderful, because the deposits are so rich in material culture, but for those inhabitants unable to buy their way to the life of the burgess or the gild-worker, the struggle to keep away from the degradation of filth was sometimes tough.

One example of such a set of deposits was a couple of burgage plots in Southgate, Hartlepool, a port town on the Durham coast of the North Sea, in north-eastern England. I have a photograph (fig. 9) of the level at which I stopped excavating in 1972. I have always used it to represent urban existence and its contrasts with the rural. The image shows dark black organic-rich deposits as the floor surfaces of small late thirteenth-century rooms within two larger buildings set either side of a small narrow alley, the classic *gasse* of north European seaports. These deposits are rich in finds of pottery and other rubbish interleaved with laminated levels of sand and dark organic material caused by the regular inundations of this inhabited area by storm surge incursions of the North Sea. Documentary sources tell us also that nearby was a large processing plant for fish which was an important money-earner for the Prior and Convent of Durham Cathedral Priory. The image then is of small dark spaces, squalor, damp, industrial processes and impermanence. We can interpret the conditions of life, but did the poor live here? We cannot be sure, but we may be able to accept that this is a viable representation of the circumstances, the structures of poverty.

Fig. 9: *Burgus squalidus*: 'An abominable smell abounding in the said city more than in any other city of the realm from dung and manure and other filth and dirt wherewith the streets and lanes are filled and obstructed' Edward III legislating for York (cited in Platt 1976. 70). Here the alleys and buildings of downtown, harbour-side Hartlepool under excavation in 1972. (Photo: author)

4. Damnation

One last image brings us to the final stripping away of all the material signs of wealth or poverty: to death itself. Archaeologists have revealed the serried ranks of skeletons in rural and urban graveyards the length and breadth of Europe. Yet these were in themselves only the residues of once corporeal existences and yet they were also a potent medieval symbol of a great transition, the separation of the soul from the body and its eventual judgement. Then there was no greater poverty than the damnation of the soul and no greater wealth than its redemption. In the photographs of cemetery excavations the skeletons are, for the most part, hard to distinguish in terms of poverty or wealth. Sometimes we may suspect that the pathology of a skeleton displaying the signs of rickets may be evidence for a deprived existence and traces of osteoarthritis an indicator of a hard life, but we actually cannot know this and the occurrence of both among the better off is known in more modern and documented medical case histories.

Fig. 10: *Mors in profundis*: The bones of a new-born child were found in this pit (lower photograph) set below the floor of a peasant house in the north row (upper photograph) at Thrislington, County Durham: once a storage pit, it was filled with rubbish in the dying days of its existence. (Photos: R. Daggett)

Yet we may among all this evidence be missing the greatest of all poverty: the poverty of the soul in certain damnation. All those interred in the excavated cemeteries will have received the sacrament of the mass for the dead and the Christian rite of burial in the 'sure and certain hope of the resurrection', as the English prayer book says. The image I produce is the photograph (fig. 10) of a stone-lined pit in a thirteenth-century peasant house in a village called Thrislington in northern England (Austin 1989). It is an elaborate storage pit, set below the floor of a room in a comfortable house, probably occupied by a freehold tenant of this small manor. The pit and its contents of grain and other food was part of the strategy of avoiding disaster and with it the onset of poverty. The irony was that in the top of the final back-filling of this pit designed to stave off poverty were laid the remains of an immediately post-foetal child, probably lost in the moment of child-birth. Laid where it was, it was unbaptised; it may also have been illegitimate; it was certainly damned by its original sin and shorn of everything both material and spiritual.

Bibliography:

Austin, David 1978. 'Excavations in Okehampton Deer Park, Devon, 1976-1978'. *Proceedings of the Devon Archaeological Society* 36, 191-239

Austin, David 1989. *Excavations at Thrislington, County Durham.* London: Medieval Archaeology Monograph 12

Austin, David 1998. 'Private and Public: an Archaeological Consideration of Things'. In *Die Vielfalt der Dinge: Neue Wege zur Analyse mittelalterlicher Sachkultur.* Ed. Helmut Hundsbichler et al. Vienna

Austin, David and Julian Thomas 1990, 'The "Proper" Study of Medieval Archaeology: a Case Study'. Chapter 2 in D. Austin and Leslie Alcock, *From the Baltic to the Black Sea: Studies in Medieval Archaeology.* London

Austin, David forthcoming. *Acts of Perception: a Study of Barnard Castle in Teesdale.* Durham

Doré, Gustave and Blanchard Jerrold 1872. *London: a Pilgrimage* London

Dyer, Christopher 1989. *Standards of Living in the Middle Ages.* Cambridge

Godfrey, Walter H. 1955. *The English Alms-House.* London

Goody, Jack 1982. *The Development of the Family and Marriage in Europe.* Cambridge

Hogarth, William 1806. *Industry and Idleness.* London

Hoskins, William George 1953-4. 'Harvest fluctuations and English economic history 1480-1619'. *Agricultural History Review* 2, 28-46

Hoskins, W.G. 1963. *Provincial England,* London

Little, Lester K. 1978, *Religious Poverty and the Profit Economy in Europe.* London

Platt, Colin 1976. *The English Medieval Town.* London

Pugin, Augustus Welby Northmore 1836 (1973). *Contrasts, A Parallel between the Noble Edifices of the 14th and 15th centuries and Similar Buildings of the Present Day. Showing a Decay of Taste.* Reprint Leicester.

Schofield, John and Vince, Alan G. 2003, *The Archaeology of Medieval Europe, 1100-1600: Medieval Towns*, 2nd ed. London

Titow, Jan Zbigniew 1962. 'Some differences between manors and their effects on the condition of the peasant in the thirteenth century', *Agricultural History Review* 10, 1-13

CLAUDE GAUVARD

Juger les pauvres en France à la fin du Moyen Âge

Depuis les travaux de Michel Mollat sur la pauvreté, les recherches en France sur ce thème sont restées rares[1]. Cela tient à plusieurs raisons, la principale étant la difficulté de cerner la notion de pauvreté à l'époque médiévale, dans une société radicalement différente de la nôtre, qu'il s'agisse des besoins individuels ou des réseaux de sociabilité qui prennent en charge les plus démunis. L'existence d'un seuil de pauvreté est par là même difficile à établir et les études récentes sur *Le petit peuple en Occident à la fin du Moyen Âge*, viennent récemment de le confirmer[2]. Je voudrais aujourd'hui rouvrir le dossier en m'appuyant essentiellement sur les sources judiciaires : nous éclairent-elles sur la façon dont la société juge ses pauvres, donc les perçoit comme une entité, et sur l'existence d'un groupe social qui peut être qualifié de « pauvre » ? La question posée n'est pas nouvelle et Bronislav Geremek y avait en partie répondu dans son ouvrage « Les marginaux parisiens aux XIVe et XVe siècles », paru en 1976[3]. Il avait alors mis l'accent sur une pauvreté associée aux marges de la société, sous la forme de mendiants et de vagabonds, de déracinés, et il avait montré le lien étroit que cette frange entretenait avec le crime comme avec l'exclusion sous la forme de châtiments extrêmes. Cette optique, qu'il ne faut absolument pas récuser car il est parfaitement exact que les mendiants valides sont exclus de la société à la fin du Moyen Âge puis à l'époque moderne, n'est pas suffisante pour donner une image globale de la pauvreté et des jugements qui sont portés sur les pauvres et j'espère avoir démontré que la criminalité ne se manifestait pas seulement aux marges de la société mais en son cœur, dans

---

[1] *Etudes sur l'histoire de la pauvreté, Moyen Âge-XVIe siècle*, dir. Michel Mollat, 2 vol.; Paris, 1974 ; Michel Mollat, *Les pauvres au Moyen Âge*, Paris, 1978.

[2] *Le petit peuple dans l'Occident médiéval. Terminologies, perceptions, réalités*, dir. Pierre Boglioni, Robert Delort et Claude Gauvard, Paris, 2002.

[3] Bronislav Geremek, *Les marginaux parisiens aux XIVe et XVe siècles*, Paris, 1976.

les populations « ordinaires »[4]. Il ne faut pas confondre pauvres et marginaux. Je voudrais donc reprendre le problème en m'attachant à des sources judiciaires, criminelles mais aussi civiles, pour évaluer quelle place la justice accorde à la pauvreté, en ayant présent à l'esprit le fait que les juges, mais aussi les parties qui engagent les procès peuvent avoir une certaine conception de la pauvreté et que cette conception révèle des normes de comportement de la société tout entière, en même temps que les rapports de force au sein de cette même société.

Les pauvres sont-ils jugés ? La question mérite d'être posée car les textes judiciaires font apparaître toutes sortes de pauvres sans qu'il soit possible de s'en tenir au seul qualificatif « pauvre » pour les retenir. Un exemple pris dans le registre d'écrous du Châtelet en 1412 peut nous le faire sentir[5]. Laurent Patin, mendiant aveugle qui opère dans la cathédrale Notre-Dame de Paris, est volé par Regnaut d'Esply qui l'a trompé sur le change de la monnaie. Lequel des deux hommes est effectivement pauvre ? Le premier est qualifié de « povre homme aveugle » et on peut s'apitoyer sur son sort comme le fait le rédacteur du registre qui le décrit aussi « querant sa vie ». Mais on apprend que ce Laurent Patin est marié, que sa femme défend ses intérêts puisque c'est elle qui engage la plainte en justice contre Regnault d'Esply, qu'il a un domicile fixe, rue des Sablons, et que la mendicité est sa profession, comme le prouve d'ailleurs sa place attitrée dans la cathédrale, derrière le chœur. Il s'agit d'un homme honorable aux activités contrôlées. L'autre est un simple « varlet servant demourant partout », donc sans domicile fixe et il occupe une place sociale subalterne, difficilement contrôlable. Il a d'ailleurs volé. La pauvreté réelle n'est-elle pas plutôt de son côté, du côté de ces populations instables qui glissent vers la délinquance ?

L'issue de cette affaire montre que le valet demeurant partout est finalement incarcéré au Châtelet où il est jugé. Mais l'est-il au même titre que le serait un autre citoyen ? Il existe incontestablement une justice de classe et les théologiens soucieux de réformer le royaume, tel Jean Gerson, ne se privent pas de répéter qu'il convient de faire justice aussi bien aux riches

---

[4] Claude Gauvard, *« De grace especial ». Crime, État et Société en France à la fin du Moyen Âge*, 2 vol., Paris, 1991.

[5] Publié par Claude Gauvard, Mary et Richard Rouse et Alfred Soman, « Le Châtelet de Paris au début du XVe siècle d'après les fragments d'un registre d'écrous de 1412 », *Bibliothèque de l'École des Chartes*, 157 (1999), p. 565-606, cas n°10, 595.

qu'aux pauvres[6]. La réalité montre que ces principes théoriques sont loin d'être appliqués. La sociologie des cas examinés au Parlement de Paris est très significative : les pauvres sont quasiment exclus de l'appel au plus grand Parlement du royaume. Les nobles sont nettement prioritaires, avec plus de 30% des cas. Il a été aussi clairement démontré, par exemple par Bernard Guenée pour le bailliage de Senlis, que la justice coûte cher et que, par conséquent, elle concerne en priorité une frange de population capable de financer la poursuite devant les tribunaux[7]. Les frais commencent avec les sergents qui portent les lettres de commission et se poursuivent par la chicane des avocats qui font traîner les choses en longueur. Dans la mesure où, encore à la fin du Moyen Âge, l'initiative du procès vient des parties plus que des juges, il est certain que la justice est discriminatoire. Il faut aussi compter avec les pots de vin qui achètent les gens de justice. Enfin, les compositions financières sont une pratique courante, y compris au criminel. Lors d'une plaidoirie, à Montpellier au début du XVe siècle, le procureur du roi n'hésite pas à dire « que les gens de Montpellier sont merveilleux et y a plus de cent ans que on ne fit justice de personne qui eust puissance car il composent tousjours a argent et ont accoustumé de menacier le juge et de le metctre au procès se il fait justice »[8]. Le soutien en justice et les accords qui arrêtent le cours des procès créent donc une justice de classe dont les pauvres sont en grande partie exclus.

Cette discrimination se poursuit jusque dans la prison où les pauvres sont incarcérés. En effet, la prison reflète les conditions inégalitaires dans lesquelles vivent les individus. L'ordonnance de 1425, qui réorganise le Châtelet, le précise : « Nous avons ordonné et ordonnons que chascun prisonnier soit mis et logié en ladite geole selon son estat, le cas de son emprisonnement »[9]. Ainsi, il existe à Rouen et à Caen une prison des chevaliers dans laquelle sont entrepris des travaux pour y construire une cheminée. La salle

---

6 Jean Gerson, *Vivat Rex*, éd. Mgr Glorieux, *Œuvres complètes*, t. 7*, Paris-Tournai-Rome-New York, 1968, 1172-1175, qui clôt son passage sur la justice du roi par ce rappel : « Dieu veuille au moins que justice soit gardee sans estre infraincte pour le grant ne pour le petit ; autrement se verifieroit le dit de Anacarsez philosophe que lez loys et arrestz jugiés sont a comparer aux telez d'araigniez ; ellez retiennent lez petitez mouchetez et laissent les grosses aller ».

7 Bernard Guenée, *Tribunaux et gens de justice dans le bailliage de Senlis à la fin du Moyen Âge (vers 1380-vers 1550),* Paris, 1963.

8 Archives nationales de France (citées ensuite ANF), X2a 14, fol. 275, août 1405.

9 François-André Isambert, *Recueil général des anciennes lois françaises*, t. 8, Paris, 1833, 724-725.

de ceux qui sont « au pain du roi », c'est-à-dire nourris par le geôlier car ils sont trop pauvres pour s'entretenir eux-mêmes, ne bénéficie pas des mêmes transformations. Remarquons néanmoins deux choses : la nature du crime influe, du moins en principe, sur le choix de la salle dans laquelle est détenu le prisonnier. Surtout, les débiteurs ont des chambres réservées qui les séparent des criminels et semblent bien entretenues, du moins à Caen et à Rouen où il y a dallage du sol, cheminée, latrines[10]. Il s'agit là d'une catégorie spéciale qui, sans être jugée, est soumise à la justice. D'ailleurs ce sont les sergents qui sont chargés par le bailli d'aller quérir les débiteurs pour les mettre en prison, comme le montrent les fragments de comptes royaux qui ont été conservés[11].

Quels liens les débiteurs et tous ceux qui, valets ou apprentis, sont incarcérés au titre de la justice civile ont-ils avec la pauvreté ? Il est bien évident que les éléments ne sont pas strictement superposables et que tous les débiteurs ne peuvent pas être considérés comme pauvres. La dette, par le rapport étroit qu'elle entretient avec le don, suppose des relations sociales autrement plus subtiles que ne le suggère la somme d'argent qui est due. Mais considérons les textes judiciaires et les écrous pour dette. Leur étude vient d'être magistralement renouvelée par Julie Mayade-Claustre qui, dans sa thèse de doctorat d'Histoire, a montré l'importance de l'incarcération pour dette dans le royaume de France à la fin du Moyen Âge[12]. Dans la Prévôté et Vicomté de Paris qui sert de cadre administratif à cette étude, la pauvreté joue un grand rôle dans cette incarcération[13]. L'étude des censiers parisiens vient le confirmer. Ils préparent en quelque sorte aux décisions d'incarcération quand ils mentionnent dans la marge des croix pour ceux qui ont certainement récidivé dans le non-paiement, ou « nichil », pour ceux qui n'ont pas payé leurs redevances peut-être pour la première fois, ou encore indiquent les modérations qui ont été nécessaires. À ces données s'ajoutent les expres-

---

[10] Description par Luc Gandeboeuf, *Prisonniers et prisons royales en Normandie à la fin du Moyen Âge (XIVe-XVe siècles)*, thèse dactylographiée, Université Paris IV, 1995, 676.

[11] Par exemple : « Pour messages envoiés a aucun des sergenz...pour envoier les debtours en prison : VIs », Bibliothèque nationale de France (citée par la suite BNF), Ms fr 25994, n°369 (bailli de Cotentin, 1327).

[12] Julie Mayade Claustre, *Le roi, la dette et le juge. Justice royale et endettement privé dans la prévôté de Paris à la fin du Moyen Âge*, thèse dactylographiée, Paris I, 2003, et récemment, ead., « Le corps lié de l'ouvrier. Le travail et la dette à Paris au XVe siècle », *Annales, Histoire, Sciences Sociales*, 2005, 383-408.

[13] Ead. « Le petit peuple en difficulté : la prison pour dettes à Paris à la fin du Moyen Âge », dans *Le petit peuple* (*op. cit. supra*, n. 2), 453-466.

sions qualitatives qu'emploient les receveurs. Ceux de la Grande Confrérie aux Bourgeois, en 1441 et ceux du Temple, à partir de 1458, parlent de « povreté », de « povre homme », de « povre femme » ou de « povres personnes, qui ne paient pas ce qu'ils doivent, voire absolument rien ». Les receveurs font de cette pauvreté l'une des raisons pour laquelle ils ont des arrérages, étant donné « la grant povreté des personnes qui n'ont de quoy payer »[14]. La dette a bien à voir avec la pauvreté. Mais les pauvres sont-ils pour autant punis ?

Un premier versant des jugements permet de fortement nuancer une vision simpliste de la justice médiévale, du moins à la fin du Moyen Âge, qui serait à la fois rigide et sévère. Considérons le vol. La notion de besoin conduit, au moins depuis Gratien, à nuancer les effets criminels du vol si celui-ci a été commis en cas d'extrême nécessité[15]. Celui qui commet un vol dans ces conditions ne peut pas être considéré comme un voleur puisque le riche a vis-à-vis du pauvre un devoir d'assistance sous peine de commettre lui-même un homicide. *Debet credere dominum permissurum* dit Huguccio. Dans le premier tiers du XIIIe siècle, Guillaume d'Auxerre donne au principe sa dimension théologique en affirmant que les biens doivent être mis en commun en cas d'extrême nécessité, sous peine de commettre un péché mortel. Thomas d'Aquin reprend cette pensée dans plusieurs écrits, dont la Somme théologique où il se demande s'il est permis de voler en cas de nécessité[16]. Après avoir montré qu'un voleur se trouvant dans la nécessité est soumis à la pénitence, donc considéré comme coupable, et avoir fait référence à Aristote qui lie le vol à la malice, ce qui laisse supposer que ce qui est mauvais en soi ne peut devenir bon même s'il est ordonné à une fin bonne, Thomas développe le *Sed contra* qui l'emporte :

> *Sed contra est quod in necessitate sunt omnia communia. Et ita non videtur esse peccatum si aliquis alterius accipiat, propter sibi factam communem.*

Et il conclut en condamnant le droit humain qui punit le vol sans distinction :

---

[14] Nombreux exemples dans Valentine Weiss, *Cens et rentes à Paris au bas Moyen Âge : documents et méthodes de gestion domaniale*, thèse dactylographiée, Paris I, 2005, 786 et suiv.

[15] Gilles Couvreur, *Les pauvres ont-ils des droits ? Recherches sur le vol en cas d'extrême nécessité depuis la Concordia de Gratien (1140) jusqu'à Guillaume d'Auxerre (1231)*, Rome, 1961.

[16] Thomas d'Aquin, *Somme théologique*, IIa IIae Question 66, 7.

> *Quod ea quae sunt juris humani non possunt derogare juri naturali vel juri divino. Secundum autem naturalem ordinem ex divina providentia institutum, res inferiores sunt ordinatae ad hoc quod ex his subveniatur hominum necessitati.*

Puis il cite saint Ambroise et les Décrets et conclut :

> *Si tamen adeo sit urgens et evidens necessitas ut manifestum sit instanti necessitati de rebus occurrentibus esse subveniendum, puta cum imminet personae periculum et aliter subveniri non potest ; tunc licite potest aliquis ex rebus alienis suae necessitati subvenire, sive manifeste sive occulte sublatis. Nec hoc proprie habet rationem furti vel rapine.*

Après saint Thomas, le principe est accepté par tous, y compris des civilistes comme Bartole et Balde : l'affamé contraint de voler est innocent.

La question est de savoir à quoi se reconnaît l'extrême nécessité qui signerait la pauvreté la plus absolue, et si les juges ont tenu compte de cette excuse en portant leurs jugements. Pour définir l'extrême nécessité qui serait un seuil de pauvreté faisant basculer vers la mort, la faim est l'élément clé. Mais il peut aussi s'agir de l'absence de vêtements. L'historien est gêné par le vocabulaire général et stéréotypé qu'emploient les théologiens et les juristes. Ils parlent du pain des affamés et des vêtements de ceux qui sont nus… Les juges sont, eux, en face de cas concrets, et il est probable que l'arbitraire dont ils disposent leur a fait tenir compte de cette excuse en cas d'extrême nécessité. Quelques cas confortent cette hypothèse. Les épaves des registres seigneuriaux de Saint-Germain-des-Prés à Paris font état d'un homme né à Provins qui, ayant volé de la viande, est relâché car il n'a pas les moyens de payer le geôlier : cette décision n'est peut-être pas seulement de simple bon sens, elle trahit de la part du juge un souci de respecter le droit canonique[17]. Il est probable que cette excuse de pauvreté entre de façon générale dans la relâche rapide de nombreux prisonniers. Il est probable aussi que la pauvreté réelle des suppliants demandeurs de la grâce royale à l'issue de leur crime a contribué à fléchir le roi quand il attribue la grâce, signe que cette fois le mot « pauvre » se colore d'une réalité sociale. Tel est le cas de Thomas Legrant du bailliage de Chartres « poure homme chargié de femme et de trois petis enfans » qui ne trouve plus le sommeil si bien que

---

[17] Cas cité par Paul Viollet, « Notes pour servir à l'histoire de la législation sur le vol », *Bibliothèque de l'École des Chartes,* 34 (1873), 331-342, ici 341, qui doute de la référence au principe du droit canonique.

« lui estans couchié en son lit en certaine nuit du moys de decembre derrenier passé, pensant en soy desconfortant en plusieurs debtes qu'il devoit (...) se leva de son lit environ heure de minuit et s'en ala au hamel de Harecourt en l'hostel de Thevenot Roussel et de Jehanne sa mere ou il embla et pris deux pourceaux »[18]. De même, Guillemette vole son maître parce qu'elle n'avait pas de linge et, à Châteauroux, un laboureur de bras, marié et père de six enfants, vole du froment, du seigle, de la viande accrochée au toit « pour avoir sa vie seulement »[19]. Un autre, en 1409, victime de la cherté des biens, envisage de demander l'aide de son voisin. Celui-ci étant absent, il le vole. La victime pense d'abord faire excommunier son voisin indélicat, puis elle lui pardonne, un pardon que confirme le roi. Le vol s'est transformé en aumône. Les documents judiciaires montrent bien que ces gens ne sont pas des professionnels du vol mais qu'ils y sont acculés. L'excuse en cas d'extrême nécessité est donc un élément qui peut, en matière de justice, permettre de cerner la véritable pauvreté. Mais pour prendre leurs décisions, les juges n'utilisent-ils que cet élément ?

On s'aperçoit que l'excuse s'accompagne d'une analyse serrée de la renommée de celui qui est coupable de vol par pauvreté. En général, le jugement qui aboutit à l'innocence suppose que le vol s'est passé en pays de connaissance où voleur et volé se connaissent. Il faut que le coupable bénéficie d'une bonne renommée au pays, à l'inverse de celui qui est considéré comme larron. Il en est ainsi de cet homme de Saint-Germain qui, quoique coupable d'un vol peu important de « poz et paailles », est pendu car il est « mal renommez » et appelé « larron »[20]. Le terme « larron » signe un sort irréversible qui se termine par la pendaison ou le bannissement. De façon générale, la récidive joue un rôle important dans l'arrestation, comme dans le cas de Regnaut d'Esply, cité précédemment. Il a agi deux fois contre le « pauvre homme aveugle » et « de ce faire il est coustumier a autres »[21]. On peut donc dire que l'extrême pauvreté peut être une excuse, mais qu'elle est réservée à des populations installées dans une renommée qui signe leur sociabilité. En conséquence, la renommée peut épargner la vie du voleur. En Normandie, en 1360, on accuse Robert Rousse d'avoir été complice d'un vol de vaches. Les juges cherchent alors à s'enfourmer de sa vie » et finalement

---

[18] ANF, JJ 165, pièce 38, janvier 1411, lettre adressée au bailli de Chartres.

[19] *Ibid.*, JJ 169, pièce 88.

[20] Louis Tanon, *Histoire des justices des anciennes églises et communautés monastiques de Paris*, Paris, 1883, 417, cas de Saint-Germain-des-Prés en 1266.

[21] *Supra* note 5.

il est dit « que informacion en ont esté faite par laquelle il fu prouvé de sa bonne vie et pour ce delivré »[22]. Même chose à Pontoise où, en 1369, des dépenses sont prévues à propos de quatre prisonniers « pour savoir et enquerir de leur estat, vie, conversacion et renommee, pour le bien de justice en la maniere que cy apres desclairié »[23].

Le sort du pauvre est alors lié plus étroitement que pour les plus riches et à plus forte raison les nobles à cette fameuse renommée que définit le regard des autres, et par conséquent à la façon dont il est perçu dans son pays de connaissance. Les riches ou les nobles refusent souvent l'enquête au pays, en prétendant que leur déclinaison d'identité suffit à prouver leur bonne renommée. Pour les pauvres, le regard des autres prime. Il peut leur être favorable, comme dans le cas de ces deux débiteurs insolvables, Sandret Gires et Henry le Pic, emprisonnés à Caen en 1409. Les habitants de la paroisse de Douvre où ils habitent déclarent « que ilz sont tous povres gens aagiés…et qu'ilz n'ont aucune chose vaillant en biens ne en heritages, mais sont vivans de omosnes »[24]. Il peut à l'inverse leur être défavorable pour des raisons qui nous échappent. En tout cas, le service et la condition subalterne, l'exercice de certains métiers en rapport avec la peau et le sang fragilisent cette renommée. Il n'est pas bon d'être « savetier » et réputé « estrangier et vagabond mal renommé et diffamé de murtres et autres malefices et moult doubté au païs»[25]. La pauvreté stricto sensu n'est plus seule en cause ici, mais elle devient redoutable quand elle se combine avec des éléments de la hiérarchie sociale. Être pauvre et servante peut conduire à la plus grande suspicion, surtout quand on a volé son maître !

Les juges s'acharnent-ils pour autant sur ceux qui ne peuvent pas prouver leur extrême pauvreté ou affirmer leur renommée ? Les cas se révèlent, là encore, extrêmement divers. Le fameux Regnaud d'Esply, arrêté au Châtelet le 24 avril, est élargi dès le 29, c'est-à-dire que son sort est tout à fait comparable à la plupart des personnes écrouées au Châtelet pour d'autres raisons et qui quittent la prison au bout de quelques jours, qu'il s'agisse de prostituées

---

[22] BNF, Ms fr. 26003, n°1058 (Falaise, 1360)

[23] BNF, Ms fr. 26008, n°644 (Pontoise, 1369)

[24] BNF, ms fr. 26037, n°4288 (Caen, 1409).

[25] ANF, X2a 14, fol. 187v-189. Pour sa défense, l'accusé, Colin le Mercier, dit qu'il est mercier et non savetier !

ou de fauteurs de troubles[26]. La pauvreté peut aussi être un élément moteur pour la libération du prisonnier ou pour le pardon d'un crime. Ainsi Perrette la Dain, accusée de meurtre, passe 194 jours dans les prisons de Rouen à la fin du XVe siècle. Elle aurait dû être exécutée, mais elle est finalement délivrée le 23 décembre sur décision des juges « Considéré que ledit cas estoit fort piteable, messires de l'Eschiquier dernier luy ont donné remission dudit cas et, pour la despence elle a esté tousjours detenue jusques a ce que, par deliberacion des officiers du roy, elle fu delivré veue la longue detencion et sa povreté, aussy pour l'onneur de la feste de Noël... »[27]. Ce cas s'apparente à la longue série des grâces accordées aux suppliants qui se disent « pauvres ». La pauvreté est l'un des premiers motifs pour que le roi accorde une lettre de rémission puisque 40% des demandeurs ayant obtenu une lettre de rémission se disent « pauvres », et dans certains cas leur situation n'est pas totalement feinte. De façon générale, les récits de crime se font l'écho des événements, en particulier de la guerre, qui ont accentué la pauvreté de ceux qui ont dû voler pour vivre car « ilz ont perdu leurs chevances et si ont esté prins prisonniers et mis a grans et excessives raençons par noz ennemis et adversaires telement qu'il ne leur est rien demouré et sont eulx, leurs femmes et enfans en adventure de delaissier le païs »[28]. On peut aussi, grâce aux lettres de rémission, mesurer comment la pauvreté s'enracine dans le tissu des relations ordinaires. Car celui qui vole n'y est pas un gueux sans loi. Au contraire, sa pauvreté est d'autant plus durement ressentie qu'elle naît du malheur de ne plus pouvoir se conformer à la norme. Elle commence quand il ne peut plus accomplir les gestes qui assurent la survie rituelle de l'espèce : relevailles des femmes, confection du vêtement de noces, enterrement décent de ses enfants en terre chrétienne, etc.[29]. L'homme s'en trouve « meu de honte et de confusion » et ce « desconfort » peut aller jusqu'à lui faire quitter le pays. La pauvreté devient un stérotype dans la série des lettres et les récidivistes l'emploient plus que les autres puisqu'ils l'évoquent trois fois plus que les autres suppliants. C'est là le signe que la pauvreté alimente la miséricorde et que, par conséquent,

---

[26] Cas cité *supra*, n. 5. Autre cas d'élargissement le lendemain de l'incarcération, *ibid.*, 599, n°32, alors que le voleur, lui aussi « varlet servant demourant partout », avait été saisi d'office pendant une effraction, avec port d'armes.

[27] BNF, Ms fr. 26105, n°1245 (Rouen, 1497-1498).

[28] Exemples cités dans Claude Gauvard, *« De grace especial »* (*op. cit. supra*, n. 4), t. 1, 404-405.

[29] *Ibid.*

elle peut être un facteur important de la grâce. De la même façon, il est rare de voir les biens des débiteurs saisis et quand ils le sont, c'est au terme d'un rituel qui signe à la fois l'archaïsme des gestes et le besoin de les insérer dans une chaîne d'exclusion qui se veut irréversible. À Paris, faute de paiement du cens, la terre peut être « brandonnée », c'est-à-dire que le sergent est chargé de ficher un brandon en terre, sorte de torche faite de paille entortillée, et de le placer aux extrémités du bien saisi[30].

Mais, à l'inverse, la pauvreté peut être un facteur aggravant qui conduit à accroître les peines qui sont prononcées, ou en tout cas à les rendre infamantes. Au civil, la dette est étroitement liée à l'excommunication que peut demander le créancier et qui est criée lors de la prière du prône. Les études les plus récentes montrent que c'est l'une des causes des excommunications les plus nombreuses[31]. À Paris, l'abandon-cession de biens semble s'être entouré de nouvelles formalités au cours des XIVe et XVe siècles. À la fin du XIVe siècle, Jean Boutillier leur consacre un long développement dans son coutumier La Somme rural. Il fait état du manteau que doit porter le débiteur le jour de l'abandon, manteau qu'il doit rituellement quitter :

> Item et selon l'usage coustumier si à ce faire il avoit mantel affublé, il le doit rapporter avec tous ses autres biens en la main de justice, et le laisser en l'ordonnance de ses creanciers : car sans leur consentement ne le r'auroit. Et la raison si est que sans mantel bien se peut vivre sans necessaire vivre, et ja a promis que outre son vivre necessaire que ce soit en paye à ses creanciers[32].

Un siècle auparavant, Philippe de Beaumanoir récusait l'idée qu'on puisse dépouiller le débiteur de ses vêtements « car vilaine chose est et contre humanité d'homme ne de fame despouiller pour dete »[33]. Mais il n'est plus suivi à la fin du Moyen Âge et la coercition semble avoir fait des progrès, même si l'offre du manteau est transformée par le rituel en un geste de re-

---

[30] Cas étudiés par Valentine Weiss (*op. cit. supra*, n. 14), 789.

[31] Véronique Beaulande, *Excommunication et pratiques sociales dans la province ecclésiastique de Reims du IVe concile de Latran au concile de Trente*, thèse dactylographiée, Université de Reims, 2000, à paraître aux Publications de la Sorbonne, 2007.

[32] Jean Bouteiller, *Le Grand Coutumier et Practique du droict civil et canon observé en France...cy-devant imprimé soubs le nom de la Somme rural*, éd. Louis Le Charondas le Caron, Paris, 1621, Livre II, titre XX, 800.

[33] Philippe de Beaumanoir, *Coutumes de Beauvaisis*, éd. Salmon, t. 2, chapitre LIV, parag. 1599.

nonciation consenti. Comme l'écrit Julie Mayade-Claustre, « la cession-abandon oscille entre la renonciation volontaire et la saisie »[34].

Le traitement de la pauvreté au pénal révèle d'autres marques discriminatoires. Les détenus des prisons du Cotentin dont nous avons conservé la trace justement grâce aux comptes du geôlier sont, comme nous l'avons vu, de vrais pauvres car nourris au « pain du roi ». Or, les chiffres donnés par Luc Gandeboeuf sont éloquents. Sur 419 prisonniers pour vol, 77 sont délivrés, un seul est gracié, 26 sont rendus comme clercs, 97 sont condamnés à mort et exécutés, 27 sont bannis, 14 sont soumis à une peine corporelle ou exposés au pilori ; le sort des autres est inconnu. Sur les 104 meurtriers, 8 sont délivrés, 6 sont graciés, 6 sont rendus comme clerc et 40 sont condamnés à mort, le sort des autres est inconnu. On ne peut qu'être frappé par la sévérité des décisions prises, car si la peine de mort n'est pas majoritaire, elle l'emporte sur toutes les autres formes de punitions. La décision des juges colle au plus prêt de la théorie que véhiculent les coutumiers qui condamnent à mort le voleur et le meurtrier. Cette tendance rejoint les chiffres que donne le fameux registre du Châtelet des années 1389-1392, qui définit une sorte de justice idéale. Or, les condamnés à mort n'y ont là aussi « aucun bien », comme le fait remarquer le clerc criminel chargé d'enregistrer leur fortune[35]. Leur profil sociologique est comparable à celui des prisonniers du Cotentin nourris au pain du roi et il se révèle profondément différent de ceux que le roi gracie par ses lettres de rémission. Ces derniers appartiennent à une population ordinaire, dont les membres peuvent se dire pour la plupart mariés, avec enfants et exercent un métier. Insérés dans la vie sociale, ils peuvent être défendus en justice par leurs proches, voire être vengés. Les deux catégories s'opposent nettement : aux premiers une condamnation radicale, aux seconds la négociation et la grâce. Ces hommes ou ces femmes entretenus au « pain du roi » et pour une grande partie d'entre eux condamnés à mort sont aussi très différents de ceux qui sont globalement écroués dans les prisons royales. Sur les 2513 personnes que recense le registre d'écrous du Châtelet à la fin du Moyen Âge ne figurent que quelques condamnations à mort[36]. Or, dans ce registre d'écrous, défilent toutes les nuances du peuple parisien, certainement pauvre, mais suffisamment riche pour payer la geôle, au moins quelques jours.

---

34 *Le roi, la dette et le juge* (*op. cit. supra*, n. 12), 539.

35 *Registre criminel du Châtelet de Paris du 6 septembre 1389 au 18 mai 1392* , éd. Henri Duplès-Agier, 2 vol., Paris 1861 et 1864.

36 ANF Y 5266a.

Incontestablement, la pauvreté la plus grande favorise les solutions radicales. Elle engendre l'infamie. Les juges n'hésitent guère à imposer l'essorillement et surtout à ordonner que le coupable soit battu de verge, en public, « par les carrefours », si possible un jour de marché, ou qu'il soit condamné au pilori.

La justice s'exerce dont selon une palette qui différencie soigneusement le pauvre du riche, et le pauvre du pauvre sans racines. Comment est-ce possible ? La justice est d'autant plus coercitive que la pauvreté a isolé l'individu, l'a retranché d'amis qui pourraient le sauver en négociant avec le juge ou en obtenant la grâce du roi. Dans une société où la vengeance reste un élément essentiel de compréhension des rapports de force, le pauvre est celui qui n'a plus les moyens de se venger et qui, de ce fait, est obligé de subir les effets les plus extrêmes de la coercition.

Jusqu'où va cette coercition ? Elle se manifeste de façon éclatante par la peine de mort qui est pour l'essentiel réservée à ceux qui peuvent être appelés des « marginaux », en rupture de biens et de solidarités. N'a-t-elle pas aussi des aspects plus insidieux qui font que la pauvreté entretient des liens étroits avec la sujétion ?

Le développement de la prison pour dette est un premier élément d'une évolution qui caractérise le développement de la royauté française aux deux derniers siècles du Moyen Âge. Sans refaire l'historique de la prison pour dette, il faut revenir sur quelques dates. En 1303, Philippe le Bel fait de la prison pour dette un privilège royal : elle est réservée aux dettes royales et aux obligations « corps et biens » de type privé qui sont obligatoirement passées sous sceau royal. Le Châtelet à Paris et les chefs-lieux de bailliages ou sénéchaussées s'engagent donc à soutenir l'accomplissement des clauses du contrat entre débiteur et créancier. L'ordonnance de 1303 est reprise en 1351, puis sous le règne de Charles V, le nombre de dettes qui peuvent entraîner la contrainte par corps est considérablement étendu. Quels sont les effets de cette législation dans la pratique ? Le Style du Châtelet, au XVe siècle, prescrit que la prise du corps n'a lieu que quand les biens meubles sont en nombre insuffisant pour rembourser la dette. L'exécution se déroule donc dans cet ordre : saisie des biens meubles, prise de corps, saisie des immeubles[37]. On voit donc que les plus pauvres ont peu de chances d'échapper à l'arrestation. Celle-ci se déroule selon un rituel confié au sergent qui somme le débiteur de payer, et à défaut de paiement lui dit : « ainse

---

[37] Julie Mayade-Claustre, *Le roi, la dette et le juge* (*op. cit. supra*, n. 12), 363.

par vertu de ceste obligation ie vous arreste prisonnier »[38]. La scène était fréquente car, au total, les prisonniers pour dettes formaient un cinquième des prisonniers du Châtelet et ils y séjournaient plus longtemps que les autres. Environ 70% des personnes incarcérées étaient délivrées au bout d'un jour, alors que cette proportion n'atteint pas plus de 40% pour les prisonniers pour dette. Leur détention ne dépasse guère plus de huit jours, mais il s'agit déjà d'un temps long pour l'époque concernée. La contrainte appliquée est donc forte, même si, comme nous l'avons vu, ces prisonniers bénéficiaient de conditions matérielles plus favorables que les autres. Elle se poursuivait à l'extérieur de la prison si le prisonnier était seulement élargi, car il restait prisonnier aux yeux de la justice. Mais les élargissements étaient beaucoup moins nombreux que les délivrances, signes que des arrangements pouvaient être pris avec le créancier, en audience ou hors audience. Ce mécanisme indique clairement que si la pauvreté a pu générer des dettes, ceux qui sont incarcérés restent quand même insérés dans le tissu social. Ce ne sont pas des exclus. La contrainte par corps s'adresse à des populations ordinaires que le roi et ses officiers maintiennent en sujétion en se faisant les défenseurs de la propriété et des biens qui sont dans le royaume. Restent ceux qui ne peuvent plus payer : l'emprisonnement pour dette est un moyen de les dénoncer et de définitivement les exclure.

Au moment où se met en place cette coercition dans le domaine civil, se développe son pendant dans le cadre de la justice retenue, la lettre de répit, selon un procédé qui est maintenant bien connu pour la justice criminelle. La justification est la même : la grâce du roi, toute puissante, est fondée sur la miséricorde que le souverain hérite de Dieu. Le vocabulaire de la grâce et du don, étroitement mêlés, se répand dans les deux types d'actes, sous la forme de l'expression « grace especial ». Il est possible, comme le montre Julie Mayade-Claustre, que le développement de la lettre de répit ait des relations étroites avec l'explosion populaire de Paris, en 1306, quand le petit peuple endetté se révolte contre la revalorisation de la monnaie, donc avec la pauvreté réelle[39]. D'autres témoignages en font foi. Cet homme en procès au Parlement à propos de sa dette dit « qu'il est povres homs et pieca se trahi devers le roy et obtint lectres de respit de non payer ses debtes jusques a un an »[40].

---

[38] *Ibid.*, 431.
[39] *Ibid.*, 621.
[40] *Ibid.*, 665, note 1938.

Certes, répit et rémission libèrent le sujet des poids qui l'oppressent : dette ou crime. Cela ne peut être nié. Mais l'octroi de la grâce ne relève pas seulement de la pauvreté réelle. Elle développe une pauvreté volontaire qui, dans le dialogue qui s'engage avec la Chancellerie, fait du bénéficiaire un assujetti. En effet, la lettre de répit comme la lettre de rémission apparaissent à peu près en même temps, au début du XIVe siècle ; l'une et l'autre ne peuvent être obtenues qu'à l'issue d'une requête qui, en principe, est examinée par le souverain et, de toute façon, les lettres de chancellerie reprennent le récit contenu dans les requêtes. L'obtention de la grâce entre donc dans un système de demande qui est soumis à une rhétorique du dialogue fondée sur la condescendance du souverain, ce qui est une façon de magnifier son pouvoir à l'image de l'empereur romain et chrétien[41].

Le sujet n'obtient ces « dons royaux » qu'au terme d'une *operosa probatio* qui le transforme en pénitent, d'où le vocabulaire de la pauvreté qui réapparaît dans la déclinaison d'identité du requérant et accompagne son humilité, et cela dès le XIVe siècle pour la lettre de rémission, plus nettement au XVIe siècle pour la lettre de répit. Que le requérant soit matériellement pauvre ou non, il faut qu'il devienne fictivement pauvre pour obtenir le don royal. Il en est ainsi des individus comme des collectivités quand celles-ci supplient le roi pour obtenir un allègement d'impôt[42]. Les exemples abondent, en particulier dans les lettres de rémission et c'est la raison pour laquelle elles ne constituent pas une source sûre pour étudier la pauvreté réelle. Être « povre et miserable » ne signifie rien, si ce n'est que l'évocation de la pauvreté permet de plus facilement gracier. Les théoriciens du politique font même de cette grâce un devoir, quand Christine de Pizan écrit dans le Livre du corps de policie, « liberalité se monstre a ceulx qui sont povres et souffreteux et qui ont mestier que on leur soit large et liberal »[43]. Au pauvre qui a fauté, répond la miséricorde du souverain. La grâce royale ne peut opérer la mutation du criminel en bon sujet que sur un terrain choisi pour sa fragilité, mais aussi et surtout pour son humilité. Le pauvre des lettres de grâce, rémission ou répit, s'apparente au pécheur.

---

41 Sur le pouvoir impérial dans l'Antiquité tardive, voir Peter Brown, *Pouvoir et persuasion dans l'Antiquité tardive : vers un Empire chrétien*, Paris, 1998.

42 Nombreux exemples dans Henri Denifle, *La désolation des églises, monastères et hôpitaux en France pendant la guerre de Cent ans*, 2 vol., Paris, 1897-1899, en particulier l'Enquête sur le diocèse de Cahors, t. 2, 821 et suiv.

43 Christine de Pizan, *Le livre du corps de policie*, éd. Robert H. Lucas, Genève-Paris, 1967, 44.

La justice du roi de France ne peut donc pas mentionner le mot « pauvre » de façon indifférente. Elle contribue à maintenir l'ambiguïté de ce qu'est le pauvre à la fin du Moyen Âge et elle peut l'excuser de crime en cas d'extrême nécessité, mais elle éclaircit aussi son statut, au moins de deux façons. D'une part, elle juge les pauvres de façon à exclure ceux qui sont considérés comme indésirables par les juges comme par la société dont le regard sur les pauvres a changé, et en ce sens elle contribue à séparer le bon pauvre du mauvais. Parmi les pauvres réputés « mauvais » sont de préférence choisis les condamnés à mort ou les condamnés aux peines infamantes, comme le sont les condamnés pour dette dont les biens sont saisis. D'autre part, en définissant pour les « bons » pauvres un moyen de réparer les infractions à la norme en se déclarant volontairement « pauvres », la justice du roi crée de nouveaux pauvres qui s'obligent à la servitude volontaire. Ainsi se construit une société politique où le don et le contre-don ne se limitent plus à l'entourage du roi, aux nobles ou aux clercs. Les partenaires – le roi et les débiteurs, le roi et les criminels- sont politiquement opposés : au puissant qui octroie la grâce est attribuée la majesté, à ceux qui reçoivent, la pauvreté. La pauvreté fait alors tache d'huile et se confond avec la sujétion.

En jouant sur la pauvreté, la justice a donc contribué à développer un pouvoir politique fondé aussi bien sur la coercition que sur la grâce, et à créer une société politique où fictivement tous les hommes sont « pauvres », donc assujettis. C'est le signe que, globalement, le statut des pauvres et leur image se sont considérablement aggravés.

Patricia Skinner

Gender and the Sign Languages of Poverty

Was medieval poverty gendered? At first sight the answer to this question might seem self-evidently, yes. It seems to be an unchanging phenomenon that women on average were and are more likely to fall into poverty, as defined by contemporaries, than men.[1] Judith Bennett has highlighted, for instance, the persistence of low pay accorded to women for the same work as men, with the rate holding remarkably steadily around the 70% level between the later Middle Ages, when such estimates are possible, and the modern day. Even in paid employment, women in the thirteenth century might not have been able to support themselves or their child/ren, according to Sharon Farmer. And this discrimination has continued: Barbara Nelson highlighted in the 1980s that women formed the majority of recipients of means-tested social welfare payments in the United States.[2] We shall return to women's poverty and responses to it later in this paper. However, our main focus here is to examine how the gender dynamics of poverty were expressed within the languages and ideologies of medieval Christian Europe, and how these compared, in some instances, with the attitudes prevalent in Jewish communities of the Mediterranean. The comparison is not a perfect one, by any means, but may point to future lines of research.

---

[1] I adduced some of the relevant early medieval evidence in my article 'Gender and poverty in the medieval community', in *Medieval Women in their Communities*, ed. Diane Watt (Cardiff, 1997), 204-221.

[2] Judith Bennett, 'Less money than a man would take', in *ead.*, *History, Patriarchy and the Challenge of Feminism* (University of Pennsylvania Press/Manchester University Press), forthcoming (I thank Judith for sharing the manuscript of her book with me prior to publication); Sharon Farmer, *Surviving Poverty in Medieval Paris* (Ithaca, 2002), 164; Barbara Nelson, 'Women's Poverty and Women's Citizenship: Some Political Consequences of Economic Marginality', *Signs: Journal of Women in Culture and Society* 10.2 (1984), 209-231.

In the space allowed, it is clearly impossible to provide a complete overview of the ways in which gender and poverty intersect; indeed, much empirical work remains to be done in order to provide illustrative examples. But it is important to recognise that the application of gender theory to the problem of poverty is particularly useful to historians because, although the term 'gender', as understood by women's and feminist historians, is traditionally used as a shorthand for the differences in status or roles of men and women, its roots in social history in fact demand that it also be used to analyse the structures of power, of which a male/female hierarchy is only a part. Poverty is gendered because the poor are, almost without exception, a powerless group and the categories thought of as poor and/or weak in medieval society correspond closely with the categories of medieval individual whom gender historians are most likely to be found studying.[3] The corollary to this, however, is that the groups of most interest to gender historians are those least likely to have left traces in the written and archaeological record (as David Austin points out, in the case of the latter). The poor, if they are recorded at all in the written record, are 'contained' within written texts generated by the medieval elite, be they sermons, records of charitable giving, lists of taxpayers (where the poorest in Paris, for example, were termed *les menus* – the least). Hence the historiography of medieval poverty has tended to focus on institutional responses, through hospitals, for example, or legislation which sought to control the 'problem' of the poor.[4] Each of these defined their version of the poor in different ways. Gender history, engaging as it does with the poststructural argument that language constitutes social reality, demands that we try to reach beyond institutional definitions of the 'poor' in medieval society, and seek to reconstruct something of the subjective and everyday lives of those individuals who fell into this all-encompassing category. In this paper I shall explore to what extent the dominant religious discourses of the Middle Ages made any distinctions between male and female poverty, and what, if any, the distinguishing signs were.

---

[3] It is regrettable, however, that the recent, otherwise excellent book of essays on early medieval gender focuses on the gender identities of the elite: Leslie Brubaker and Julia H. M. Smith, ed., *Gender in the Early Medieval World* (Cambridge, 2004).

[4] See for example, Miri Rubin, *Charity and Community in Medieval Cambridge* (Cambridge, 1987), John Henderson, *Piety and Charity in Later Medieval Florence* (Oxford, 1994) and Sheila Sweetinburgh, *The Role of the Hospital in Medieval England: gift-giving and the spiritual economy* (Dublin, 2004).

Who fell into the category of 'poor'? Other contributors to this round table have identified a real problem in even determining what 'poverty' meant to medieval people, with a continuum stretching from the destitute with no basic sustenance all the way to a perceived loss of status in comparison with one's normal social position, which might have been comfortably off. To put it another way, the 'poverty line' was a moveable one. Bronislaw Geremek's classic study of late medieval Paris appears to include only those for whom begging was a means of subsistence as the true poor.[5] However, even the term 'beggar' was fluid: it was used, in the documents discarded by the medieval Jewish community of Old Cairo, not for the mendicant poor but to describe smaller merchants, artisans and craftsmen.[6] This ambiguity is a product of our sources, for economic deprivation, it seems, was only a part of the equation which made someone 'poor'. If we briefly review the biblical models underpinning the medieval discourse on poverty, we find the poor as one of four groups defined in the Old Testament as needing justice and special compassion: the others were widows, orphans and the sojourner (a foreigner living in Israel). In the agrarian society of the ancient Near East, the lack of an adult male was understood as an involuntary accident of life which deprived the family of its major bread-winner in the sense of cultivator of the land.[7] It was thus contingent, and could be temporary: widows might remarry and/or find husbands for their orphaned daughters, orphan boys would grow into adult males themselves. And their poverty was relative: it did not have to mean total destitution, just a loss of former social

---

5 Bronislaw Geremek, *The Margins of Society in Late Medieval Paris* (Cambridge, 1987), 193.

6 Shelomo Dov Goitein, *A Mediterranean Society*, vol. 1 (Berkeley, 1967), 79. This expression is only one example of the rather different social perspectives of the Jewish community revealed by this invaluable source – even paid employment, rather than autonomous entrepreneurship, was seen as degrading: *ibid.*, 92-99.

7 Donald E. Gowan, 'Wealth and Poverty in the Old Testament: the Case of the Widow, the Orphan and the Sojourner', *Interpretation* 41.4 (October 1987), 341-353, at 343. It is notable that the Jewish community of Old Fustat in Egypt continued to help these categories of people, as medieval alms lists from the genizah or document store there reveal: besides widows and orphans, the most numerous group was poor foreigners: Goitein, *A Mediterranean Society* (*op. cit. supra*, n. 6), vol. 1, 56. The strong sense of public philanthropy among the Jewish community, it seems, encouraged people to travel in search of help, *ibid.*, 57.

status and power.[8] Katharina Simon-Muscheid's contribution to this round table demonstrates clearly that the discourse of loss and lack of status continued into the Middle Ages. The theme of powerlessness is continued in New Testament sources. Bruce Malina's study of this subject reveals an opposition between the greedy rich and the powerless poor but, as he states, these are not exact opposites.[9] Poverty is again not wholly about economic lack. The four groups outlined in Old Testament sources are joined by numerous physically disabled persons who, similarly, were unable to work and might suffer from injustices. For all of these groups the necessity was not to become rich - indeed, extreme wealth was viewed as negatively as extreme poverty - but simply to receive help from those who were in a position to give it. As developed by the Church Fathers and Jewish legal sources, the economic duty of giving of alms to such needy groups would lead to divine reward. As the Talmud put it 'he who gives alms to the poor beholds the countenance of God',[10] whilst canonists of the twelfth and thirteenth century devoted much attention to the problem of what to do with superfluous property, and what right the poor had to receive alms.[11] It is possible, therefore, to see a subtle shift towards the definition of poverty as economic lack in the promotion of such charitable activity, on which the self-identity of the medieval church is held to have been based.[12] This may of course be due to the fact that a material contribution to temporarily alleviate the problem was much easier than addressing the underlying causes of poverty: the inevitable presence of the poor in society seems not to have been challenged.[13] Indeed,

[8] Michel Mollat, *The Poor in the Middle Ages: An Essay in Social History*, tr. A. Goldhammer (New Haven and London, 1986) [orig. French edition Paris, 1978], 6, usefully discusses this loss of status.

[9] Bruce Malina, 'Wealth and Poverty in the New Testament and Its World', *Interpretation* 41.4 (October 1987), 354-367, at 355. A similar opposition is seen in tenth-century Byzantine legislation: Rosemary Morris, 'The Powerful and the Poor in Tenth-Century Byzantium: Law and Reality', *Past and Present* 73 (1976), 3-27.

[10] Church Fathers: Rebecca H. Weaver, 'Wealth and Poverty in the Early Church', *Interpretation* 41.4 (October 1987), 368-381; Jewish law: Shelomo Dov Goitein, 'The Mediterranean Mind in the High Middle Ages (950-1250) as Reflected in the Cairo Geniza Documents', in *Amalfi nel Medioevo: Convegno Internazionale 14-16 giugno 1973* (Salerno, 1977), 177-192, quote at 189.

[11] Brian Tierney, *Medieval Poor Law: a Sketch of Canonical Theory and Its Application in England* (Berkeley, 1959), 37.

[12] Weaver, 'Wealth and Poverty' (*op. cit. supra*, n. 10), 381.

[13] It is a social issue which has of course challenged successive generations of thinkers. For example, Richard Teichgraeber, 'Hegel on Property and Poverty', *Journal of the History*

their visibility reminded those who were well-off to give alms, and thereby earn a spiritual reward.

But the issue was not simply one of access to economic resources. Regardless of the place or period, all studies agree that almost more debilitating for the poor was and is the 'enormous scorn for their public dependency',[14] or the loss of status, whether temporary or permanent, which accompanied poverty.[15] Poverty could therefore mean a loss of power relative to one's normal social status, and it was not inevitable for all people. St Basil of Caesarea, preaching in response to a famine which hit Cappadocia in Asia Minor in the 360s, castigated the congregation at a penitential service for walking past the starving poor (*penetes*) rather than opening up their hoarded stores of food.[16] The theme of the well-off refusing to aid the poor is a common one, and Basil's words are echoed by Peter of Blois in 1194 when he took bishop Raoul of Lisieux to task for speculating on grain prices rather than distributing his stores to the poor.[17] Both sources highlight again the temporary, and *unnecessary* nature of the poverty afflicting the area. If those who had food shared it, they imply, the poor would not starve. We should note in passing that neither writer makes any distinction between male and female suffering.

This lack of distinction recurs in modern treatments of medieval poverty. As Sharon Farmer has recently acutely observed, 'our understanding of the medieval poor is incomplete in part because modern medievalists have failed to address the multiplicity of medieval gender categories ...'[18] Certainly it

---

of Ideas 38 (1977), 47-64, explores how Hegel dealt, inconclusively, with the political implications of the permanent presence of the poor in society, reducing the issue to the individual's personal responsibility and refusing to allow that the state should intervene. Robert Fatton Jnr., 'Hegel and the riddle of poverty: the limits of bourgeois political economy', *History of Political Economy* 18 (1986), 579-600, reaches similar conclusions, suggesting, p. 580, that Hegel resigned himself to the inevitability of a 'penurious rabble'.

14 Nelson, 'Women's Poverty' (*op. cit. supra*, n. 2) , 221.

15 Gowan, 'Wealth and Poverty' (*op. cit. supra*, n. 7), 352. The shame caused by poverty is summed up by a bequest of the Jew Jacob Boniac in 1398 to the 'abashed poor': Robert .I. Burns, *Jews in the Notarial Culture: Latinate Wills in Mediterranean Spain* (Berkeley, 1996), 121.

16 Susan R. Holman, 'The Hungry Body: Famine, Poverty and Identity in Basils' *Hom.* 8', *Journal of Early Christian Studies* 7.3 (1999), 337-363, at 343. Geremek, *Margins of Society* (*op. cit. supra*, n. 5), 202, also notes the use of children by beggars to excite the pity of passers-by.

17 Quoted in Michel Mollat, *Poor in the Middle Ages* (*op. cit. supra*, n. 8), 108.

18 Farmer, *Surviving Poverty* (*op. cit. supra*, n. 2), 1-2.

was not an analytical tool used in (or available to) earlier studies: Geremek's work on Paris, for example, uses such categories only when his sources made the distinction between the 'true' and 'false' poor, the former including the crippled, sick, old, widows and orphans, that is, those for whom work was impossible and who thus had the right to seek assistance.[19] Such categories had a long history. But there is an inherent tension between the discourses of the Church, which explicitly labelled those likely to need help as 'miserable persons', and the subjective, personalised and thus differentiated histories of poor people, which scholars such as Farmer are now attempting to reconstruct.[20] For certain women and their children the route out of poverty rested upon their lack of social status in comparison to adult males. They were recognised in both Christian and non-Christian cultures as requiring special care, especially in the cases of widows and orphans. Poor through no fault of their own, they were deemed worthy of help since they did not have the means to help themselves.

Remaining unmarried, too, could be a sign of poverty in a society which expected brides to come with dowry payments. Assistance was manifested in a gendered way in the frequent charitable bequests found in medieval wills: the provision of dowries for poor girls. Such bequests were common in Christian wills, particularly after the inflation of dowries from the twelfth century onwards,[21] and are found also in the Latinate Jewish wills of medieval Spain studied by Robert Burns, which acknowledge explicitly the vulnerability of women remaining single. The example he cites, the 1286 will of Sara, the widow of Davi, resident in Perpignan, provides not only dowries for Jewish poor girls, but in fact leaves almost her entire estate for the education of poor Jewish children. It is unclear whether 'children' should be read as 'boys' in this instance, but highly likely.[22] Women's fortunes, therefore, rested upon marriage, and they received support to achieve this goal. The idea was a powerful one, based on an assumption of women's primary

---

[19] Geremek, *Margins of Society* (*op. cit. supra*, n. 5), 169.

[20] On gender's welding of the 'subjective and personal' onto history, see Penelope J. Corfield, 'History and the Challenge of Gender History', *Rethinking History* 1.3 (1997), 241-258, at 244.

[21] See the discussion by David Herlihy and Christiane Klapisch-Zuber, *Tuscans and their Families* (New Haven and London, 1985), 224-226.

[22] Robert I. Burns, *Jews in the Notarial Culture* (*op. cit. supra*, n. 15), 87-89. In another example cited by Burns, 111, the Jewish widow Reina, of Valls in Catalonia, similarly left 500 *solidi* to marry off Jewish girls.

role as mothers, and it would persist into modern welfare legislation.[23] Yet even such explicit bequests in wills may not bring us to the realities of poverty as experienced in the Middle Ages. The provision of a dowry was part and parcel of a public ritual, signifying the marriage and the union of two families, but did its importance diminish further down the social scale? Does the term 'poor girl' in wills represent a truly destitute single woman? Or is it in fact coded language for a girl of similar or slightly lower social status to the testator, whose reputation or that of her family were threatened by temporary or permanent financial difficulty? Or are such bequests in fact a product of their age, when the flourishing urban society of twelfth-century and later medieval Europe had thrown up the phenomenon of more young girls migrating away from their families to seek work as domestic servants? If so, the bequests might be read as much as a moral judgement as a charitable impulse.

But not all single women, widows and orphans were poor; poverty was not confined to these groups and disabled, non-working men. An approach to poverty taking gender as its main category of analysis exposes the inadequacy of formal lines of charity to help, for example, working men with large families or single women with children.[24] The contention that patriarchy is as much a issue between higher and lower status men (Robert Connell's concept of 'hegemonic masculinity' has been influential here)[25] has been influential in moving gender history away from a focus simply on women's issues. The application of gender theory to the history of poverty, whilst perhaps creating a low-key epistemological shift in the way the latter is studied, also exposes the multiplicity of interpretations within gender theory itself.[26] For some feminist historians, the realisation that poverty and powerlessness were *not* women-centred issues may be troubling, undermining the theory of patriarchy as the dominance of men over women's produc-

---

23 A parallel here is the Mothers' Aid pension, developed in 1911 after the 1909 White House conference on dependent children found that 'children of parents of worthy characters, suffering from temporary misfortune, and children of reasonably efficient and deserving mothers who are without the support of the normal breadwinner should, as a rule, be kept with their parents, such aid being given as may be necessary...' Quoted in Nelson, 'Women's Poverty', (*op. cit. supra*, n. 2), 229.

24 Farmer, *Surviving Poverty* (*op. cit. supra*, n. 2), 63 and 164 respectively.

25 Robert W. Connell, *Masculinities* (Cambridge, 1995).

26 Corfield, 'History and the Challenge of Gender History' (*op. cit. supra*, n. 20), 254, argues that pluralist inclusivity is the hallmark of current gender history.

tive and reproductive lives.[27] After all, the formula found most often in medieval documents was 'widows, orphans *and* the poor', that is, a more subtle analysis of the Church's language regarding the poor also offers support for a more inclusive study of the history of poverty which incorporates men's as well as women's experiences. A major difference, already highlighted, was the expectation, at least by the later Middle Ages, that men should work to feed themselves and/or their families, and that those who were able to and did not did not in turn deserve the generosity of others. This stipulation, which had been expressed by Augustine and was taken up again the 13th-century *Glossa Ordinaria*,[28] does not appear to have ever been applied to women (although the use of children to invoke the pity of passers-by surely suggests that female beggars might not necessarily attract help if seen alone).

This difference, and the example cited earlier of provision of dowries for poor girls, suggest that further work is needed to tease out the specifics signs of poverty as they relate to men and women. A fruitful line of enquiry may be that of dress. As a quite literally material sign of economic well-being, dress was the subject of some scrutiny in medieval society, and women's dress even more so. The Old Testament's description of the proud women of Jerusalem provided ample ammunition for those who inveighed against women's love of adornment,[29] and we are familiar with the notion of elite women's dress ostentatiously expressing the material wealth and status of their natal and marital families, if only through the numerous and repeated examples of sumptuary legislation attempting to curb such excess. But such legislation, ironically, points up the ambiguity of expensive dress - according to some regulations, it could equally mark out a prostitute.[30] And shabbiness

[27] See the discussion of the tension between women's and gender history in Laura Lee Downs, *Writing Gender History* (London, 2004), 73-74.

[28] Tierney, *Medieval Poor Law* (*op. cit. supra*, n. 11), 58. He notes increasingly harsh statements along these lines in later glosses.

[29] Isaiah 3.16-24 narrates how the Lord would punish women through shaving their heads, removing the jewellery around their heads (including nose rings), necks, fingers and ankles, and depriving them of their fine veils, robes, gowns, cloaks, purses, revealing garments and long veils on their heads. But crucially, the passage ends with the ultimate punishment, deprivation of their menfolk, at which point the women plead (4.1) that they are capable of feeding and clothing themselves but cannot endure the shame of remaining unmarried.

[30] On sumptuary laws, Catherine Kovesi Killerby, *Sumptuary Law in Italy, 1200-1500* (Oxford, 2002). For the fine line between the richly-dressed woman and the prostitute, see Ruth Mazo Karras, '"Because the other is a poor woman she shall be called his wench":

of dress is even more tricky to interpret. Secondhand clothing was a thriving business in medieval Europe, and many women in fact made their living from this trade,[31] so the possession of old clothes did not necessarily indicate poverty as such.[32] When in 1398 the Jew Jacob Boniac of Puigcerda in the Pyrenees left 'all my clothing to my poor relations',[33] his impulse may have been, literally, to keep up family appearances, rather than indicating desperate need on the part of the recipients. Women, too (and more frequently), took care to pass on items of dress in their wills:[34] does this indicate a heightened consciousness on their part of the symbolic power of clothing to indicate social status or, at the least, respectability? It is difficult to judge in transactions between adults, but certainly the language of widows' documents from southern Italy emphasises the need to clothe and put shoes on their children.

This brings us full circle to the incontrovertible fact that poverty among medieval women is most visible among widowed mothers, for they had the backing of the church as an institution in demanding assistance, and therefore some vestige of their voices is preserved.[35] But how do we identify the

---

Gender, Sexuality and Social Status in Late Medieval England', in *Gender and Difference in the Middle Ages*, ed. Sharon Farmer and Carol Braun Pasternak (Minneapolis, 2003), 210-229, at 213-214; see also James Brundage, 'Sumptuary Laws and Prostitution in Late Medieval Italy', *Journal of Medieval History* 13 (1987), 343-355. The extremes to which regulation of dress could go is shown by the detailed regulations of Amedeus VIII of Savoy in 1430, discussed in Françoise Piponnier and Perrine Mane, *Dress in the Middle Ages* (New Haven and London, 1997), 83-86.

[31] David Herlihy, *Opera Muliebra: Women and Work in Medieval Europe* (New York and London, 1990), cites examples of female old-clothes-dealers in late medieval Toulouse (p. 95), Paris (p. 146) and Bologna (p. 155).

[32] An interesting but altogether exceptional example of the differing significance of old and tattered clothing is given by Liutprand of Cremona, ambassador for the German Emperor Otto I to the Byzantine court in the late tenth century, who (deliberately or otherwise) misinterprets the revered but ancient garments used the imperial procession he witnessed: Liudprand of Cremona, *The Embassy to Constantinople*, chapter 9, in *The Embassy to Constantinople and Other Writings*, tr. F. A. Wright, ed. John Julius Norwich (London, 1993), 181.

[33] Burns, *Jews in the Notarial Culture* (*op. cit. supra*, n. 15), 121.

[34] E.g. the wills of the Anglo-Saxon woman Wulfwaru: *English Historical Documents* I, ed. Dorothy Whitelock (Oxford, 1954), 524, and that of Bellenda of Genoa: Steven Epstein, *Wills and Wealth in Medieval Genoa, 1150-1250* (Cambridge, Mass. and London, 1984), 125-6.

[35] See, from a later period, the cases studied by Pamela Sharpe, 'Survival Strategies and Stories: Poor Widows and Widowers in Early Industrial England', in *Widowhood in Me-*

truly poor among them? In an earlier paper I identified the surrender of their own children as an extreme measure.[36] In the Latin examples from southern Italy, however, beyond an assurance that the children would be cared for and receive some material benefit at the end of a fixed term, implying a period of service to those receiving them, there is no overt indication of extreme poverty. But the documents of the Jewish community in Old Cairo seem to be far more explicit: here we see children being pledged in return for services or loans by a widow and a blind woman (whom it may be suggested was also widowed) in al-Mahdiyya (Tunisia) and Fustat respectively. Taken together with Goitein's assertion that child labour is rarely mentioned in the genizah documents and may have been obviated by the Jewish community's concern for education, the mortgages of children by women must, I think, be a reliable sign of poverty in these cases.[37]

What is striking, but to be treated with some caution, is that explicit expressions of women's poverty are almost always made by widows, fulfilling the expectation raised by the church's ideology that this was indeed a vulnerable group. Widowhood as a status has received much recent attention from medieval historians, emphasising it both as a time of vulnerability and loss of male protection, but also, sometimes, as a period of emancipation from male control in terms of property management.[38] Regional and cultural variations, however, serve to challenge the idea that widows shared common experiences.[39] Michel Mollat's helpful distinction between the *conjunctural*

---

dieval and Early Modern Europe, ed. Sandra Cavallo and Lyndan Warner (London, 1999), 220-239.

[36] Skinner, 'Gender and Poverty' (*op. cit. supra*, n. 1), 211.

[37] Goitein, *Mediterranean Society* (*op. cit. supra*, n. 6), vol. 1, 259 (mortgages) and 98 (child labour).

[38] Cavallo and Warner, ed., *Widowhood* (*op. cit. supra*, n. 35); Louise Mirrer, ed., *Upon My Husband's Death: Widows in the Literature and Histories of Medieval Europe* (Ann Arbor, 1992); Emmanuelle Santinelli, *Des femmes eplorées? Les veuves dans la société aristocratique du haut moyen age* (Lille, 2003); Robert A. Wood, 'Poor Widows, c. 1393-1415', in *Medieval London Widows, 1300-1500*, ed. Caroline Barron and Anne Sutton (London, 1994), 55-69; Ariel Guiance, 'El costo social de la muerte: viudas y huérfanos en la Castilla medieval', *Historía (São Paulo)* 19 (2000), 37-53.

[39] For example, legal variations between regions might mean that widows enjoyed very different rights over their own and their husbands' property, as in the contrast between French and Flemish customs highlighted by David Nicholas, 'Of Poverty and Primacy: Demand, Liquidity and the Flemish Economic Miracle, 1050-1200', *American Historical Review* 96 (1991), 17-41, at 37. Jewish widows, too, might enjoy different

poverty of the temporarily distressed and the *structural* poverty of those who would never be able to ameliorate their circumstances enables us to reflect further on the fluid status of the medieval widow. He draws heavily on similar distinctions made by late antique commentators, even if the Greek terms used, *penes* and *ptochos*, seem to have been somewhat fluidly applied.[40] The poverty of widows falls within both categories: they were believed to be *structurally* vulnerable as lone women, regardless of their access to resources, and thus in need of protection by the Church or, by extension, medieval rulers responsible for the well-being of their subjects. This accords with a feminist perspective of the medieval Church as a paternalistic institution reinforcing the subjection of women to male-centred hierarchical codes organised around the centrality of marriage or paternal supervision, but at the same time presents a generic view of widows-as-a-group, undifferentiated by their actual economic circumstances.

But the *conjunctural* poverty of widows, the accident of life which drew them into the sphere of the Church's protection and might well be a temporary status, attracts the gender historian keen to reconstruct the subjective experience of those women. Failing remarriage or other familial support, the poor widow was accepted as a deserving case for charity. The wealthy widow, on the other hand, might come under conflicting pressures as to her remarriage, and seek the Church's protection through retirement to a contemplative life. Here we see the inadequacy of an economic definition of 'poor' – widows were counted among the weak whatever their economic circumstances. For the gender historian addressing poverty, however, this does not adequately reflect the *agency* of widows in addressing their situation: their discursive vulnerability was not always played out in reality. The case of the wealthy widow Juliana, refused a hearing in a church court on account of the fact that she was not poor, shows that there was some attempt to discern the technically 'wretched' (under which category her widowhood placed her) from the genuinely vulnerable.[41] In medieval southern Italy, there are a number of examples of widows *adopting* the discourse in order to

---

rights to their Christian neighbours: Cheryl Tallan, 'Medieval Jewish Widows: Their Control of Resources', *Jewish History* 5 (1991), 63-74.

40 Mollat, *Poor in the Middle Ages* (*op. cit. supra*, n. 8), 26; cf. Morris, 'Powerful and the Poor' (*op. cit. supra*, n. 9), 17 and Holman, 'Hungry Body' (*op. cit. supra*, n. 16), 342, n.20.

41 Pope Innocent IV also addressed this problem in his *Decretals* in c.1250: on this and Juliana see Tierney, *Medieval Poor Law* (*op. cit. supra*, n. 11), 17-18.

get around legal obstacles, arguing their poverty, or that of their children, to allow them to access resources which the law prevented them from managing alone.[42] These are not economically poor widows, clearly, but nor do they conform to the stereotype of women seeking male protection: the implication of their actions is that, given permission to liquidate land to raise money, they will maintain their own and their children's independence. And the Church's focus on widows also conceals the lack of provision made for other vulnerable groups, such as lone single women whose status, as we have already seen, was often ambiguous.[43]

I want now to move on to the case of orphans, again identified as a vulnerable group by both Jewish and Christian ideology, but also receiving considerable attention from gender historians as part of the wider revision of ideas about the experiences of medieval childhood.[44] A case study from southern Italy, in which the orphans are without both parents,[45] serves to underline the issues I have highlighted here about the fluid definition of 'poverty', and provides a corrective to the image of the Church as idealised protector. In 1181 in the small Italian town of Atrani on the Amalfitan peninsula, a certain John son of Manso and his wife Mosica acted on behalf of their grandsons Roger and Manso in returning a piece of property to the convent of St Laurence in nearby Amalfi. They acted, they say, because the two

---

42 Skinner, 'Gender and Poverty' (*op. cit. supra*, n. 1), 208-210.

43 See Ann Kettle, 'Prostitutes and Servant Girls in Later Medieval England', in *Matrons and Marginal Women in Medieval Society*, ed. Robert R. Edwards and Vickie Ziegler (Woodbridge, 1995), 19-32; the pressures incumbent on single girls in service are also discussed in Christiane Klapisch-Zuber, *Women, Family and Ritual in Renaissance Italy*, tr. Lydia Cochrane (Chicago, 1985), pp. 165-177.

44 See the discussion of Shulamith Shahar, *Childhood in the Middle Ages* (London, 1990), 155-161.

45 It should be noted that the term, deriving from the Greek for loss, was also often used to describe those without a father, but with a surviving mother. The most famous example is abbot Guibert of Nogent, who states that the death of his father 'made me an orphan' at the age of eight months: John F. Benton, *Self and Society in Medieval France: the Memoirs of Abbot Guibert of Nogent (1064?-1125)* (New York, 1970), 44. See also Dominique Gangler-Mundwiler, 'Enfants sans père: orphelins et écriture dans le roman cyclique français du Moyen Age', *Littérature, médecine, société* 8 (1986), 5-39 and Marie-Claude Struyf, 'Les orphelins de père dans l'oeuvre romanesque de Jean Renart', in *Les relations de parenté dans le monde médiéval: XIVe colloque du Centre universitaire d'Études de Recherches médiévales d'Aix* (Aix-en Provence, 1989), 273-285.

boys *non illa laborabant quia non potuebant quia sunt parvuli et pauperes.*[46] This document is a useful way to explore the practical experiences of medieval poverty, but as we shall see, it is highly conditioned by the discursive model of poverty outlined above. For a start, we can only surmise, but do not know for sure, that the two young children were being cared for by their grandparents. Secondly, although they had access to a piece of landed property and thus to economic support, their physical inability to work it led to it being relinquished and the boys being described as 'small and poor'. However, the circumstances leading up to the surrender reveal that the church's view had been ambivalent at best. For the convent had pursued the boys for their neglect of the land (*caluniastis ipsi predictis nepotibus nostris* [*sic*]); now, it agreed not to pursue them further. Whether it offered any further support to these poor children is not stated, but it is unlikely: the only benefit they were to receive from their grandparents' action was the cessation of litigation over the land. The ecclesiastical institution had finally accepted that they were, indeed, 'pauperes'. Their poverty was not their own fault, and yet the convent's acceptance of the remission of its land back into its hands was represented as a merciful act (the document states that it is an act of *misericordia*). Thus we see that even those who fell comfortably into the category of the vulnerable deserving of the church's support might in reality face difficulty in obtaining it. Furthermore, the economic requirements of the convent seem to have taken precedence here: there appears to have been no possibility of allowing the land to lay unproductively until the boys were of an age to cultivate it themselves, nor of the grandparents themselves taking it on (we do not, of course, have any idea about their physical capability, but they cannot have been older than their 40s).

We have no further documentation to find out what happened to these two boys next. What were the options for young orphans in medieval society? For the purposes of this paper I exclude at this point abandoned babies, although their existence is again surely an indirect piece of evidence about the desperate poverty of their mothers.[47] Were we to classify the fatherless children discussed above in this category, some kind of indentured or semi-free service in another household was an option, although the vulnerability of young girls in such a situation has been highlighted in more than one

---

46 *Il Codice Perris, Cartulario amalfitano sec. X – XV*, ed. Jole Mazzoleni and Renata Orefice, vol. 1 (Amalfi, 1985), 323-324, document no. 168.

47 John Boswell, *The Kindness of Strangers: the Abandonment of Cildren in Western Europe* (London, 1988).

study.[48] Children might also be given as oblates to the church, whether orphans or not, although there developed a significant debate over the religious vocation of these young people.[49] That the care of orphans was a meritorious act is expressed in the byname Parnas, visible in the Cairo genizah documents and denoting one who cares for both orphans and the poor.[50] But most frequently, surely, they were simply taken in by other family members. At this point there would be no need for them to appear in the written record except in the circumstances outlined at Atrani, when the church was recovering its property. Orphans, in any case, appear most frequently in the written record alongside their widowed mothers, rather than in the context outlined above.

In conclusion, this discussion has highlighted that the ecclesiastical categories of widow, orphan and the poor are simply a starting point in our understanding of the gender dynamics of poverty as experienced in the Middle Ages. They do, however, shape the type of evidence we are likely to meet about the experiences of the poor, since much documentation is concerned with the alleviation of distress, and thus conforms to the accepted ideologies of who should and should not receive help. A major contribution of gender analysis to the discussion of medieval poverty is the fact that the concept of the 'deserving poor', understood to be a later medieval phenomenon and based largely on legislative materials, should perhaps be interpreted as a way of distinguishing among mostly men, whose physical fitness was the subject of scrutiny. Women, it could be argued, enjoyed a less exacting test of their circumstances, and mothers of children even more so. But their access to charity was predicated on external judgements as to their moral state: a never-married mother received little sympathy, and perhaps this explains why we find mothers forced to give up their children from economic necessity. Thus the ideology of charity limited the groups who had a right to receive assistance: we might wish to look *outside* these categories to find the truly impoverished. And even those who technically fulfilled the criteria of 'miserable persons' might not always receive help, as the unhelpful treatment of the orphans of Atrani illustrates.

To return to my opening question – was poverty gendered? Yes, but we need to acknowledge that the problem extends beyond male-female di-

---

[48] See above, note 43.

[49] Mayke de Jong, *In Samuel's Image: Child Oblation in the Early Medieval West* (Leiden, 1995).

[50] Goitein, *Mediterranean Society* (*op. cit. supra*, n. 6), vol. 1, 145.

chotomies, and delve deeper than the prescriptive language of much ecclesiastical writing to unpick the groups defined therein and to identify others suffering poverty whom the Church did not recognise. In particular, it has proven instructive to compare the respective measures of Christian and Jewish communities in the face of poverty: the vulnerable groups identified by each share common roots, but there are interesting differences in the responses to poverty and the languages used to describe it. More cross-cultural work may serve to reveal further divergences;[51] clearly, however, our attempts to document 'the poor', as a first stage in reconstructing their lives, must avoid the tendency to universalise that experience. Rather than an undifferentiated group, 'poor' men, women and children might belong to a wide variety of categories, and manifest different signs of their distress.

[51] Ephraim Shoham Steiner's paper at this round table has revealed the important evidence that disability in the Jewish community did not necessarily lead to impoverishment. Does this mean that the physically disabled Jewish man could maintain his status, perhaps through scholarly achievement, in contrast to his Christian contemporary, for whom physical incapacity threatened a status rested on either military capability or fitness to till the land? Such a distinction would have important implications for our understanding of the categories of medieval masculinity.

EPHRAIM SHOHAM-STEINER

Poverty and Disability: A Medieval Jewish Perspective*

In 1760 Rabbi Naphtali Hirsch Gössler wrote to his son in Halberstadt from his fund raising "road trip" to Amsterdam. The letter has many insightful and somewhat sarcastic remarks; in one of them Rabbi Naphtali Hirsch relates to the priorities in almsgiving common among wealthy Spanish-Portuguese Jews of the mid eighteenth-century Amsterdam Jewish community:

> The Portuguese Jews here are very wealthy and they are also very generous when it comes to matters of charity and alms giving. However they prefer supporting the lame the sick and the blind rather then supporting poor scholars of the Torah. It appears that like the Jews in Poland they are well aware of the fact that there are greater chances they might become lame, sick or blind than of becoming scholars of Torah.[1]

Rabbi Gössler was what we, in modern day English, referred to as a professional or semi-professional fundraiser. In Yiddish, the medieval and early modern German dialect common among Jews and spoken to date by some Ultra Orthodox communities, these fund raisers are still referred to as "Schnorrers". As such, Rabbi Gössler had enough experience in his own background to easily compare two relatively large Jewish communities in two rather distant parts of Europe from two very different backgrounds. His cynical remark rings true for it contains some fundamental truths regarding issues of poverty, charity, the social language of poverty, and the connection between poverty and physical disability. Although Rabbi Gösslar wrote in the eighteenth century these truths reach back into the Middle Ages.

* This research was made possible by funds from the Blechner and Friends Career Development Chair in East European Jewish Culture in the Department of Jewish History at Ben-Gurion University of the Negev – Be'er Shevah.

1 Jacob Rader Marcus, *Communal Sick Care in the German Ghetto* (Cincinnati, 1947), 15.

By the eighteenth century, and especially in a large, prosperous and well established community such as Amsterdam, Rabbi Gösslar was not alone in his attempt to raise charity for his cause. Furthermore, by the eighteenth century the charitable foundations for the sick and the needy, as well as other "non-profit organizations" such as the *Chevrah Kaddisha* (a term literally meaning the "holy society" referring to the undertakers charitable organization) were well established and many prominent and affluent community members were involved in them as trustees.[2] This of course did not altogether cause the disappearance of "regular" sick, needy and disabled beggars wandering the streets. Handicapped beggars were still a very common sight in synagogues and by the households of the wealthy and other members of the community, in constant search for both charity and shelter.[3] According to Rabbi Gösslar, this phenomenon was common in both Amsterdam and Poland. Poverty, charity and disability are interwoven and almost inseparable. A handicapped individual was, and in many cases still is, more likely to touch the "purse opening mechanism" of most human beings because of either empathy, pity, compassion or for exactly the opposite reasons, trying to fend the beggars off by giving them a petty donation so that they will trouble one no more.

In his fundamental study on Poverty and the Poor in the Middle Ages, Michel Mollat has already shown the high correlation between poverty and

---

[2] One of my teachers, Yosef Kaplan of the Hebrew University in Jerusalem, has dedicated a life time of research and writing to the social aspects of the early modern, predominantly Spanish-Portuguese (*Sepharadi*), Jewish community in Amsterdam, its social stratification and its institutions. I want to cite two of his chief works in this field: Y.Kaplan, *From Christianity to Judaism: The Life of Isaac Orobio de Castro*, tr. R. Loewe (Oxford, 1989); *idem, An alternative Path to Modernity: The Sephardi Diaspora in Western Europe* (Leiden, 2000). On the relationship between Jews of Sephardi decent and their eastern European co-religionists in Amsterdam see *idem*, 'The Portuguese Community in 17th-Century Amsterdam and the Ashkenazi World', *Dutch Jewish History* 2 (1989), 23-45; *idem*, 'Amsterdam and Ashkenazic Migration in the Seventeenth Century, *Studia Rosenthaliana* 23 (1989), 22-44. *idem*, The self-definition of the Sephardic Jews of Western Europe and Their Relation to the Alien and the Stranger', in *Crisis and Creativity in the Sephardic World 1391-1648*, ed. Benjamin R. Gampel (NewYork, 1997), 121-145.

[3] On this issue see Elliott Horowitz, 'Charity, the Poor and Social Control in European Jewish Communities between the Middle Ages and the Early Modern Period,' in *Religion and Economy – Connections and Interactions*, ed. Menahem Ben-Sasson (Jerusalem, 1995), 209-232 (Hebrew). On similar Jewish organizations in other parts of Europe see: Bracha A. Rivlin, *Mutual Responsibility in the Italian Ghetto 1516-1789* (Jerusalem, 1991) (Hebrew).

physical disability. Mollat argued that this connection is multi-faceted. Among those people who earned their livelihood from manual labor or craftsmanship a physical impairment often led to an inability to earn an income.[4]

In many cases even men and women who were once able bodied and earning were driven to poverty due to physical misfortunes that caused them to stop being part of the work force and thus stop earning their livelihood. Mollat further argued that being needy and poverty stricken had a tremendous effect on one's diet and as a result on the ability to recover from disease. Long lasting diseases, poorly treated bone fractures, sores, ulcers and other illnesses, even if not debilitating in themselves, often culminated in permanent physical impairment, and reduced those suffering from them to a state of permanent physical disability. This made the chance of a change for the better scant.

For obvious reasons, the poor were also less immune to illness a priori; once down with a disease the prospects of a speedy recovery in poor living conditions were either low or altogether impossible. We should also bear in mind that the lives of beggars involved a constant struggle against the elements of nature. Itinerant beggars were a part of society that was constantly "on the move"; beggars took to the roads where they were literally "exposed" to the perils of wayfaring travelers with very little for comfort and shelter. We should also remember that in many medieval European societies the value of stability was considered very high and the image of the wayfaring beggar was therefore a problematic one.

The above, therefore, demonstrates Mollat's observation that poverty and disability were in many respects interchangeable. However most, if not all the sources that Mollat in his profound study made use of are almost solely medieval Christian sources. This statement is true for other scholars of medieval studies like Robert Jötte and Bronislav Geremek, who's studies have enriched our knowledge and understanding of the medieval poor and poverty.[5]

---

[4] Michel Mollat, *The Poor in the Middle Ages*, tr. A. Goldhammer (New Haven and London, 1986), 4-12.

[5] Bronislav Geremek, *The Margins of Society in Late Medieval Paris*, tr. J. Birrell (Cambridge, 1987) *idem*, 'The Marginal Man', in *The Medieval World*, ed. Jacques L Goff, tr. L. G. Cochrane (London, 1990), 347-373; *idem*, *Poverty: A History*, tr. A. Kolakowska (Oxford, 1997); Robert Jütte, *Poverty and Deviance in Early Modern Europe* (Cambridge, 1994).

In this short article I wish to bring forth some of the evidence found in medieval Jewish writings, especially in Rabbinic sources that are often regrettably overlooked by medievalists. Language barriers, cultural and at times religious and political biases have prevented medievalists from delving into this relatively large corpus. I propose to look at this material regarding disability and its almost inseparable and very visible connection to poverty, and draw attention to the unique viewpoint these sources supply with regard to European Middle Ages – a viewpoint from the religious margins of 'mainstream society'.

It is at this point that I should voice some remarks of a methodological nature. First we must bear in mind that much of the data found in Rabbinic sources is of a different nature then the sources used by medievalist studying poverty and its institutional relief in the Middle Ages (or for that matter any other social issue). The sources in question are by the most part restricted to either the ethical genre or are of legal nature typical to the rabbinic literature of medieval Europe. This is true of both printed editions of the Jewish material as well as the data still in manuscript form.

The reason for this difference in genre between the Jewish and non-Jewish sources is closely associated with the nature of the medieval European Jewish experience. When we compare the Modern Jewish Studies scholarship about medieval poverty and poor relief to that of medieval studies on similar issues a striking difference emerges. While medievalists have, relatively speaking, many sources, scholars of Jewish Studies have very few sources, if any, from the European Middle Ages that can give a detailed picture of the establishment, upkeep and donations to charitable institutions. To illustrate this point I wish to give an example from medieval England.

In her study of hospitals and sick care in medieval England published almost a century ago, Rotha Mary Clay used a rather large number of medieval charters granted and lists of donations made to English hospitals.[6] In more recent studies on the same topic, Nicholas Orme and Margaret Webster have surveyed almost six hundred establishments, from as early as the eleventh century up until the mid-sixteenth century, using records of these establishments that have survived to date in both local regional and national archives. Orme and Webster's study addressed issues regarding the organiza-

[6] Even in an article of an overview nature like that written by Martha Carlin we find reference to a large number of sources of an archival nature; see M. Carlin, 'Medieval English Hospitals' in *The Hospital in History*, ed. Lindsay Granshaw and Roy Porter (London and New York, 1989), 21-40.

tion, administration, financing, and even evidence concerning the inhabitants and inmates of the institutions they had investigated.[7] Looking for similar material among the Jews of medieval European communities is an extremely frustrating task and it is not surprising that we can hardly find it. It is also not surprising that most of the works mentioned earlier in the footnotes regarding Jewish charitable organizations are based on sources not earlier than the sixteenth century. The reason for this is twofold, first of all size. Even the larger Jewish communities in medieval Europe didn't come close in size to their Christian contemporaries. Fewer people leave behind fewer evidence of a smaller number of institutions and a smaller number of documents reflecting these institutions activity. But there is also a second reason, related to the nature of Jewish existence as a persecuted minority in the Middle Ages. When Emily Taitz had surveyed the Jewish charitable establishments in northern France she wrote the following:

Hospitals were established both by the Church and the Jewish Community for the benefit of their own people exclusively. Lepers were provided with separate facilities. A large leprosarium for Christians was built just outside Troyes and was already in place in 1123 when Count Hughes left for the Holy Land. Although there is no record of a parallel facility for Jews in Troyes, it is not impossible that there was such a hospital since other towns had them.[8]

---

[7] Nicholas Orme and Margaret Webster, *The English Hospital, 1070-1570* (New Haven, 1995). In her study of hospitals and communal sick care in medieval Cambridge situating charitable activity within contexts of religious sentiment and social observation and experience Miri Rubin used similar archival sources to the ones used by Orme and Webster. See M. Rubin, *Charity and Community in Medieval Cambridge* (Cambridge, 1987).

[8] Emily Taitz, *The Jews of Medieval France: The Community of Champagne* (Westport Conn. and London, 1994), 125-126, n.44-46. We shouldn't be misled by the last sentence. The proof Taitz brings from hospitals in "other towns" refers to one piece of evidence from a non-Jewish source concerning a possible Jewish *leprosarium* in Provins in 1244. She begins with an account of the chronicler Geoffrey de Courlon relating that in 1146 the king of France "misled by his desire for money" conceded to the Jews the right to build a *leprosarium* in the area of Sens as well as synagogues and cemeteries; see Gustave Julliot (ed.), *Chronique de l'abbaye St. Pierre le-Vif de Sens par Geoffroy de Courlon* (Sens 1876), 476. By 1244 Taitz declares that documents indicate a Jewish *leprosarium* in Provins. On this establishment see also Heinrich Gross, *Gallia Judaica Dictionnaire géographique de la France d'après les sources rabbiniques (*with supplement by: Simon Schwartzfuchs) (Amsterdam, 1969), 493-495. It is also mentioned in Gilbert Dahan, 'Quartiers juifs et rues des juifs', in Bernhard Blumenkranz (ed.), *Art et archéologie des juifs en France medievale* (Toulose, 1980), 26, n. 81. Dahan quotes two sources, one re-

Even if we accept Taitz's assumption that such institutions existed, the troubles of persecution and expulsion led Jews in many instances to leave behind rather then to hold on to dossiers of documents regarding institutions that might have existed but from the time of expulsion will no longer survive in that format.

In light of these reservations we will have to deduce our conclusions with regard to poverty, its institutional relief and the relationship between poverty and disability from sources less common to this kind of research.

The second methodological remark aims at restricting the generalization mentioned earlier regarding the innate connection between poverty and disability. Many poor people suffered from disability, but not all disabled people were poor. The Jewish sources speak of disabled people who are not poverty stricken but rather either influential members of the community or even religious functionaries that continue to hold leading religious position although they are physically disabled. Several entries in medieval rabbinic writing describe disabled individuals who are clearly not poor but on the contrary, prominent members of society, affluent and economically well off.[9]

---

ferring to a *locus ubi Judei leprosi solent morari* and the other *locus ubi quondam fuisse dicebatur domus Judeorum leprosorum*. In his book on the French monarchy and the Jews, Bill Jordan refers to these establishments and states that they were evacuated in 1306 when Jews were expelled from France. William C Jordan, *The French Monarchy and the Jews From Philip August to the Last Capetians* (Philadelphia, 1989), 215 and n. 17, and 309, n. 94. This establishment was recently mentioned by François-Olivier Touati, 'Domus Judaeorum leprosorum: Une léproserie pour les juifs à Provins au Moyen Âge', in *Fondations et oeuvres charitables au Moyen âge. Congrès national des sociétés historiques et scientifiques (121e, Nice, 26–31 octobre 1996). Section d'histoire médiévale et philologie*, ed. Jean Dufour and Henri Platelle (Paris, 1999), 34-35. It seems that all the evidence points to probably one establishment whose own documentation dossier did not survive.

9 Up until the 13th century Jews were almost always members of the urban social component of society and were usually economically affiliated with trade, commerce, finances or in fewer cases craftsmanship. This enabled even those members of Jewish society who were disabled and couldn't perform manual labor to still earn a living. Furthermore, community employees, communal leaders, scholars and even those holding ritual positions could at times go on holding their respective vocations and socio-religious position even when they were for some reason handicapped. Thus we hear of a community who turned to Rabbi Meir of Rothenburg asking him if a cantor hold on to his position although his arms have "fallen off" (perhaps as a result of leprosy). R. Meir ruled unequivocally that not only can the cantor remain in his position but rather that his "broken heart" – a result of the handicap – is considered an advantage to his trade rather than an impairment for his vocation. The fullest version of this responsa is found in MS London (*Beit Hadin*) no. 14

To mention but one example, the famous late twelfth- and early thirteenth-century Rabbi Simcha of Speyer lost his eyesight in his older age. This did not seems to prevent him from continuing to serve as a revered sage and supra communal leader.

In an eye opening article written some years back, Elliot Horowitz pointed out that in the late thirteenth century and later on in the fourteenth and fifteenth centuries we hear of more and more attempts to regulate begging and to verify that those individuals seeking public support and communal alms are, in fact, who they claim to be: impoverished individuals.[10] This specific communal scrutiny intensified in the aftermath of the Black Death, when an overwhelming number of Jews (as their Christian neighbors in many parts of Western Europe) were left with very little means to support their families.[11] The attempts at regulation of begging date back to the early thirteenth century and probably correspond, as Horowitz points out, with the contemporary Christian custom of distributing tokens to known beggars as a means of identification and authorization.[12] It is as early as the late twelfth century or early thirteenth century that we hear Rabbi Yehudah "the Pious" of Regensburg (d. 1217) attacking, in his ethical work *Sefer Hassidi*m – "The Book of the Pious" those Jewish beggars who, in an attempt to win compassion and eventually charity funds, put on a feigned act of physical disability.[13] In a sharp and didactic manor Rabbi Yehuda suggests the fol-

---

(in the Adler list) fol. 156 col. D § 1066. This MS itself dates back to 1391, but the responsa collection in it is 90 years older. It was edited by Meir's brother Abraham following his famous brother's passing in 1293. I used a photograph of the original MS found at the *Institute for Hebrew Microfilmed Manuscripts at the Jewish National and University Library in Jerusalem* (film # 04685).

10 See note 3.

11 Yacov Guggenheim, 'Von den Schalantjuden zu den Betteljuden. Jüdische Armut in Mitteleuropa in der Frühen Neuzeit', in *Juden und Armut in Mittel und Osteuropa*, ed. Stefi Jersch-Wenzel, François Guesnet et. al. (Cologne, 2000), 55-69.

12 See Horowitz, 'Charity' (*op. cit. supra*, n. 3), 215, n. 12.

13 In the course of work I refer several times to The Book of the Pious (*Sefer Hassidim*). This extraordinary source of Jewish culture in the medieval Franco-German area survived in a few manuscripts. The largest is MS Parma Palatina Heb.3280. In 1891 this MS was copied and published in Berlin by J. Wistinezki. In 1924 a better edition based on Wistinezki's work was published in Frankfurt am Main. [In this article I refer to it as SHV. The second version of the Book of the Pious survived in an early print from Bologna (1538) based on this early printed edition R. Margaliyot published this version again in Jerusalem in 1957. In this article I refer to it as SHM.] Alfred Haverkamp, Peter Schäfer, and Israel Yuval are currently leading a team of researchers (Saskia Dönitz, Rami Reiner, René

lowing: "He who feigns lameness or blindness or any other disability should know that he will not leave this world until his assumed misfortune will turn into his life's reality."[14]

The literary roots of this remark, and the idea behind it, can be traced back to a Talmudic ethical ruling form the sixth century found in the Babylonian Talmud tractate Ketubot. However, Rabbi Yehudah the Pious probably wouldn't have mentioned it with such force and threatening manner among other rulings regarding charity unless it happened to be a pressing issue in his time.

Fear of deception was not the only matter in need of regulation. In another rather enigmatic entry in the same *Book of the Pious* we hear of Jews giving charity to non-Jews.[15] Jews, while naturally feeling more obligated to their brethren and fellow co-religionists, did however give charity to non-Jews who asked for it, if not for any other reason than to maintain a good and neighborly relationship with their immediate surroundings[16]. This practice is probably based on ethical rulings dating back to late antiquity, if not earlier, advising the readers to be charitable even to those non-Jewish beggars who menace the Jew with threats of supernatural nature and demonic retribution if they fail to give charity. By way of concluding this remark, the author mentions in passing that this is true "to madman as well". It appears to have been common among medieval European folk to give even symbolic charity to those deemed mad in order to appease the spirits that possessed them and divert them from attacking the giver.

Richtscheid and others) who are working on Sefer Hasidim. This project will eventually lead to a better edition and translation. It is called "Juden und Christen im 'Buch der Frommen' (Sefer Hasidim) – Edition, Übersetzung und Kommentierung ausgewählter Texte zur Geschichte der Juden und der jüdisch-christlichen Beziehungen im mittelalterlichen Deutschland."

14 SHM §125, reference to Babylonian Talmud (BT) Ketubot 68a.

15 SHV § 381.

16 To illustrate this point, let us look at one example: One of the ritual obligations of the Jewish festival of Purim is to give charitable donations to the poor. This ruling is based on a verse in the book of Ester (9:22). In a ruling attributed to the northern French Jewish sage Rabbi Shlomo Yizhaki, know better by his acronym RaSHI (1040-1105), he reprimands those Jews who give this obligatory charitable donation associated with the festival to their own non-Jewish household servants. By doing so, says RaSHI, they withhold potential charity from their needy Jewish brethren. The Hebrew phrasing of the ruling makes it quite clear that this practice was common among Jewish urban circles in this time period. Shlomo Buber and Yacov Freimann (ed.), *Sidur Rashi* (Berlin, 1912), §346 (Hebrew).

This casual remark catapults us to a whole other aspect of the link between poverty and disability: the bond between poverty, charity and what we would today refer to as mental disability, another aspect of the visual sign language of poverty.

Insane individuals in the European Middle Ages were roughly classified according to two distinct categories: the harmless and the raving mad[17]. The harmless, calm, though at times hilarious fools were left to wander about the public sphere in relative freedom, collecting alms and charity. Judith Nemann in her *Suggestion of the Devil* described this common medieval non-violent variety as "**barefoot and breadless beggars**"[18]. Recently, James Brodman in his book on *Charity and Welfare – Hospitals for the Poor in Medieval Catalonia* noted that:

> People whose behavior we would now characterize as disturbed were not differentiated from the run of beggars until the 14th century, when society began to sort the poor into various categories.[19]

In an *exemplum* from the aforementioned *Book of the Pious* we hear of a man who decided to feign madness while in captivity in order to conceal his Jewish identity.[20] The story describes him wandering the streets appearing

---

17 I mention but a few outstanding works: Traugott Konstantin Oesterreich, *Possession, Demoniacal and Other: Among Primitive Races, in Antiquity, the Middle Ages, and Modern Times*, tr. D. Ibberson (New York, 1930); George Rosen, *Madness and Society: Chapters in the Historical Sociology of Mental Illness* (Chicago, 1968); Judith S. Neaman, *Suggestion of the Devil: The Origins of Madness* (New York, 1975); Bernard Chaput, 'La Condition Juridique et Sociale de l'aliéné mental', in *Aspectes de la Marginalité au Moyen Age*, ed. Guy H. Allard (Montréal, 1975), 39-47; Penelope B. R. Doob, *Nebuchadnezzar's Children: Conventions of Madness in Middle English Literature* (New-Haven, 1974); M. Laharie, *La folie au Moyen Age: XIe-XIIIe siècles* (Paris, 1991) and, more recently, Barbara Newman, 'Possessed by the Spirit: Devout Women, Demoniacs and the Apostolic Life in the Thirteenth Century,' *Speculum* 73 (1998), 733-770. See also Catherine J. Kudlick, 'Disability History: Why We Need Another Other', *American Historical Review* 108 (2003), 763-793, esp. n. 4. On madness and madmen in medieval Islam see Michael W. Dols, *Majnun: The Madman in Medieval Islamic Society*, ed. Diana E. Immisch (Oxford, 1992); Boaz Shoshan, 'The State and Madness in Medieval Islam', *International Journal of Middle East Studies* 35 (2003), 329-340.

18 Neaman, *Suggestion of the Devil* (*op. cit. supra*, n. 17), chapter 2.

19 James William Brodman, *Charity and Welfare: Hospitals for the Poor in Medieval Catalonia* (Philadelphia, 1998), 85.

20 For an analysis of this *exemplum* see Ephraim Shoham-Steiner, 'The Humble Sage and the Wondering Madman: Madness and Madmen in an exemplum from "*Sefer Hassidim*"', *Jewish Quarterly Review* 96 (2006), 38-49.

foolish, receiving food donations that sustain him and spending his time in the company of children both playing with them and ridiculed by them. Indeed, Sander Gilman points out that harmless madman were represented both in literature and in the visual arts as part of the world of children, being of "lesser mind" than a "normal" adult.[21]

The raving mad, on the other hand, were considered a menace, a threat to themselves and to society. Physical as well as textual evidence points to the segregation and at times imprisonment of these individuals, and even to their grave physical mistreatment.[22] With these distinctions in mind let us look at a case from the mid or late thirteenth century from the Responsa of Rabbi Meir ben Baruch of Rothenburg, a man considered by many to be the most prominent religious leader of German Jewry during the second half of the thirteenth century.[23]

---

[21] Sander Gilman, *A Cultural History of Madness and Art in the Western World from the Middle Ages to the Nineteenth Century* (New York, 1982). A similar notion appears in the medieval European Jewish homiletic exegetical collection called *Yalkut Shimoni* attributed to the thirteenth-century Rabbi Shimon of Frankfurt. This collection is generally heavily reliant on earlier works and homiletic material dating from late Antiquity to the early Middle Ages. This is also the case in a passage relating to David's feigned madness in the court of the Philistine King Achish of Gath (1 Samuel 21). In *YS* passage we find a dialogue between David and God regarding the nature and purpose of madness. David describes a madman's behavior and its social resonance in the public sphere. The description quoted in *YS* relies heavily on the early medieval *Midrash Shoher Tov* (*MST*) on Psalm 34. However, when we compare the description in the earlier MST with Rabbi Shimon's 13th-century version we find several remarks in Rabbi Shimon's version of the text, absent from the original *MST*. I suggest that part of the description was inserted either by R. Shimon or by an unknown medieval contemporary: "… A man walks in the market place tearing his clothes *and the children mock him and chase him* and the crowd laughs at his dismay…" See Shimon of Frankfurt, *Yalkut Shimoni,* ed. Dov Hyman and Yitchak Shiloni (Jerusalem, 1999), vol. 6, par. 131 (Hebrew).

[22] See Alfred Sander, 'Die Dollen in der Kiste – Zur Behandlung von Geisteskranken in den spätmittelalterlichen Städten', in *Festschrift für Peter Berghaus zum 70 Geburtstag*, ed. Thorsten Albrecht (Münster, 1989), 147-167.

[23] On Rabbi Meir's life and work see Ephraim Kanarfogel, 'Preservation, Creativity, and Courage; the Life and Works of R. Meir of Rothenburg', *Jewish Book Annual* 50 (1992), 249-259. See also Joel Berger, 'Rabbi Meir ben Baruch von Rothenburg – sein Leben und Wirken', in *Zur Geschichte der mittelalterlichen Jüdischen Gemeinde in Rothenburg ob der Tauber: Rabbi Meir ben Baruch von Rothenburg zum Gedenken an seinen 700. Todestag*, ed. Hilde Merz et al. (Rothenburg ob der Tauber, 1993), 201-208.

The case, found in the large collection of responsa edited by Rabbi Meir's students, tells of a situation in which a married woman became insane.[24] The disputed issue concerns the financial responsibility for the upkeep of the woman who, though not yet divorced, no longer cohabited with her husband and probably resided with her own kin and folks. We must bear in mind that according to the *halakha* (code of Jewish law), two opposing restrictions governed such a case. On the one hand, a man could not divorce his insane wife or, for that matter a woman her insane husband; such a procedure was not valid unless the insane spouse regained his or her senses or, at the very least, had a lucid interval when consenting to the legal procedure.[25] Marriage to a second wife was also impossible. Since the early eleventh century the famous "Ban of Rabbenu Gershom" made the already practiced monogamy among Jews in medieval Europe into a formal rule.[26] On the other hand, for as long as the woman remained irrational, her husband was forbidden to have any form of sexual relations with her because of the assumption that a madwoman was unable to observe the strict Jewish ritual purity laws concerning menstruation.

In the above case that came before R. Meir, the man argued that since he and his wife no longer cohabited, and because she was currently residing with her kin due to her mental state, he should be exempt from paying for her upkeep. R. Meir, however, ruled otherwise. In his mind, even though the couple no longer had marital relations, the husband had to provide for his wife. Furthermore, Rabbi Meir explicitly rules that when necessary, in case the husband is pressed for cash, he should hire himself out as a manual laborer or even go as far as taking to the road to beg for charity in order to

---

[24] The responsa can be found in MS Moscow (Ginzburg collection) No.155, fol. 174b-181b.This fragment was first published by Simcha Emanuel in 1993: S. Immanuel, New Responsa by MaHaRam of Rothenburg, *Ha'meayen* 33 (1993), 18-19 (Hebrew). Simcha Emanuel is a leading authority on medieval German Jewish rabbinics in general and the writings of Rabbi Meir of Rothenburg in particular. See his recent article 'Unpublished responsa of R. Meir of Rothenburg as a source for Jewish history', in *The Jews of Europe in the Middle Ages (tenth to fifteenth centuries): Proceedings of the International Symposium Held at Speyer, 20-25 October 2002*, ed. Christoph Cluse (Turnhout, 2004), 283-293.

[25] On the Jewish law of divorce see David Wewrner Amram, *The Jewish Law of Divorce* (New York, 1968).

[26] On this and other issues concerning the marriage and divorce of Jewish women in medieval Europe see Avraham Grossman's fundamental study *Pious and Rebellious: Jewish Women in Medieval Europe* (Waltham MA, 2004), 51-64 and 70-78.

provide for his wife! This ruling is aimed to prevent, at all costs, even the hypothetical possibility that the wife at her deranged mental state might take to the streets, compelled by need to beg for her livelihood. R. Meir ruled that great care must be taken by all parties involved (the husband, the wife's kin, and, for that matter, even rabbinic and communal authorities), to safeguard the deranged wife's personal dignity and to spare her the degrading humiliation of begging in the streets in her mental state.[27]

The rationale for this ruling is twofold. First of all, I believe that true compassion and understanding for the woman's condition were exercised in this case. However, we must remember that contemporary Christian religious sources expressed similar concern, as some scholars have noted:

> Although evangelical poverty and mendicancy were permitted by Innocent III and obtained an officially approved status in the mendicant orders, female mendicancy was never acceptable to the official church and had to be discouraged.[28]

Thus, even when religious individuals like St. Catherine of Sienna asked to permit her order to assume apostolic poverty and mendicancy, following the rule of St. Francis, her request was denied on these very grounds – the prevention of female mendicancy. Judging from a potentially polemical point of view, Jewish leaders and especially supra-communal legal authorities like R. Meir did not want to fall short in piety from their immediate counterparts and permit female mendicancy.[29] In the Jewish mind, even if not in reality, Jewish actions came under constant non-Jewish scrutiny. Due to the wife's state of mental health and given the perils of the streets Rabbi Meir feared that the woman might be subjected not only to ridicule, but to harassment

---

[27] Although Jewish women in medieval Western Europe enjoyed a relative freedom of movement, especially by comparison to their co-religionists in Iberian and Muslim countries, there were some restrictions on female movement in Medieval Europe as well. See Grossman, *Pious and Rebellious* (*op. cit. supra*, n. 26), 114-121.

[28] Anke E. Passenier, 'The Life of Christina Mirabilis: Miracles and the Construction of Marginality', in *Women and Miracle Stories: A Multidisciplinary Exploration*, ed. Anne-Marie Korte (Leiden, Boston and Cologne, 2001), 156.

[29] On Rabbi Meir's role as a supra-communal leader and spiritual leader for Ashkenazi Jewry of his time see Israel Meir Levinger, 'Rabbi Meir von Rothenburg als Halachist und geistiger Führer', in *Zur Geschichte der mittelalterlichen Jüdischen Gemeinde in Rothenburg*, ed. Hilde Merz (*op. cit. supra*, n. 23), 217-222.

and possible sexual abuse from Jews and what in his mind was even worse, from non-Jews as well, thus violating the groups' social boundaries.[30]

The very explicit and unequivocal tone of the ruling regarding the husband's obligation to provide for the insane wife economically even at the cost of begging for their livelihood is therefore telling.[31] However, another look at the specific phrasing used in the responsum suggests an even deeper under-current with an implied message. It seems that for as much as the Jewish religious leaders were concerned with the woman's mental state and even with the possible violation of group boundaries the thought of prevention of female mendicancy altogether is also present. Upon conclusion Rabbi Meir uses this responsum to argue that the general rule should be that if anyone should take to the streets in cases of poverty, regardless of mental state, it is the male and not the female.[32] Due to R. Meir's prominence, this specific

---

[30] The attitude towards this madwoman was reconstructed using a gendered perspective, leading R. Meir and later Jewish sages to prefer an enforced inner exile within the safe haven of the Jewish home to married woman who were deemed mad rather then having a woman roam the streets begging in a mentally disabled state. Rabbi Meir says explicitly of the woman: "*she is not fit for human company*". One should not underestimate the hardships involved in such a situation. With the absence of communal institutions to hospitalize mentally disturbed patients the only place they could be kept was at home. This hardship is emphasized in two quotes: the first from the Jewish 12th-century philosopher and codifier Moses Maimonides (1138-1204) who wrote that "the sane are unable to dwell with the insane in the same quarters" (The Maimonidian Code, The Rules of Divorce, ch. 10 ruling 23). A similar description appears in the 14th-century account of a madwoman in The Book of Margery Kempe: Book I, ch. 75: "*Sche roryth and cryith so that sche makith folk evyl afeerd. Sche wyl bothe smytyn and bityn, and therfor is sche manykyld on hir wristys.*"

[31] Recently some scholars have convincingly argued that interfaith sexual relations resonated much more strongly than violation of intra-group sexual norms. It seems that as long as sexual relations reflected the balance of power between religious groups, group-enforced sanctions were less harsh than in cases where the group perceived the relations as not correctly expressing the "true", even if imagined, power relationship. Jews of course had no true power over the surrounding Christian majority, but they had an imagined state of affairs in mind. A Jewish woman, even a mad one, still symbolized the Jewish collective in their eyes, explaining their concern with aimless female wandering and begging, a situation that might invite sexual harassment. See David Nirenberg, 'Religious and sexual boundaries in the medieval Crown of Aragon', in *Christians, Muslims, and Jews in Medieval and Early Modern Spain*, ed. Mark D. Meyerson and Edward D. English (Notre Dame, 2000), 141-160.

[32] By this, Rabbi Meir had also voiced his own opinion in an old dispute between two prominent northern French Jewish sages of the mid 12th century, Rabbi Eliyahu of Paris and Rabbi Jacob ben Meir "Tam" of Rempro on this matter. Rabbi Meir had studied in

ruling was not only followed but it became the standard rule among Jews in both western Europe, the realm known among Jews as Ashkenaz, as well as among the Jews of the Iberian peninsula known as *Sefarad*.[33]

It would seem that this case demonstrated another point. To members of a minority group, the "sign language" or "symbolic interaction analysis" can, at times, be of extreme importance and significance. Members of minority groups and especially their communal leaders are extremely aware of their image and very sensitive to how they are perceived by others. To the Jews of medieval Europe, poverty and disability as a sign of poverty were a problem not only because of their obvious implications. Visible poverty and physical and mental disability associated with it projected an image Jews were extremely reluctant to expose to their surroundings. I would like to suggest that a conscious attempt was made to project an image without poverty or, at the very least, with minimal signs of poverty and need to the surrounding society.

This attempt was made not only because Jews didn't want to be associated with poverty and disability as such but rather because it had and impact on the "working arrangement" they had with their surrounding society. Jews owed their partial acceptance and fragile religious tolerance in medieval Western Europe, especially between the eleventh and thirteenth centuries, to a very delicate economic equilibrium. This equilibrium was embedded in charters and privileges granted to Jewish communities all over medieval Western Europe. If not in reality, then in the imagined state of affairs that Jews had in mind, visible signs of poverty and disability so strongly associated with it posed a challenge, if not to say a threat, to their very position as members of an urban society. As early as the mid-eleventh century, in close

---

Paris with the renowned Rabbi Yechiel of Paris in the 1230s and had sided with the supporters of Rabbi Eliyahu ben Judah of Paris. On this controversy that predates Rabbi Meir by almost a century see Ephraim Elimelech Urbach, *Ba'aLei Hatosafot* (Jerusalem, 1980), 123 (Hebrew).

33 Rabbi Meir's close disciple Rabbi Asher ben Yeh'iel (RoSH) fled Germany in the aftermath of his master-Rabbi Meir's imprisonment (1286) subsequent death (1293) and the Ritter Rindfleisch Riots in Germany in 1298. He immigrated through France to Iberia and setteled there. His son, Rabbi Jacob had compiled in the mid-14th century many of his father's and his father's master's scattered teachings into one comprehensive legal compendium that in many ways still governs halachic law to the present time (The Book of Four "Turim" – lit. columns). See Israel M. Ta-Shma, 'Between East and West: Rabbi Asher b. Yehi'el and his son Rabbi Ya`akov', in *Studies in Medieval Jewish History and Literature*, ed. Isadore Twersky, vol. 3 (Cambridge Ma., 2000), 179-196.

temporal proximity to the charting of some of the early communal privileges granted to Jews in the Rhineland, famous Jewish sages expressed this notion in a subtle way.

Rabbi Gershon ben Yehuda (960-1028) known also by his title : *Meor Hagola* (lit. the luminator of the diaspora) is well known by his famous edict. One of the articles of the edict reads as follows: "The members of the community can draw up ruling regarding the poor or any other ruling. If these articles are based on a majority of supporters the others can not disregard this ruling and say: I will go to court and defend my objection, for one cannot summon a court hearing for these matters rather the matter is in the hands of the community's 'betters' as was in the early days."[34] Apart from a very early demonstration of what seems to be a majority-based ruling typical of the Rhineland Jewish communities in the eleventh century we have a ruling regarding an example of an internal community issue that can not be turned over in court. Furthermore Rabbi Gershom explicitly states that such issues not only cannot be resolved in court but rather a court cannot be summoned to deal with them and the only authority in which one can appeal against a "poor law" designed to levy a communal tax for the benefit of the poor is with the highest communal authorities, the "communities' betters" (*Tovei Ha'ir*). I believe the reason Rabbi Gershom chose the poor law as the example for an edict that can not be overturned by a court is highly significant. It probably raised resentment from those members of the small eleventh-century Rhineland communitis that saw it as another economical burden. Unlike many other cases in Jewish legal history Rabbi Gershom's edicts are a fine example of rulings that were very strictly observed by the Ashkenazi Jewish community because of their association to Rabbi Gershom's personal gravitas and the reverence to his legal input. Later in the eleventh century we hear that Rabbi Shlomo ben Yizchak, better known by his acronym RaSHI, and Rabbi Meshulam ben Kalonimus of Luca, who lived his later life in Mainz, both comment on a pre-Talmudic ruling from the *Mishna* in tractate *Avot* that states, quoting Yossi ben Yochanan of Jerusalem, a first century B.C sage, that one should house the poor in ones house (*Avot* chp.1, article 5).

The simple understanding of the ruling is that one has to feed and house passing beggars. With regard to this ethical ruling the two eleventh-century

[34] My translation based on: Ben-Zion Dinur, *Yisral Ba'gola*, vol. A (3) (Tel Aviv, 1961), 270 (Hebrew).

sages understand the ruling rather differently. Rabbi Meshulam says "they (the beggars) should be employed in your household and you should prefer them to non-Jewish servants."[35] RaSHI, following R. Meshulam's lead, writes: "I rather provide for those poor Israelites by providing them with work in my house hold" (commentary on BT Baba Metzia 60b) and elsewhere: "do not employ many (non-Jewish) servants in your house hold but rather bring in the poor in their stead, they will serve you and you shall get a heavenly reward for it" (RaSHI's commentary on the abovementioned verse from Avot). A twelfth-century century commentary on the aforementioned quote from *Avot* associated with RaSHI's disciples in northern France expresses a similar opinion almost verbatim.[36] This interpretation expresses not only an attempt to minimize non-Jewish presence in the Jewish household and to maintain and support impoverished Jews, but at the same time it seems as an attempt to minimize the visible presence of Jewish poor in the streets. When read together with Rabbi Gershom's ruling on the irreversibility and inability to even consider appealing against the communal "poor laws" in the Rhineland Jewish communities, it seems the issue of the poor was of great importance to medieval European Jewish leadership. I believe that Jews did not only exercise empathy towards their impoverished co-religionists, they were also extremely uncomfortable with explicitly visible signs of poverty like begging and physical disability. These signs undermined, in Jewish eyes, some basic guidelines of the Jewish existence in medieval Europe. Since charity is obligatory by biblical law and further enforced in Talmudic law, driving away the poor or disregarding them was never an option, especially in light of Jewish existence as a minority society during the European Middle Ages.

Looking back at the privileges granted by Christian rulers to Jews in the eleventh and twelfth centuries it is the economic, financial and mercantile issues that stand out as the most important components of these arrangements.[37] The privileges facilitated a situation, in which economically capable communities and individuals became not only a part but, at times, a crucial

---

[35] Both sources appear in Horowitz, 'Charity' (*op. cit. supra*, n. 3), 218-220.

[36] Rabbi Shimcha of Vitry, *Machsor Vitry*, ed. Simon Hurwitz (Nuremberg 1923), vol. 2, 468 (Hebrew).

[37] Such as the famous privilege granted to the Jews by William the Conqueror "imported" from Roan to England as well as the privilege granted to the Jews of Speyer by Bishop Rudigerus Hausman see Julius Aronius, *Regesten zur Geschichte der Juden in Deutschland* (Berlin, 1893), § 168.

part of the economic urban fabric.[38] With that in mind, there is little wonder that Jews tried as hard as possible to conceal impoverished individuals and resented begging and other obvious signs of poverty. It was this attempt and probably its partial success that enabled a Jewish thirteenth-century polemist like the anonymous author of *Sefer Nizahon Vetus* to make the following remark:

> we thank God for saving us from being afflicted with impure issue, leprosy and skin disease as they [= the non-Jews] are, for the Lord is the one who cures us.[39]

At first glance there is nothing in this statement to suggest that it might refer to poverty or poverty stricken individuals, however at a second glance there might be a hint in this direction in the word "skin disease". The Hebrew source with regard to the skin disease reads *Serufei Esh* which literally means burnt by fire. However, from the contextual reference to leprosy Berger's translation *skin disease* is accurate although not specific. It is my belief that the Jewish anonymous polemist of *Nizahon Vetus* referred by this phrase to the notorious skin disease known as Ergotism or St. Anthony's Fire. This is one of the poverty related diseases mentioned by Mollat as a by-product of consuming poor quality cereal grains infected by fungus *(Claviceps purpurea*, called ergots**)**.[40] Such a statement, claiming that Jews are not afflicted with poverty associated diseases could have been easily discredited by a mere glance around, let alone appearing in a polemic work, unless people thought it rung partially true.

As the fourteenth century approached, these attempts at "hiding" the poor proved futile, for the numbers of the poor were becoming too big. What be-

---

[38] In his book on the Jewish wine industry creditors in France and Germany, Haim Soloveitchik has pointed out the paradox between the hatred to Jews and continuous attacks against them during the mid and the late 13th century on the one hand, and the quick resettlement and rehabilitation of Jewish life in these same areas after riots on the other. Soloveitchik explains the paradox with the formative if not the crucial role Jews played in the wine crediting business that was of great economical importance to that local population. This in turn led to Jews becoming virtually indispensable, even if by the 13th century they were popularly resented. See: H. Soloveitchik, '"Halakhah", Taboo and the Origin of Jewish Moneylending in Germany', in *The Jews of Europe in the Middle Ages*, ed. Chr. Cluse (*op. cit. supra,* n. 24), 295-304.

[39] David Berger, *The Jewish Christian Debate in the High Middle Ages: A Critical Edition of the Nizzahon Vetus* (Philadelphia, 1979), § 217 (p. 211).

[40] Mollat, *The Poor* (*op. cit. supra*, n. 4), 63.

gan as a constant trickle in late twelfth and early thirteenth century was by the fourteenth century a flood. The late thirteenth century saw a rise in the number of Jewish poor as it has seen the rise in the number of non-Jewish individuals reduced to poverty. The Jewish situation, although not very different from the surroundings, has been attributed to various causes. The economic changes that affected the whole population took a special toll on Jews as they had fewer legal "shock absorbers" and means of power against economic perils in medieval society. The rising power of the Christian urban elite, and the growing awareness within urban circles to their religious and social identities contributed to the erosion in the legal status of the Jews, who were perceived as competing economically with the rising burger class. These in turn caused growing intolerance toward Jews, pushing many of them from trade and craftsmanship to the non-guild regulated ventures like pawn broking, crediting and the money lending business. These vocations, though providing, required economical prerequisites in the form of hard currency cash available only to the more affluent members of the community who could compete and survive in these occupations economically. Thus, a growing number of one time providers were slowly reduced into poverty. Essential parental duties such as marrying off the children became a huge burden on income. If in the twelfth century most of the Jews traveling the roads were merchants, from the beginning of the thirteenth century we find more evidence of Jews whose travels were driven by sheer economic need. Fathers traveling from one community to another in an attempt to raise funds to marry off their daughters (a task considered worthy of charity among observant Jews) and more people drifting from town to town in order to earn a few coins for their livelihood.

Jewish rabbinic sources from the turn of the thirteenth century, especially responsa literature, reflect the growing number and high visibility of people referred to in the sources as "lodgers", or in Hebrew *achsanaim.* As Israel Yuval demonstrated some years ago, this term was used in the thirteenth century to describe those inter-community travelers who lacked the mercantile connections in the towns they arrived at. The *achsanaim* relied in their travels either on the hospitality of community members or, particularly in large communities, on a communal facility similar in nature to the thirteenth-century *domus hospitium* – again a link between poverty and disability. This institution known in Hebrew as the *A-chsania*, usually adjacent to the local synagogue, was home to itinerant beggars as well as to the sick and disabled in the community.[41] The term clearly resonates the Greek root *xenoi* meaning foreigner, stranger but also guest. The growing number of itinerant beggars posed a problem to communal authorities. Rabbinic leadership found itself caught between an attempt to regulate the distribution of charity among a growing number of needy and disabled people, while attempting to verify their true identity without violating their dignity, which was threatened in any case. Escalating competition over diminishing resources caused some beggars to assume the identity of disabled poor men and women in the hope of enlarging their share or by attracting more attention to their needy state by means of deception.

To conclude: Jacob Guggenheim has shown that during the fourteenth and especially the fifteenth century transalpine Jewish communities experienced a 100% rise in the number of their poor compared to the previous century: "a growing number of individuals did not have a fixed residence, a secure roof over their heads or a regular source of income." The *Betteljuden* or *Schalantjuden*, as they are referred to in German sources of the period, testify by their mere names to the fact that what appeared to be the Jewish attempt of the eleventh century to "conceal" the poor became virtually impossible[42]. Poverty and physical as well as mental disability of the Jewish poor folks could no longer be concealed.

In our short discussion we showed how attempts were made to verify that the poor were indeed who they claimed to be. Furthermore, we saw how even if attempts to conceal poverty altogether were impossible for gender based reasons, Jewish leaders tried as best they could to prevent female mendicancy and female exposure altogether to life on the roads. Compassion as well as the interests of safeguarding the group boundaries were involved in this effort. Michael Toch pointed out that in the early fifteenth century in a community like Nuremberg it was but a handful of affluent Jewish financiers that served as the virtual and at times only economic backbone of the entire community. However, this phenomenon did not restrict itself to Nuremberg

41 Israel Jacob Yuval, 'Hospices and Their Guests in Jewish Medieval Germany', in *Proceedings of the Tenth World Congress of Jewish Studies*, Division B, vol. 1 (Jerusalem, 1989), 125-129 (Hebrew).

42 Yacov Guggenheim, 'Meeting on the Road: Encounters between German Jews and Christians on the Margins of Society', in *In and Out of the Ghetto: Jewish-Gentile Relations in Late Medieval and Early Modern Germany*, ed. Ronnie Po-Chia-Hsia and Hartmut Lehmann (Cambridge, 1995), 125-136. esp. 126-127.

and can be found elsewhere[43]. By this time, the intolerance towards the Jews was so great that in the mid-fifteenth century many German towns had demanded the relocation and expulsion of their Jewish population. The *Regnum Teutonicum* was by no means unique, Jews were increasingly not tolerated in many western European regions: Expelled from England as early as 1290, Jews were since then "on the move" to find other places where their business would be appreciated and their very existence tolerated. In almost all cases prior to their expulsion Jews were extorted by the local authorities to a point that some historians tagged this phenomenon fiscal "milking cows". Once impoverished in large numbers, Jews were no longer inclined as before to conceal beggars and disabled impoverished individuals, and they were more visible to the public eye.

---

[43] Michael Toch, 'Der jüdische Geldhandel in der Wirtschaft des deutschen Spätmittelalters: Nürnberg (1350-1499)', *Blätter für deutsche Landesgeschichte* 117 (1981), 283-310; *idem*, 'Geld und Kredit in einer spätmittelalterlichen Landschaft; zu einem unbeachteten hebräischen Schuldenregister aus Niederbayern (1329-1332)', *Deutsches Archiv für Erforschung des Mittelalters* 38 (1982), 499-550.

KATHARINA SIMON-MUSCHEID

Sozialer Abstieg im Mittelalter

1. Prämissen

Unter dem neutralen Begriff der „sozialen Mobilität" werden verschiedene gesellschaftliche Transformationen zusammengefasst, nämlich die horizontale und vertikale Mobilität. Was uns hier ausschließlich interessiert, ist die sogenannte vertikale Mobilität und zwar in Form des sozialen Abstiegs.[1] Da diese Richtung der vertikalen Mobilität letztlich in Situationen des Mangels und der Armut führt, soll zuerst der mittelalterliche Begriff „pauper" auf seine Verwendbarkeit hin untersucht werden, bevor wir uns fragen, was sozialer Abstieg bedeutet, welche Veränderungen er für bestimmte Gruppen und die beiden Geschlechter nach sich zieht, durch welche Zeichen er sich manifestiert, wie er von den Betroffenen selbst wahrgenommen wird und wie das Umfeld darauf reagiert. Für die folgenden Überlegungen zum Problem des sozialen Abstiegs im Mittelalter sind zwei Prämissen vorauszuschicken:

1.1. Die Bedeutungsvielfalt von „pauper"

Zum ersten ist der mittelalterliche Begriff „pauper" („arm"), der sich jedem eindimensionalen Definitionsversuch entzieht, mehrdeutig. Er deckt zwar die moderne Bedeutung von „arm" ab, umfasst aber Bereiche, die heute nicht mehr primär mit „arm" assoziiert sind, und ist deshalb erklärungsbedürftig. Weil er von verschiedenen Akteuren zu unterschiedlichen Zwecken in unterschiedlichen diskursiven Zusammenhängen verwendet wurde, lässt sich das

[1] Pierre Bourdieu (Hg.), La misère du monde, Paris 1993; Winfried Schulze (Hg.), Ständische Gesellschaft und soziale Mobilität (Schriften des historischen Kollegs, Kolloquien 12), München 1988; siehe auch Hans-Peter Müller (Hg.), Sozialer Wandel. Modellbildung und theoretische Ansätze, Frankfurt a.M. 1995.

spezifische Bedeutungsfeld mit seiner impliziten positiven oder negativen Bewertung nur aus dem jeweiligen Kontext erschließen. Die Bedeutungsfelder von „pauper“, die für moderne Menschen nur schwer miteinander in Einklang zu bringen sind, decken materielle, rechtliche, soziale, spirituelle und physische Bereiche ab. [2] Der gemeinsame Nenner ist das Defizit in einem oder mehreren dieser Bereiche gemessen am Gegenpol „dives“, der – je nach Kontext – ausreichende tägliche Nahrung, Reichtum, Macht, Status bis hin zu physischer Stärke und Gesundheit bedeutet. Auf die geschlechtsspezifischen Konnotationen von „paupertas“ werden wir gleich eintreten.

– Auch wenn im folgenden der Begriff „pauper“ ausgeweitet und seine vielfache Einsetzbarkeit in unterschiedlichen Argumentationszusammenhängen diskutiert wird, so ist es wichtig, als erstes die konkrete materielle Not zu benennen, die für die betroffenen „pauperes“ die Beschaffung der Grundbedürfnisse (Nahrung, ein Dach über dem Kopf) zum täglichen Überlebensproblem werden ließ.[3] Diese elementaren Form der „paupertas“, die – wie in der Literatur immer wieder betont wird – das weibliche Geschlecht und insbesondere alleinstehende Frauen in besonderem Ausmaß betroffen habe[4], wurde von Männern und Frauen als konkrete Altersperspektive gefürchtet.[5]

---

[2] Michel Mollat, Les pauvres au Moyen Âge, Paris 1978, bes. die Einleitung 9-21; Otto Gerhard Oexle, Armut, Armutsbegriff und Armenfürsorge im Mittelalter, in: Christoph Sachβe, Florian Tennstedt (Hg.), Soziale Sicherheit und soziale Disziplinierung, Frankfurt a. M. 1986; Pierre Boglioni u. a. (Hg.), Le petit peuple dans l'Occident médiéval: terminologies, perceptions, réalités, Actes du Congrès international tenu à l'Université de Montréal, 18-23 octobre 1999, Paris 2003; Otto Gerhard Oexle (Hg.), Armut im Mittelalter (Vorträge und Forschungen 58), Ostfildern 2004, darin Franz J. Felten, Zusammenfassung. Mit zwei Exkursen zu „starken Armen“ im frühen und hohen Mittelalter und zur Erforschung der pauperes der Karolingerzeit, 349-401, mit weiterführender internationaler Literatur über die verschiedenen Aspekte von "Armut“.

[3] Helmut Bräuer (Hg.), Arme – ohne Chancen? Kommunale Armut und Armutsbekämpfung vom Spätmittelalter bis zur Gegenwart, Leipzig 2004; Hans-Jörg Gilomen u.a. (Hg.), Von der Barmherzigkeit zur Sozialversicherung. Umbrüche und Kontinuitäten vom Spätmittelalter bis zum 20. Jahrhundert/De l'assistance à l'assurance sociale. Ruptures et continuités du Moyen Âge au XXe siècle (Schweizerische Gesellschaft für Wirtschafts- und Sozialgeschichte 18), Zürich 2002; Ernst Schubert, Erscheinungsformen der Armut in der spätmittelalterlichen deutschen Stadt, in: Helmut Bräuer, Elke Schlenkrich (Hg.), Die Stadt als Kommunikationsraum, FS Karl Czok, Leipzig 2001, 659-697.

[4] Zur Problematik der Witwenschaft siehe weiter unten.

[5] Zur Altersarmut und Vorsorge sehr materialreich Gabriela Signori, Alter und Armut im späten Mittelalter. Überlegungen zu den lebenszyklischen Dimensionen von sozialem Ab-

– „Arm" in seiner zweiten Bedeutung ist gleichzeitig standesbezogen und geschlechtsspezifisch konnotiert: Wer in einer Ständegesellschaft – als Mann oder Frau – einem niederen Stand angehörte, verfügte über einen minderen Rechtsstatus. Dies galt ebenso für sämtliche Angehörigen des weiblichen Geschlechts aufgrund ihrer Geschlechtszugehörigkeit. Die Begründung dafür hatte die Bibel mit Evas leichter Verführbarkeit geliefert. Bis in die tiefe Neuzeit gab dies Basis und Legitimation für eine asymmetrisch konzipierte Geschlechterhierarchie ab, die Frauen den Männern unterordnete. Da sich im Fall des weiblichen Geschlechts die rechtliche Unterordnung mit geistiger Schwäche als weibliche „Geschlechtscharaktere" legitimierte, verbinden sich hier zwei frauenspezifische Formen der „paupertas".[6]
– Als „arm" galt drittens, wer selbst schwach und schutzlos auf die Hilfe der Starken (an physischer Kraft oder politischem Einfluss) angewiesen war. Dies umfasste ursprünglich alle nicht waffenfähigen Gruppen der Gesellschaft, das heißt den Klerus als Stand, das weibliche Geschlecht insgesamt, Kinder sowie alte und schwache Männer. Auch in diesem Fall wird eine doppelte „paupertas" mit „weiblich" konnotiert, es sind dies die physische und geistige Schwäche, die das weibliche Geschlecht zum Objekt des männlichen Schutzes und gleichzeitig der männlichen Bevormundung werden ließen.[7] Wenn wir diese Kategorie von Armen und ihren potentiellen Beschützern für unsere Überlegungen nutzbar machen wollen, müssen wir das reine „Waffenhandwerk" ausweiten auf juristischen Beistand und die vielfältigen Schutzfunktionen einer Klientel, in die Männer direkt und Frauen indirekt über ihre männlichen Verwandten eingebunden waren.

---

stieg und den formellen und informellen „Strategien" der Überwindung, in: Oexle (Hg.), Armut (wie Anm. 2), 213-257.

6 Elisabeth Kari Børresen, Subordination and Equivalescence. The Nature and Role of Women in Augustinus and Thomas Aquinas, Washington D.C. 1981; Gerhard Dilcher, Die Ordnung der Ungleichheit. Haus, Stand und Geschlecht, in: Ute Gerhard (Hg.), Frauen in der Geschichte des Rechts. Von der Frühen Neuzeit bis in die Gegenwart, München 1997, 55-72; Karin Hausen, Die Polarisierung der „Geschlechtscharaktere". Eine Spiegelung der Dissoziation von Erwerbs- und Familienleben, in: Werner Conze (Hg.), Sozialgeschichte der Familie in der Neuzeit Europas, Stuttgart 1976, 363-393.

7 Dieses Konzept weiblicher Schwäche bot armen Bittstellerinnen und Witwen insbesondere ein gesellschaftlich akzeptiertes Argumentationsmuster, das einer gängigen Armutsdefinition entsprach und als unterstützungswürdig galt. Frauen spielten mitunter die ihrem Geschlecht anhaftende Hilflosigkeit und „geistige Armut" geschickt aus.

- Viertens waren physisch und psychisch Kranke sowie Invalide arm gemessen an Gesundheit und Stärke. Die „armen Siechen", wie die Leprösen genannt wurden[8], galten im 12. und 13. Jahrhundert als Inbegriff der Kranken, deren entstellte Gesichter und verkrüppelte Glieder ihnen einen ambivalenten Status eintrugen. Lepra wurde einerseits als sichtbares Zeichen der göttlichen Auserwähltheit, andererseits als Zeichen der Sünde verstanden, die erste Interpretation verhalf ihnen zum Status besonders einflussreicher Fürbitter, die zweite trug ihnen (zusammen mit den Juden) 1321 in Frankreich die Verfolgung wegen angeblicher Verschwörung und Brunnenvergiftung ein.[9] Die „Spitzenvertreter" der Armutsbewegung wie Elisabeth von Thüringen und Franz von Assisi pflegten Lepröse nicht nur in unserm Sinn, sondern identifizierten sich mit ihnen als mit den elendesten Geschöpfen in gewählter Selbsterniedrigung.[10] Im Fall der Leprösen lässt sich wie bei den materiell Armen und Nichtsesshaften der Prozess der Marginalisierung verfolgen, der im späten Mittelalter abgeschlossen war.
- Als fünfte und letzte Kategorie, auf die wir eintreten, sind die Fremden zu nennen. Als Armut galten der Mangel an vertrauten Sozialbeziehungen sowie der geminderte Rechtsstatus (gemessen an Bürgern), der sie für die Dauer ihres Aufenthalts in der fremden Stadt oder im fremden Land zu schutz- und rechtlosen Personen werden ließ.[11]

Die verschieden konnotierten Bedeutungsfelder von „pauper" machen es schwierig, „das mittelalterliche Konzept" von Armut zu fassen. Außerdem wurde „pauper" als Fremd- oder Selbstbezeichnung mit unterschiedlichen Bedeutungsinhalten gefüllt je nach Absicht der Sprechenden oder Schrei-

---

[8] Auch „Sondersieche" oder nach ihren Behausungen außerhalb der Siedlungen „Feldsieche", euphemistisch auch „die guten Leute".

[9] Zum Wandel der Bewertung der Leprösen Nicole Bériou, François-Olivier Touati, Voluntate dei leprosus. Les lépreux entre conversion et exclusion aux XIIe et XIIIe siècles, Spoleto 1991; Jean-Olivier Touati, Maladie et société au Moyen Âge: la lèpre et les léproseries dans la province ecclésiastique de Sens jusqu'au milieu du XIVe siècle, Paris 1998; zur Lepra vor allem im deutschen Reich und in England Kay Peter Jankrift, Mit Gott und schwarzer Magie. Medizin im Mittelalter, Darmstadt 2005, 119-140.

[10] Zu Hospitalgründung, Hagiographie und Ikonographie vgl. Sankt Elisabeth: Fürstin, Dienerin, Heilige. Ausstellung, Dokumentation, Katalog, hg. v. d. Philipps Universität Marburg in Verbindung mit dem Hessischen Landesamt für geschichtliche Landeskunde, Sigmaringen 1981; als typischer Buchtitel etwa Norbert Ohler, Elisabeth von Thüringen: Fürstin im Dienst der Niedrigsten, Göttingen 1997, 3. Aufl.

[11] Die Wörter „alienus" und das deutsche „elend" sind etymologisch verwandt.

benden: Die „pauperes“ wurden von Predigern theologisch überhöht, von Schriftstellern und Dichtern negativ oder positiv stilisiert, von Chronisten als gefährlicher Unruheherd geschildert und von den Obrigkeiten zu Administrationszwecken in verschiedene Kategorien unterteilt: Die „pauperes Christi“ sahen sich als die Nachfolger Christi und seiner Jünger, die die wahre Kirche verkörperten. Bittstellerinnen und Bittsteller bezeichneten sich in ihren Appellen um Unterstützung, Rechtshilfe oder Gnade selbst als „Arme“, was einerseits als notwendige und erwartete Demutsgeste galt, andererseits aber auch auf ihre Notsituation verwies. Was der Begriff „pauper“ beinhaltet oder beinhalten sollte, wird somit durch die unterschiedlichen Diskurse und ihre Adressaten determiniert.

1.2. Zeitliche Dimension

Zum zweiten verändert sich in der zeitlichen Dimension von der Antike bis zum Hochmittelalter die gesellschaftliche Bewertung der „pauperes“, sie schwankte zwischen der antiken Verachtung von Armut und christlichem Mitleid, bis sie im 11./12. Jahrhundert als besonderer spiritueller Wert verklärt wurde. Die vor allem von Laien, darunter vielen Frauen getragene hochmittelalterliche Armutsbewegung hatte der „reichen“ Kirche und dem „unrechtmäßig erworbenen Reichtum“ ihre Vision einer Nachfolge Christi entgegengesetzt und ein Leben in Armut und Bescheidenheit auf ihre Fahnen geschrieben. Die frühen Beginen, die aus bürgerlichen und adeligen Häusern stammten, Franz von Assisi und Elisabeth von Thüringen verzichteten freiwillig auf die Privilegien ihres Standes und auf materielle Güter und verteilten ihre Habe an die „Armen“. Zeichen des veränderten, freiwillig gewählten niederen Standes war (wie in regulären geistlichen Gemeinschaften) eine Neueinkleidung als Teil der „rites de passage“.[12] Es bleibt zu betonen, dass es sich in der Frühzeit der Bewegung mehrheitlich um Angehörige der höheren Stände handelte, die auf Rang und materielle Güter verzichteten, die sie selbst (oder ihre Familie) besaßen. Nur diese Form von Armut wurde spirituell überhöht und als Gewinn an „spirituellem Reichtum“ gepriesen, nicht aber die „gewöhnlichen“ Mangel- und Notsituation der eigentlichen „pauperes“, die nichts besaßen und deshalb auch auf nichts verzichten konnten. Von

---

[12] Von zentraler Bedeutung war ihre Vision von freiwilliger Besitz- und Bedürfnislosigkeit („Nacktheit“ und „Einfalt“ nach dem Verständnis von Franz von Assisi), die sogar einen festen Wohnsitz ausschloss. Für Frauen blieb allerdings die „stabilitas loci“ die verbindliche Norm.

ihnen wurde erwartet, dass sie ihre Armut geduldig und ohne zu murren ertrugen.

Das Konzept von Armut in Theorie und Praxis, das die katharischen „perfecti“ im Unterschied zur kirchlichen Orthodoxie vorlebten, muss auf die Gläubigen im Südwesten Frankreichs und andern „häresieverseuchten“ Gebieten attraktiv und glaubwürdig gewirkt haben; es wurde deswegen auch von den Bettelorden übernommen.[13] Doch die „pauperes Christi“, die ihren Lebensunterhalt durch das Sammeln von Almosen bestritten, forderten schon die zeitgenössische Kritik heraus: Der Pariser Kanoniker Guillaume de Saint Amour, der zu ihren vehementesten Gegnern im Umkreis der Pariser Universität zählte, denunzierte die Bettelorden schon um die Mitte des 13. Jahrhunderts als arbeitsscheue Schmarotzer. Grundsätzlich wandte er sich gegen die Existenzform der Bettelorden und der Beginen, die für ihn den Typus der „valides mendicantes“ verkörperten, weil sie als arbeitsfähige Männer und Frauen von Bettel und Almosen lebten.[14]

Das Konzept der freiwilligen Armut hatte im hohen Mittelalter dem spirituellen Bedürfnis wohlhabender und hochgestellter Männer und Frauen entsprochen, das es ermöglichte, Kirchenkritik mit (semi-)religiöser Lebensführung in der Nachfolge Christi in Einklang zu bringen. Doch im Verlauf des Spätmittelalters veränderte sich das gesellschaftliche Wertesystem definitiv unter dem Einfluss der Scholastik. Allerdings ist die Abwertung von „Armut“ nicht die Folge eines geradlinig verlaufenen Prozesses zu verstehen, vielmehr standen sich lange Zeit unterschiedliche Bewertungen der Armut gegenüber. Doch im Verlauf des Spätmittelalters setzten sich das neue gesellschaftlich relevante Wertesystem und damit eine definitive Trendwende durch. Sobald Arbeit und Arbeitsfähigkeit sich als einzige akzeptierte Werte etabliert hatten, wurde konsequenterweise jede Existenzform, die nicht darauf gegründet war, als parasitär denunziert. Damit geriet auch das Konzept der freiwilligen Armut definitiv in Misskredit. Das ursprünglich aus der religiösen Polemik stammende Schlagwort der „valides

---

[13] Malcolm Barber, The Cathars: Dualist Heretics in Languedoc in the High Middle Ages, Harlow 2000; Jean Duvernoy, Cathars, Vaudois et Béguins, dissidents du pays d'Oc, Toulouse 1994; Gerd Melville u. a. (Hg.), In propositio paupertatis: Studien zum Armutsverständnis bei den mittelalterlichen Bettelorden (Vita regularis 13), Münster 2001.

[14] Michel-Marie Dufeil, Guillaume de St.-Amour et la polémique universitaire parisienne 1250-1259, Paris 1972; Jean-Claude Schmitt, Mort d'une hérésie. L'Eglise et les clercs face aux béguines et aux béghards du Rhin supérieur du XIVe et XVe siècle, Paris 1978, 56-59.

mendicantes“, das auf die Lebensform der Franziskaner und der Beginen abzielte, wurde ausgeweitet und in den politisch-administrativen Diskurs der spätmittelalterlichen Obrigkeiten integriert.[15] Einbezogen wurden jetzt alle arbeitsfähigen Männer, Frauen und Kinder ab acht Jahren, die – aus welchem Grund auch immer – keiner Arbeit nachgingen, sondern von Bettel und Almosen lebten. Sie alle fielen jetzt in die große Kategorie der „Müßiggänger“ und der „starken Bettler“, die sich dem neuen Wertesystem verweigerten.[16]

Diese Tendenz verschärfte sich zunehmend bis zu einer völligen „Entidealisierung“ von Armut in ihren unterschiedlichen Formen. Damit lösten öffentlich zur Schau gestellte Bedürftigkeit, Krankheit und Gebrechen einen neuen ordnungspolitischen Diskurs aus, der die Armenunterstützung grundsätzlich in Frage stellte und Kriterien für die Vergabe von Almosen neu definierte. Die städtischen Behörden unterteilten die Flut der „Armen“ zu verwaltungstechnischen Zwecken in verschiedene Kategorien und entschieden aufgrund rechtlicher sowie moralisch-sittlicher Kriterien, wer Anspruch auf Unterstützung habe.[17] Ausgeschlossen waren im Prinzip alle „Arbeitsfähigen“, außerdem Fremde, Nichtsesshafte, Männer und Frauen, die ihre Armut „selbst verschuldet“ hatten und Frauen „von unmoralischem Lebenswandel“. Die Restkategorie, die nach diesen wesentlichen Einschränkungen noch

---

[15] Hans-Jörg Gilomen, Eine neue Wahrnehmung arbeitsloser Armut in der spätmittelalterlichen Eidgenossenschaft, in: Traverse 1992/2, 117-129; zur Polemik gegen die Franziskaner und Beginen von seiten der Dominikaner vgl. Sabine von Heusinger, Johannes Mulberg († 1414). Ein Leben im Spannungsfeld von Dominikanerobservanz und Beginenstreit (Quellen und Forschungen zur Geschichte des Dominikanerordens N. F. 9), Berlin 2000; Schmitt, Mort (wie Anm. 14).

[16] Bronislaw Geremek, Le refus du travail dans la société urbaine du bas Moyen Âge, in: Jacqueline Hamesse, Colette Muraille-Samaran (Hg.), Le travail au Moyen Âge Une approche interdisciplinaire, Louvain-la-Neuve 1990, 379-394; zur „neuen“ Polemik gegen die Bettelorden Christopher Ocker, „Rechte Arme“ und „Bettler Orden“, in: Bernhard Jussen, Craig Koslofsky (Hg.), Kulturelle Reformation, Sinnformation im Umbruch 1400-1600 (Veröffentlichung des Max-Planck-Instituts für Geschichte 145), Göttingen 1999, 129-157.

[17] Ernst Schubert, „Hausarme Leute“ und „starke Bettler“, in: Oexle (Hg.), Armut (wie Anm. 2), 283-348; Helmut Bräuer, Almosenausteilungsplätze – Orte der Barmherzigkeit und Selbstdarstellung, des Gesprächs und der Disziplinierung, in: Bräuer, Schlenkrich (Hg.) Die Stadt (wie Anm. 3), 57-100; Katharina Simon-Muscheid, La fête des mendiants. Fictions et réalités au Bas Moyen Âge (Bâle et Cologne), in: Marc Boone, Peter Stabel (Hg.), Shaping Urban Identity in Late Medieval Europe: The Use of Space and Images, Leuven-Apeldoorn 2000, 183-200.

verblieb, umfasste nicht oder nicht mehr arbeitsfähige und „unverschuldet" in Not geratene Bürgerinnen, Bürger (mitunter noch Hintersassen), die über einen guten Leumund und festen Wohnsitz verfügten und deren Lebensweise den moralisch-sittlichen Kriterien entsprach.

Außer den rechtlichen Einschränkungen boten die Kategorien „selbstverschuldete Armut" und „unmoralischer Lebenswandel" einen weiten Spielraum für den Ausschluss derjenigen Armen, deren Lebensweise im Widerspruch zu den sittlich-moralischen Normen gestanden hatte oder stand. Schlüsseln wir dies geschlechtsspezifisch auf, so ergibt sich die folgende Liste negativer Aktivitäten und Verhaltensweisen für Männer, nämlich Wirtshausbesuch, Trinken, Fluchen, Spielen, Verschleudern der Mittel, „unstete" Lebensweise. Ledige Schwangerschaft, Konkubinat, Verlassen der ehelichen Gemeinschaft, eine „Argwohn erregende Lebensweise" sowie „unökonomisches Haushalten" schlossen Frauen vom Kreis der Unterstützungsberechtigten aus. Männer und Frauen, die im späten Mittelalter und in den späteren Jahrhunderten aus irgendeinem Grund die sozialen Stufenleiter hinunterfielen und in Not gerieten, mussten sich als „gute Arme" legitimieren können, auch wenn sie nach rein rechtlichen Kriterien Anspruch auf Unterstützung hatten.

Das weite oben skizzierte Bedeutungsfeld von „pauper" verengte sich im obrigkeitlichen Diskurs des Spätmittelalters und implizierte vor allem materielle Not. Auch wenn die städtischen Obrigkeiten mit Misstrauen auf „die Armen" blickten und sich bemühten, durch Restriktionsmaßnahmen die „wahren Bedürftigen" aus der Menge der „valides mendicantes" herauszufiltern, so wurden doch noch immer Gegenstimmen laut. Der berühmte Strassburger Münsterprediger Geiler von Kaysersberg, der sich für eine Reform und gleichzeitig für Transparenz des Almosenwesens einsetzte, betonte dennoch den Vorrang des Almosens vor der Unterscheidung in „würdige" und „unwürdige" Arme.[18] Die traditionelle Vorstellung der „Jenseitsökono-

[18] Während Geiler von Kaysersberg in seinen *21 Artikeln* zur Reform der Armenpolitik und Krankenfürsorge verhindern wollte, dass Almosen anstatt den „wahren Bedürftigen" den „starken" Bettlern zugute kämen, wandte er sich in seiner Predigt *De arbore humana* gegen ein strikte Kontrolle der Armen: „Und ob dir ynfiel ein gedankck, du solltest in [den Bettler] schelten, er ist ful, er mag nit wercken, er ist gesunt, gat müssig, ist ein lügner [...]", so dürfe man ihm eine Gabe nicht verweigern; auch wenn er ein recht sündhafter Mensch sei, so sei er immer noch einen Bissen Brot wert, da Gott noch die Sonne über ihn scheinen lasse; zitiert nach Thomas Fischer, Städtische Armut und Armenfürsorge im 15. und 16. Jahrhundert. Sozialgeschichtliche Untersuchungen am Beispiel der Städte Basel, Freiburg i.Br. und Strassburg, Göttingen 1979, 153; zur Entstehung der *21 Artikel* vgl.

mie", die Spender und Arme über ihre jeweiligen Gaben verband, ließ sich von der neuen kommunalen Fürsorgepolitik noch nicht aufbrechen, die Almosen nur an „würdige" Arme vergeben wollte, – trotz Bestrafung der Spender. Sogar in reformierten Gebieten, wo die Reformatoren den Almosen jeglichen Wert zur Erlangung des Seelenheils absprachen, dauerte es lange Jahre, bis diese Botschaft ankam. „Pauperes" blieben somit für das Seelenheil der „potentes" weiterhin von Bedeutung.

2. Literarische Fiktionen und „historische Realitäten"

Das Motiv des sozialen Abstiegs lässt sich besonders drastisch in literarischen Fiktionen darstellen, wenn der Autor König, Dame oder Ritter im Verlauf der Erzählung „Alles" verlieren lässt, was ihre herausragende Position ausmacht. Die Diskrepanz zwischen der hohen Abkunft und dem (temporären) Verlust von Status, Ehre, Reichtum und gewohnter Umgebung bietet Raum für detaillierte Beschreibungen des veränderten sozialen Umfelds.

Im Roman vom Grafen von Anjou zum Beispiel trauert die vom Hof ihres Vaters geflohene Tochter, die bei einer armen Frau Zuflucht gefunden hat, den Delikatessen und erlesenen Weinen des gräflichen Hofes nach und klagt über das steinharte, schwarze und verschimmelte Brot und das Wasser, das sie jetzt mit der armen Frau teilt. Der soziale Abstieg vom höfisch raffinierten Genießen und dem reichen Angebot an kulinarischen Köstlichkeiten zur kärglichen Speise der Armen, die gerade zum Überleben dient, wird durch die Kontrastierung typischer, „statusgebundener" Nahrungsmittel sichtbar gemacht: Fülle und Mangel, Raffinesse und Roheit (Wasser ist kein Kulturprodukt wie Wein) charakterisieren die beiden Pole der Gesellschaft.[19]

Uwe Israel, Johannes Geiler von Kaysersberg, (1445-1510): der Strassburger Münsterprediger als Reichsreformer (Berliner historische Schriften 27), Berlin 1995, 222-232; neuerdings Rita Voltmer, Wie der Wächter auf dem Turm, ein Prediger und seine Stadt: Johann Geiler von Kaysersberg (1445-1510) und Strassburg (Beiträge zur Landes- und Kulturgeschichte 4), Trier 2005; Francis Rapp, L'église et les pauvres à la fin du Moyen Âge, l'exemple de Geiler de Kaysersberg, in: Revue d'histoire de l'Eglise de France 52 (1966), 39-46.

[19] Nancy B. Black, Medieval Narratives of Accused Queens, Gainesville 2002, 66-87; die Liste der erlesenen Weine, deren Verzicht die junge Frau beklagt (Gewürzweine, mit Honig gekochter Wein, mit Ingwer und Rosen gewürzte Weine, Weine aus der Gascogne mit den schönen Farben, Weine von Beaune und Saint Pourçain etc.) entspricht der Hierarchie der besonders geschätzten Spitzenweine in andern literarischen Fiktionen und ist historisch belegt, Michel Zink, Autour de la bataille des Vins d'Henri d'Andeli: le blanc du

Das zweite Beispiel thematisiert eine besondere Art von Abstieg und Ausgrenzung, die hier unter dem Aspekt des sozialen Abstiegs betrachtet werden sollen: Der „arme" Heinrich, der als Ritter über alle höfischen Tugenden außer Demut verfügt, wird vom Aussatz (Lepra) befallen. Als Lepröser verliert er sein gesellschaftliches Umfeld und seinen Status. Er verschenkt sein Gut und zieht sich auf seinen letzten Meierhof zurück, nachdem er erfahren hat, dass die ärztliche Kunst machtlos sei und dass ihn nur Gott oder das Blut einer Jungfrau heilen könne. Weil der Ritter im letzten Moment auf das angebotene Opfer des jungen Mädchens verzichtet, wird er von Gott geheilt.[20] Lepra war im 12./13. Jahrhundert ein Thema, das Literaten, Prediger, Mediziner, kirchliche und weltliche Obrigkeiten gleichermaßen beschäftigte. Die ambivalente Bewertung zwischen den Polen „Auserwähltheit" und „Sündhaftigkeit" manifestiert sich einerseits in der Darstellung des armen Lazarus und Hiobs als Lepröse (z.B. in Moissac) anderseits der Lepra als Strafe für die mangelnde Demut des Ritters und damit als Stigma seiner Sünde. In scharfem Kontrast steht das gute Aussehen des Ritters mit dem von Lepra zerstörten Körper des Kranken, der dadurch zum „armen Siechen" wird. Die räumliche und soziale (in diesem Fall freiwillig vorgenommene) Ausgrenzung manifestiert sich im „Abstieg" von der höfischen Gesellschaft mit ihren Vergnügungen zum schlichten Meierhof. Da die ärztliche Kunst versagt, stehen dem Kranken zwei Alternativen offen: entweder ein heidnisch-magisches Ritual, das das Blut unschuldiger Jungfrauen (oder Kinder) erfordert[21], oder die christliche Ergebenheit in sein Schicksal als unheilbarer Lepröser. Diese als Art Konversion verstandene Einsicht des Ritters führt schließlich zur Heilung durch göttliche Gnade.

Während in der Literatur die ursprüngliche Ordnung nach dramatischen Verwirrungen wieder hergestellt wird, endet der „reale" soziale Abstieg selten mit der völligen Wiedererlangung des ursprünglichen Zustandes (als Ausnahme können vielleicht hochstehende Gefangene genannt werden, die

---

prince, du pauvre et du poète, in: Max Millner, Martine Chatelain (Hg.), L'imaginaire du vin (Actes du Colloque de Dijon), Marseille 1983, 111-122; zur Speise der Armen der Beitrag von Melitta Weiss Adamson in diesem Band.

[20] Hartmann von Aue, Der Arme Heinrich, hg. v. Hermann Paul, 16. neu bearbeitete Auflage, besorgt von Kurt Gärtner, Tübingen 1996 (Altdeutsche Textbibliothek 3, Ed. 16).

[21] Die südfranzösische Literatur, die im Unterschied zur deutschen Literatur die Negativstereotypen der Leprösen stark ausspielte, rückte diesen Aspekt besonders in den Vordergrund, Paul Rémy, La lèpre, thème littéraire au Moyen Âge, in: Le Moyen Âge 52 (1946), 195-242.

in den Verließen ihrer Gegner schmachten, bis sie gegen ein hohes Lösegeld ihre Freiheit, ihren Status und ihre ursprüngliche Machtposition wieder erlangen). Doch im Unterschied zur Literatur beschränkt sich das Phänomen auch keineswegs auf die oberen Stände, vielmehr handelt es sich um ein allgemein gesellschaftliches Problem. Vom sozialen Abstieg bedroht und betroffen waren gleichermaßen die städtische Bürgerschaft und die Landbevölkerung, Männer wie Frauen. Sogar in der heterogenen und stark hierarchisierten Gruppe der Armen lässt sich dieses Phänomen beobachten. Hier wird die Tendenz fassbar, mit allen zur Verfügung stehenden Mitteln gegen ein weiteres Abgleiten nach unten zu verhindern. „Unten" bedeutete in diesem Fall die letzte Stufe, nämlich mobile Bettelarmut, die seit dem 14. Jahrhundert tendenziell stigmatisiert und kriminalisiert wurde.[22]

3. Sozialer Abstieg in der spätmittelalterlichen Gesellschaft

Den geographischen Raum für unsere Untersuchung über die Gründe, Formen und Zeichen des sozialen Abstiegs bilden die oberrheinischen Städte Strassburg, Colmar, Basel sowie die kleineren Städte Mülhausen (Mulhouse) und Freiburg i. Br. Wir haben vor allem Quellenmaterial aus dem Gebiet der oberrheinischen Städte beigezogen, um herauszuarbeiten, was sozialer Abstieg bedeutet, welche Veränderungen er für bestimmte Gruppen und die beiden Geschlechter nach sich zieht, durch welche Zeichen er sich manifestiert und wie er von den Betroffenen selbst wahrgenommen wird. Die oberrheinische Städtelandschaft bietet eine reichhaltige Quellenbasis für das späte Mittelalter, das von Verfassungstexten und Chroniken über Predigtliteratur und Gerichtdokumenten (darunter Inventarlisten, die auch die „arme" Bevölkerung erfassen) bis hin zu einer literarische Produktion reichen, als deren Ausgangspunkt für unser Thema Sebastian Brants *Narrenschiff* (gedruckt in Basel 1494) betrachtet werden kann.

Funktionstüchtige Netzwerke halfen mit, temporäre wirtschaftliche Engpässe und Notlagen zu entschärfen. Ihre Mitglieder streckten das notwendige Bargeld vor, leisteten Rechtshilfe verbargen Wertgegenstände vor der drohenden Konfiskation bei sich zu Hause, vermittelten Kontakte und organisierten auch eine Flucht. Als Netzwerke, die auf verschiedenartige Weise

---

[22] František Graus, Randgruppen in der städtischen Gesellschaft des Spätmittelalters, in: Zeitschrift für historische Forschung 8 (1981), 385-437; Bronislaw Geremek, Truands et misérables dans l'Europe moderne (1350-1600), Paris 1980; derselbe, Le refus (wie Anm. 16).

Hilfe leisteten, verstehen wir die Familie, die Nachbarschaft, Bruderschaften, Zünfte und Gesellenorganisationen. Dies soll nicht darüber hinwegtäuschen, dass diese mehr oder minder formalen Strukturen von hierarchisch strukturierten Beziehungsnetzen in Form von Klientelen überlagert waren. Auch der „Patron“ gewährte den Mitgliedern seiner Klientel Schutz, Unterstützung und Darlehen gegen bestimmte Gegenleistungen wie etwa Loyalität.[23] Das Fehlen solcher Netzwerke oder ihr Verlust machte die Überwindung von Notsituationen ungleich schwieriger, ohne das Eingebundensein war die Position eines Individuums schwach und gefährdet.

3.1. Gründe für den sozialen Abstieg

Außer den makrohistorischen krisenhaften Einbrüchen, die mit Missernten und Teuerungen korrelierten und so zur Verarmung weiter Kreise führten, waren es vor allem die alltäglichen, unspektakulären und individuellen Fälle von Verschuldung, die die mittleren und unteren Bevölkerungsgruppen bedrohten. Konnte die Spirale von Verschuldung, Mangel an Bargeld oder Wertobjekten, Rückforderung der Gläubiger und schließlich die Konfiskation von Hab und Gut durch städtische Amtleute zugunsten der Gläubiger nicht unterbrochen werden, so drohte als schlimmstes Szenario die Zwangsversteigerung von Hab und Gut der Schuldner oder das Schuldgefängnis.[24] Nur wer über Kreditfähigkeit oder soziale Netzwerke verfügte, konnte sich das notwendige Geld beschaffen, um die Schulden zu begleichen und die konfiszierte Ware rechtzeitig wieder auszulösen.

---

[23] Zu den verschiedenartigen Netzwerken in den oberrheinischen Städten Katharina Simon-Muscheid, Die Dinge im Schnittpunkt sozialer Beziehungsnetze. Reden und Objekte im Alltag (Oberrhein 14.-16. Jahrhundert), (Veröffentlichungen des Max-Planck-Instituts für Geschichte 193), Göttingen 2004; Katherine I. French u. a. (Hg.), The Parish in English Life 1400-1600, Manchester 1997; Christian Giordano, Von der Familie zur Klientel. Die Aktivierung personalisierter Netzwerke in mediterranen Gesellschaften, in: Traverse 1996/3, 33-51; Claude Gauvard, Violence citadine et solidarités au Moyen Âge, in: Annales E.S.C. 48 (1993), 1113-1126; Andrea Zorzi, Contrôle social, ordre public et répression judiciaire à Florence à l'époque communale: éléments et problèmes, in: Annales E.S.C. 45 (1990), 1169-1188; John Henderson, The Parish and the Poor in Florence at the Time of the Black Death, in: Continuity and Change 3 (1988), 247-272; Christiane Klapisch-Zuber, Parenti, amici e vicini: il territorio urbano d'una famiglia mercantile nel XV secolo, in: Quaderni storici 33 (1976), 973-982.

[24] Julie Mayade-Claustre, Le petit peuple en difficulté: La prison pour dettes à Paris à la fin du Moyen Âge, in: Boglioni (Hg.), Le petit peuple (wie Anm. 2), 453-466.

Verschuldung und gerichtliche Konfiskation von Hab und Gut durch die Gläubiger werden in den oberrheinischen Gerichtsdokumenten als ständige latente Bedrohung für die mittleren und unteren Bevölkerungsgruppen manifest, auch die Armen mit ihrer geringen Habe waren davon nicht ausgenommen. Fehlten kleine Geldsummen, so ließ sich der momentane Mangel durch den Gang zur „Käuflerin", die mit Altkleidern und Gebrauchtwaren handelte, oder zu jüdischen Pfandleihern, die außerhalb der Städte in den elsässischen Dörfern lebten, beheben.[25] Die oberrheinischen Inventare reflektieren diese vorübergehende oder zur Regel gewordenen Notsituationen in Form kleiner Randbemerkungen, mit denen der Schreiber versetzte Kleidungsstücke, Wertgegenstände, Hausgerät und Werkzeug auflistet. Ein besonders eindrückliches Beispiel dafür ist das Inventar eines Rebknechts aus dem früheren 15. Jahrhundert, aus dem hervorgeht, dass seine Frau ein Rebmesser und eine Säge verpfändet hatte, um Brot kaufen zu können.[26] Das Beispiel dieses Ehepaars steht für einen großen Teil der zünftigen und unzünftigen Männer und Frauen der oberrheinischen Städte, die im Reb- und Ackerbau tätig waren und deren wirtschaftliche Balance durch jede kleine Teuerung aus dem Gleichgewicht gebracht wurde.

In den Druckereizentren Strassburg und Basel lässt sich außerdem für das 15. und 16. Jahrhundert – am anderen Ende der sozialen Skala – eine eindrückliche Anzahl von Bankrotten unter den Druckereiunternehmern und den von ihnen anhängigen Druckern belegen, deren Güter zuhanden ihrer Gläubiger konfisziert wurden. Diese Beschlagnahmeinventare widerspiegeln den hohen Lebensstandard der Druckereiunternehmer, gleichzeitig dokumentieren sie (zusammen mit andern Gerichtsakten) das hohe finanzielle

---

25 Auch Wirtsleute, Arbeitgeber von Mägden und Gesellen, Nachbarinnen und Nachbarn und Kollegen liehen Geld gegen Pfänder, Simon-Muscheid, Die Dinge (wie Anm. 23); Gustav Schmoller, Die öffentlichen Leihhäuser sowie das Pfandleih- und Rückkaufsrecht überhaupt, in: Jahrbuch für Gesetzgebung, Verwaltung und Volkswirtschaft NF 4 (1880), 87-123; Gerd Mentgen, Studien zur Geschichte der Juden im mittelalterlichen Elsass, Hannover 1995, 542-557.

26 Zur wirtschaftlich prekären Situation der im Reb- und Ackerbau tätigen Männer und Frauen, die als potentielle Arme bei der geringsten Preisschwankung vom sozialen Abstieg bedroht waren, vgl. Fischer, Städtische Armut (wie Anm. 18); ein Drittel bis die Hälfte der zünftigen und unzünftigen ansässigen Bevölkerung lebte vom Reb- und Ackerbau; die mobilen Lohnarbeiterinnen und -arbeiter, die sich für die Erntzeit verdingten, sind zahlenmäßig nicht fassbar, Katharina Simon-Muscheid, Ein Rebmesser hat sine frowe versetzt für 1 ß brotte. Armut in den oberrheinischen Städten des 15. und 16. Jahrhundert, in: Helmut Bräuer (Hg.), Arme (wie Anm. 3), 39-70.

Risiko. Wer nicht über ausreichende finanziellen Reserven oder Kreditfähigkeit verfügte und nicht rechtzeitig einen Profit erwirtschaftete, der die Bezahlung der ausstehenden Schulden ermöglichte, musste aufgeben und damit den Verlust von Status, Prestige und hohem Lebensstandard hinnehmen.[27] Von solchen Konkursen waren gleichermaßen die von ihnen angestellten Drucker, Korrektoren, Schriftgießer und anderen in der Buchproduktion beschäftigten Handwerker betroffen. Ihre Beschlagnahmeinventare zeichnen sich durch auffällige Unvollständigkeit aus, die nur den Schluss zulässt, dass diese wesentlich mobilere Gruppe bereits vor der drohenden Konfiskation geflohen war und ihr wichtigstes Arbeitsgerät und möglichst viel von ihrem Besitz mitgenommen hatte. Als Spezialisten des Buchdrucks konnten sie hoffen, in einem andern Druckereizentrum Arbeit zu finden.

Greifen wir auf die Geschichte des armen Heinrich zurück, denn am Beispiel der Lepra lässt sich für das Spätmittelalter der Zusammenhang von Krankheit und sozialer Ausgrenzung (nicht nur Abstieg) am deutlichsten zeigen. Dies hängt zusammen mit der Ambivalenz der Krankheit, die sich in der Literatur wie in den medizinischen Aitiologien und den populären Deutungsmustern manifestiert. Im Fall der Lepra überlagerten sich die Kategorien „unrein" (nach biblischer Tradition) und „krank" (im medizinischen Sinn), außerdem galt diese Krankheit als unheilbar und ansteckend. Aus diesem Grund hatten kirchliche und weltliche Autoritäten seit dem frühen Mittelalter Maßnahmen zur Absonderung der Leprösen und zu ihrer materiellen Unterstützung ergriffen. Leprosorien außerhalb der Siedlungen sollten die doppelte Ansteckungsgefahr verringern und verhindern, dass umherziehende Lepröse ihre Krankheit verbreiteten. Einer hochmittelalterlichen Phase der Identifizierung der „guten Leprösen" mit Christus (ähnlich wie die Idealisierung der freiwilligen Armut) folgte eine definitive Umdeutung, die die lepraspezifischen Negativstereotypen hervorhob und Leprösen an den Rand der Gesellschaft rückte.[28] Das Übergangsritual, mit dem die kranken

---

[27] Diese Beschlagnahmeinventare listen vollständige Druckereiwerkstätten mit Pressen, Papiervorräten und gedruckten Büchern sowie exklusiven Kleidern und Hauseinrichtungen auf, Simon-Muscheid, Die Dinge (wie Anm. 23); aus der Fülle der Literatur zum oberrheinischen Buchdruck Miriam U. Chrisman, Printing and the Evolution of Lay Culture in Strasbourg, in: Ronnie Po-Chia Hsia (Hg.), German People and the Reformation, Ithaca/London 1988, 74-100; Pierre Louis van der Haegen, Der frühe Basler Buchdruck: ökonomische, sozio-politische und informationssystematische Standortfaktoren und Rahmenbedingungen, Basel 2001.

[28] Der veränderte Tenor der Predigten widerspiegelt die veränderte Haltung gegenüber den Kranken: Waren die „leprosi deo voluntate" während des 13. Jahrhunderts die Adressaten

Männer und Frauen nach einer positiv verlaufenen Lepraschau ins Leprosorium aufgenommen wurden, kann durchaus unter der Perspektive der sozialen Ausgrenzung betrachtet werden. Mit einer Predigt wurden sie aus der Welt der Lebenden verabschiedet und durch eine Neueinkleidung in den Stand der „Leprosi" aufgenommen.

Wenn sich auch, wie etwa in Strassburg oder in andern großen Städten, zwei Leprosorien mit unterschiedlichem Standard nachweisen lassen[29], in denen wohlhabende Lepröse und arme Lepröse untergebracht wurden, so bedeutet dies doch die definitive Entfernung aus dem gewohnten Umfeld, das Einfügen in eine nicht freiwillig gewählte Gemeinschaft, die nach dem Muster religiöser Gemeinschaften geführt wurde, und den unfreiwillige Verzicht auf Handlungsfreiheit. Aus der Perspektive der notleidenden umherziehenden Leprösen mochte die Aufnahme in ein Leprosorium die erfreuliche Perspektive auf Nahrung und ein Dach über dem Kopf bedeuten. Von außen betrachtet gehörten beide in die Kategorie der „armen Siechen". Während bessergestellte Lepröse, die mit dem erzwungenen Übertritt ins Leprosorium ihre bürgerliche Existenz verloren, den Entscheid der lokalen Lepraschau anfochten und positive Gutachten aus andern Städten beibrachten, suchten Bettelnde als „falsche" Lepröse in den Leprosorien unterzukommen.[30]

Vor allem die englischsprachige Literatur fokussiert auf die prekäre Situation der Witwen. Die Situation von Witwen wird seit einigen Jahren international diskutiert; aufgeworfen wurde dabei die grundsätzliche Frage nach dem Zusammenhang von Witwenschaft, Armut und sozialem Abstieg. Dass der Witwenstand zu wirtschaftlichen Einbußen und einer sozial schwächeren Position führen konnte (durch Erbteilung, Erbstreitigkeiten, Verschuldung, ausstehende Schulden, Wegfall einer Einkommensquelle, (Wieder-) Aufnahme einer Erwerbstätigkeit etc.) ist unbestritten, doch bedeutete Heirat keineswegs eine sichere materielle Versorgung für Frauen.[31] Was sich hinge-

---

von Predigten gewesen, so richteten sich die Predigten mit dem ausgehenden 13. Jahrhundert an die „leprosos et abjectos", Bériou, Touati, Voluntate (wie Anm. 9).

[29] Jürgen Belker, Aussätzige: „Tückische Feinde" und „Armer Lazarus", in: Bernd-Ulrich Hergemöller (Hg.), Randgruppen der spätmittelalterlichen Gesellschaft, Warendorf 1990, 200-231, hier 212f.; Jankrift, Mit Gott (wie Anm. 9).

[30] Jankrift, Mit Gott (wie Anm. 9), 136.

[31] Karl Bücher hat dies in seiner einflussreichen Schrift *Die Frauenfrage im Mittelalter*, 2. verbesserte Aufl. Tübingen 1910, dargelegt. Seither schwingt dieser Tenor auch in der Forschung mit; Helmut Bräuer, Elke Schlenkrich, Armut, Verarmung und ihre öffentliche Wahrnehmung. Das sächsische Handwerk des ausgehenden 17. und 18. Jahrhunderts, in: Karl Heinrich Kaufhold, Wilfried Reininghaus (Hg.), Stadt und Handwerk, Köln-Weimar-

gen feststellen lässt, ist, dass die kumulierten Formen der „paupertas", nämlich fehlende Protektion, Verlust von Netzwerken, Fremdheit, Alter und abnehmende Arbeitskraft die Problematik der Witwenschaft verschärften. Als besonders eindrückliches Beispiel ist Christine de Pizan zu nennen, die als Witwe vergeblich um die Herausgabe der Güter ihres Mannes kämpfte. Doch nach dem Tod ihres Mannes verfügte sie am französischen Königshof über keine einflussreichen Freunde mehr oder solche, die es wagten, ihrem Widersacher entgegenzutreten, wie sie bitter beklagte. Doppelt schutzlos als junge Witwe und als Fremde gab sie schließlich den aussichtslosen Kampf um das Erbe auf. Fortan stand für sie das Problem, sich und ihre Familie zu ernähren, im Vordergrund.[32]

Was sich aus dem oberrheinischen Material herausarbeiten ließ, ist ein Phänomen, das unter bestimmten Umständen auch als frauenspezifische Form des sozialen Abstiegs interpretiert werden kann, nämlich als Magd dienen zu müssen. Magddienst wird in den gängigen Life-Cycle-Modellen als Durchgangsphase für junge Mädchen bis zur Heirat verstanden.[33] Was

---

Wien 2000, 93-117, verweisen nachdrücklich auf die Verarmung von arbeitenden Handwerkern, Lohnarbeitern und Dienstboten, welche die betroffenen Männer und Frauen zu „Überbrückungsbettel" oder zur Bitte um Unterstützung zwang; zu Existenzproblemen und Überlebensstrategien (verheirateter und verwitweter) Frauen im Handwerk vgl. Katharina Simon-Muscheid (Hg.), „Was nützt die Schusterin dem Schmied". Frauen und Handwerk vor der Industrialisierung, Frankfurt-New York 1998; gegen den automatisch gedachten Zusammenhang zwischen dem Verlust des männlichen Beschützers/Ernährers und einem unausweichlichen sozialen Abstieg der Witwen vgl. Patricia Skinner, Gender and Poverty in the Medieval Community, in: Diane Bornstein Watt (Hg.), Medieval Women in Their Communities, Toronto 1997, 204-221; zu weiblichen Netzwerken als Überlebensstrategie Sharon Farmer, Surviving Poverty in Medieval Paris. Gender, Ideology, and the Daily Lives of the Poor, Ithaca 2002; bereits Annette Winter, Studien zur sozialen Lage der Frauen in der Stadt Trier nach den Steuerbüchern von 1364. Die Unterschichten, in: Kurtrierisches Jahrbuch 15 (1975), 20-46, hat auf solche Frauenhaushalte aufmerksam gemacht.

32 Dazu ihre autobiographische Schrift L'Avision Christine, hg. v. Liliane Dulac, Christine M. Reno, Paris 1998; die schwere Krankheit ihres Vaters, der als Arzt und Astrologe von Venedig an den Hof König Karls V. berufen worden war, hatte die finanziellen Reserven der Familie aufgezehrt; nach dem Tod ihres Ehemanns blieb sie als 25jährige Witwe mit drei kleinen Kindern zurück und musste auch für ihre Mutter und ihre Nichte aufkommen; zu ihrer Furcht vor der drohenden Armut Otto Gerhard Oexle, Christine et les pauvres, in: Margarethe Zimmermann, Diana de Rentiis (Hg.), The City of Scholars. New Approaches to Christine de Pizan (European Cultures 2) Berlin/New York 1994, 206-220.

33 Gegen dieses statische Modell, das die (unfreiwillige) Flexibilität weiblicher Lebensläufe nicht berücksichtigt, unter Einbezug der unterschiedlichen Arbeitssituationen und Le-

sich hier hingegen abzeichnet, ist eine Erwerbs- und Überlebensform, die Frauen aller Altergruppen, jungen Mädchen, ledigen Müttern, aber auch verheirateten, entlaufenen, verlassenen, geschiedenen Ehefrauen und Witwen eine Art Auskommen bot.

Um zu verhindern, dass ihre langjährigen Mägde nach dem Tod ihrer Herrin in die Armut abglitten, und um sich gleichzeitig eine Pflegerin bis ans Lebensende zu sichern, vermachten Erblasserinnen ihren getreuen Mägden Kleider, Betten, Hausrat unter der Bedingung, dass sie bis zu ihrem Lebensende in ihrem Dienst blieben. Auch die oberrheinischen Nachlassinventare enthalten oft Hinweise auf mündlich zugesagte Legate, allerdings lässt sich in solchen Fällen das Alter der betreffenden Magd nicht eruieren. Dennoch erlaubt die Bandbreite der Mägdeinventare Rückschlüsse auf die unterschiedlichen Lebenssituationen dieser Frauen, die durch „Dienen" ihren Lebensunterhalt verdienen mussten.[34]

Aus den oberrheinischen Gerichtsdokumenten des 15. und 16. Jahrhunderts werden weitere Gründe für einen sozialen Abstieg ersichtlich, die Männer und Frauen in verschiedener Weise trafen: Wenn die städtische Justiz Mörder, Verräter und Stadtfeinde hinrichten ließ und ihr Vermögen konfiszieren, so schuf sie damit gleichzeitig eine weitere Kategorie von sozialen Absteigern, nämlich die Frauen und Kinder der Verurteilten als sekundäre Opfer. Waren diese auch unschuldig, so traf sie die Strafe dennoch mit, denn durch die Konfiskation verloren Frau und Kinder ihre Existenzbasis, und die Kinder gingen ihres väterlichen Erbes verlustig. Die Verurteilung des Ehemannes führte somit zu einem Verlust der Perspektive für die folgende Generation. Griffen in solchen Fällen die erwähnten Netzwerke nicht ein, so war ihr Abgleiten in die Armut – oder zumindest die Unmöglichkeit, weiter-

---

bensperspektiven Dorothee Rippmann, „Frauenwerk" und Männerarbeit, Gesinde, Tagelöhner und Tagelöhnerinnen in der spätmittelalterlichen Stadt, in: Basler Zeitschrift für Geschichtswissenschaft und Altertumskunde 95 (1995), 5-42; Barbara Hanawalt, Growing up in Medieval London. The Experience of Childhood in History, Oxford-New York 1993; Mireille Vincent-Cassy, Dedans et dehors: les domestiques à la fin du Moyen Âge, in: Gerd Melville, Peter von Moos (Hg.), Das Öffentliche und das Private in der Vormoderne, Köln-Weimar-Wien 1998, 498-527.

[34] Beispiele für solche bedingte Legate an Mägde in Paul Baur, Testament und Bürgerschaft im spätmittelalterlichen Konstanz (Konstanzer Geschichts- und Rechtsquellen 31), Sigmaringen 1989, 202-205; Gabriela Signori, „wann ein früntschaft die andere bringt". Kleriker und ihre Mägde in spätmittelalterlichen Testamenten (13.-15. Jahrhundert), in: Eva Labouvie (Hg.), Ungleiche Paare. Zur Kulturgeschichte menschlicher Beziehungen, München 1997, 11-32; Simon-Muscheid, Die Dinge (wie Anm. 23).

hin standesgemäß zu leben – vorprogrammiert. Dasselbe galt für die politischen Auseinandersetzungen zwischen den einzelnen Städten oder den Fehden zwischen dem umliegendem Adel und den Städten, bei denen die unterlegene Partei verbannt oder getötet wurde. Wurden die Besitzverhältnisse neu geregelt oder ihr Hab und Gut zuhanden der Sieger eingezogen, gingen Ehefrauen und Kinder der Unterlegenen wiederum leer aus. Flucht und Verbannung bedeutete für Männer und Frauen insofern einen sozialen Abstieg, als Flüchtlinge ihren Rechtsstatus verloren und als Fremde einen neuen Beschützer und eine neue Existenzbasis suchen mussten.

Diese frauenspezifische Form des sozialen Abstiegs quasi als „Nebeneffekt" politischer Ereignisse hatte ihrerseits weitreichende Auswirkungen auf die nächste Generation. Denn der Verlust des Erbes veränderte die Lebensperspektiven der Kinder, er beeinflusste den künftigen Lebensstandard, den Sozialstatus der Erben, die Heiratschancen der Erbinnen und – nicht zu unterschätzen – im stadtbürgerlichen Milieu die Ausbildungschancen der Knaben.

Was diesen Aspekt so interessant macht, sind Prozesse, die einige der betroffenen Ehefrauen gegen die Städte anstrengten, die ihre Männer verurteilt hatten. Sie prozessierten oft über Jahre hinweg, um ihr eigenes Hab und Gut und das Erbe ihrer Kinder zurückzuerlangen. Dabei beschränkten sie sich nicht auf die Rolle der armen Bittstellerin und der hilf- und schutzlosen Frau, die aus ihrer weiblichen Schwäche heraus agiert.[35] Sie verliehen ihren Forderungen Nachdruck, indem sie Söldner anheuerten, die in ihrem Namen Fehden gegen die betreffende Stadt führten.

3.2. Der feine Unterschied

Wenn Filme über das Mittelalter Armut bildlich umsetzen, so greifen sie in den Fonds populärer Vorstellungen: Arme sind als Arme kenntlich, wenn sie zerfetzte Kleidung tragen und wenn sie ungekämmt und schmutzig daherkommen. Doch dies trifft nur auf die unterste Stufe, die Bettelarmut zu. Genau diese Sichtbarkeit der Armut wollten die andern Armen durch Verhalten

---

[35] Katharina Simon-Muscheid, Der weite Weg zur Erbschaft. Weibliche Rechtswege und Strategien im späten Mittelalter, in: Jens Flemming u.a. (Hg.), Lesarten der Geschichte. Ländliche Ordnungen und Geschlechterverhältnisse, FS Heide Wunder, Kassel 2004, 402-417; zu einem besonders prominenten Fall weiblicher Selbsthilfe Dorothee Rippmann, Königsschicksal in Frauenhand. Der „Kronraub" von Visegrád im Brennpunkt von Frauenpolitik und ungarischer Reichspolitik, ebenda 377-401.

und Kleidung um jeden Preis vermeiden, weshalb wir auch vom „feinen Unterschied“ sprechen können. Die Analyse der oberrheinischen Inventare des 15./16. Jahrhunderts hat eine große Bandbreite unterschiedlicher Existenzformen armer Männer und Frauen zu Tage gefördert. Sie belegt nachdrücklich die verschiedenen Armutsstufen von sichtlich verarmten handwerklich-bürgerlicher Haushalten, über Bezieherinnen und Bezieher städtischer Almosen, Randständigen bis hin zur mobilen Bettelarmut.

Der soziale Abstieg war kein standes- oder geschlechtsspezifisches Phänomen. Er hatte jedoch für die verschiedenen Stände, sozialen Gruppen und die beiden Geschlechter unterschiedliche Auswirkungen. Zu den „pauperes“ im weiteren Sinn zählten ebenso die Notleidenden in unserm Sinn wie die veramten Adeligen und reichen Bürger, die aus Mangel auf die standesgemäße Lebensweise verzichten mussten, zu der sie ihr Stand verpflichtete. Der schon erwähnte Pariser Kanoniker Guillaume de Saint Amour hatte diese sozialen Absteiger in seinen Schriften auch berücksichtigt. Sosehr er gegen die „valides mendicantes“ polemisierte, so plädierte er für eine standesgemäße Behandlung von Angehörigen höherer Stände, die in die Armut abgeglitten waren. Diese sollten bei der Unterstützung privilegiert werden, denn, so argumentierte er, mit dem Verlust ihrer Habe hätten die Betroffenen auch einen empfindlichen Statusverlust erlitten. Auf diesen verlorenen Status, der sie vor den andern Armen auszeichne, müsse Rücksicht genommen werden.[36]

Eine weitere privilegierte Kategorie bildeten – auch nach den Kriterien der spätmittelalterlichen Fürsorge – die „verschämten Armen“ (auch Hausarme). Diese Bezeichnung, die Armut mit Scham verbindet, setzte ein Ehrgefühl voraus, dass sie die öffentlich sichtbare Kennzeichnung als „arm“ und „unterstützt“ als stigmatisierend empfinden ließ.[37] Zu diesen zählten Männer

---

[36] Dufeil, Guillaume de St.-Amour, (wie Anm. 14).

[37] Zur Diskussion des Begriffs „verschämte Arme“ vgl. Felten, Zusammenfassung (wie Anm. 2), 381f.; nach Definition eines Frankfurter Arztes von 1428: „Personen, welche heimlich Hauskummer leiden und doch ihre Tage mit Ehre zugebracht haben. Hausarme, die sich mit ihrer getreuen Arbeit nähren und doch keinen ausreichenden Verdienst haben, solche Menschen, die sich früher ihren Bedarf erworben haben, jetzt aber Alters oder Krankheits halben es nicht mehr zu tun vermögen, ferner fromme Hausarme, welche mit Kindern überladen sind und dieselben nicht ernähren können, und endlich fromme hausarme Frauen, welche Kindbetterinnen sind oder ihrer Entbindung entgegensehen“, zitiert bei Erich Maschke, Die Unterschichten der mittelalterlichen Städte Deutschlands, in: Erich Maschke, Jürgen Sydow (Hg.), Gesellschaftliche Unterschichten in den südwestdeut-

und Frauen aus handwerklich-bürgerlichen Kreisen, die „ohne eigenes Verschulden" in eine Notlage geraten waren. Es waren Menschen, die ihr Leben lang gearbeitet hatten und – modern ausgedrückt – „working poors", deren Einkommen nicht ausreichte, um ihre Familie zu ernähren. Auch sie hatten Anspruch auf Rücksichtnahme, die in diskreter Unterstützung bestand und damit ihr Ehrgefühl nicht verletzte. In den oberrheinischen Inventaren wird diese privilegierte Gruppe sichtbar. Es sind Männer und Frauen, deren Inventare obrigkeitliche Tuch- und Kleideralmosen enthalten und deren Hausrat zumindest Reste handwerklich-bürgerlicher Ensembles sowie „anständige" Kleidung aufweisen.[38]

Zu den Privilegierten zählten – zumindest aus obrigkeitlicher Perspektive – diejenigen armen Männer und Frauen, die durch ein obrigkeitliches Zeichen zum Almosenheischen berechtigt waren.[39] Dieses Abzeichen aus Metall, das ihre Trägerinnen und Träger in der Öffentlichkeit als unterstützungswürdige Arme kennzeichnen sollte, musste gut sichtbar an der Kleidung befestigt werden. Doch diese gut gemeinte Auszeichnung erwies sich mitunter als kontraproduktiv, denn es wurde von der Bevölkerung mit den gängigen vestimentären Stigmasymbolen assoziiert, die Angehörige verschiedener Randgruppen zu tragen gezwungen waren.[40] Die derart Privilegierten, deren Umgebung diese feinen Unterschiede nicht zur Kenntnis nahm, baten denn auch ihre Obrigkeiten, ihnen das Tragen dieses Zeichens zu erlassen.

Beziehen wir die „armen Siechen" wieder ein, so können wir auch in ihrem Fall seit dem späten Mittelalter von obrigkeitlich vorgeschriebenen Zei-

---

schen Städten (Veröffentlichungen der Kommission für geschichtliche Landeskunde in Baden-Württemberg, Reihe B 69), Stuttgart 1967, 1-74, hier 63.

38 Zur Hierarchie der Armen und ihren Möglichkeiten, sich gegen „weiter unten" abzugrenzen Simon-Muscheid, Die Dinge (wie Anm. 23), 209-242.

39 Zur Problematik dieser Zeichen, die erstmals in der zweiten Hälfte des 14. Jahrhunderts fassbar werden, Helmut Bräuer, Bettel- und Almosenzeichen zwischen Norm und Praxis, in: Gerhard Jaritz (Hg.), Norm und Praxis im Alltag des Mittelalters und in der frühen Neuzeit (Forschungen des Instituts für Realienkunde des Mittelalters und der frühen Neuzeit. Diskussionen und Materialien 2), Wien 1997, 75-93.

40 Danièle Sansy, Marquer la différence: l'imposition de la rouelle au XIIIe et XIVe siècles, in: La rouelle et la croix, destins des juifs en Occident (Médiévales 41, 2001), 15-36; Robert Jütte, Stigma-Symbole. Kleidung als identitätsstiftendes Merkmal bei spätmittelalterlichen und frühneuzeitlichen Randgruppen (Juden, Dirnen, Aussätzige, Bettler), in: Neidhart Bulst, Robert Jütte (Hg.), Zwischen Sein und Schein. Kleidung und Identität in der ständischen Gesellschaft (Saeculum 44), Freiburg-München 1993, 65-89; Graus, Randgruppen (wie Anm. 22).

chen zur Unterscheidung von den Gesunden sprechen. Ihr Statuswechsel wurde bei ihrem Eintritt ins Leprosorium durch die Einkleidung sichtbar gemacht wurde, sie erhielten einen grauen Mantel, einem breiten Hut sowie Handschuhe. Dazu kam das Attribut, das durch akustische Signale auf die als gefährlich betrachteten Leprösen aufmerksam machen sollte, nämlich die Klapper.[41]

3.3. Emotionen

In literarischen Fiktionen lamentieren die Protagonistinnen und Protagonisten über ihre Situation, in historischen Quellen sind direkte Äußerungen und verbal ausgedrückte Emotionen wesentlich seltener zu finden. Doch werden auch hier Gefühle im Zusammenhang mit dem (befürchteten) sozialen Abstieg manifest. Scham war nicht nur ein Gefühl, das den „guten" Armen als Attribut von außen zugewiesen wurde, sondern der konkrete Gegenpol von Ehre, die auch im handwerklich-bürgerlichen Kontext den „verhaltensleitenden Code" abgab.[42] Aus den direkten und indirekten Zeugenaussagen vor Gericht geht hervor, dass der Verlust von Ehre, Sozialstatus und materieller Sicherheit Scham- und Angstgefühle auslösten. Eindrücklich ist die Klage einer Frau, deren Mann wegen eines Mordes aus der Stadt geflohen war, und deren Hab und Gut von obrigkeitlichen Beamten zum Zweck der Konfiskation inventarisiert wurde. Was sie als konkrete Perspektive beklagt, ist die Vertreibung aus ihrem Haus, der Verlust von Hab und Gut, die zerstörte Lebensperspektive für ihre Kinder und die beschämende Vorstellung, um Almosen bitten zu müssen. Es ist die bedrohliche Vorstellung des sozialen

---

[41] Belker, „Tückischer Feind" (wie Anm. 29); Jütte, Stigma-Symbole (wie Anm. 40), 75-77; die Ausgrenzung in Frankreich ging wesentlich weiter: Das Konzil von Lavaur bestimmte 1368 „il est normal de choyer par compassion et d'enserrer dans les bras de la charité fraternelle due par tout bon chrétien ceux que le jugement divin à touché par la lèpre corporelle, toutefois comme leur maladie apparaît contagieuse et gagne le corps des bien-portants par contact, nous, voulant prémunir contre les dangers de leur fréquentation, décidons que les lépreux demeureront ainsi écartés des valides, et ne pourront entrer dans les églises ordinaires, ni fréquenter les places publiques, les marchés, les échoppes ou tout autre endroit commun aux gens sains [...]. Ils porteront un insigne sur leurs vêtements, grâce auquel on les différenciera des personnes valides", Touati, Maladie (wie Anm. 9), 755.

[42] Klaus Schreiner, Gerd Schwerhoff, Verletzte Ehre. Überlegungen zu einem Forschungskonzept, in: Klaus Schreiner, Gerd Schwerhoff (Hg.), Verletzte Ehre. Ehrkonflikte in Gesellschaften des Mittelalters und der Frühen Neuzeit, Köln-Weimar-Wien 199, 1-28.

Abstiegs, den die ehrbare junge Ehefrau eines Handwerkers in relativ gesicherten Verhältnissen vor sich sieht.[43] Zorn über ungerechte Gerichtsurteile ist ein anderes Gefühl, das in den Gerichtsdokumenten deutlich fassbar wird. In den meisten Fällen macht er sich in Beschimpfungen und leeren Drohungen Luft. In den oben erwähnten Prozessen hingegen setzen ihn die zornigen, vom Gericht gedemütigten Ehefrauen in Taten um und kämpfen hartnäckig um Rehabilitation und Rückgabe ihres Besitzes.[44]

4. Sozialer Abstieg: Synthese

Endgültiger oder bloß temporärer Verlust ist ein Schlüsselwort, das den sozialen Abstieg charakterisiert. Sozialer Abstieg verändert die Position im Koordinatennetz subjektiv und objektiv, ideell wie materiell. Er reduziert den sozialen und rechtlichen Status, vernichtet Machtpositionen und tangiert die Ehre. Außerdem wirkt er sich auf das Umfeld aus, das die soziale Position mitdefiniert, und verändert damit auch die Qualität von Beziehungsnetzen. In der literarischen Fiktion sieht sich die Grafentochter gezwungen, bei einer armen Frau Schutz zu suchen und der leprös gewordene Ritter muss sich aus der höfischen Gesellschaft zurückziehen. Die Herrin wird zur Bittstellerin, der Ritter zum stigmatisierten Außenseiter. Ändert sich die Situation nicht, so verschlechtern sich künftige Heiratschancen, Erbschaftsaussichten sowie der Status der Kinder, das heißt, die folgende Generation ist direkt mitbetroffen.

Sozialer Abstieg manifestiert sich gegen außen durch Verhaltensweisen und Zeichen. Auf der Ebene der Verhaltensweisen kann die direkte Folge der freiwillige oder erzwungene Abbruch von familialen, politischen, sozialen, spirituellen, nachbarschaftlichen, geschäftlichen Beziehungen sein. Damit verbindet sich der freiwillige Wechsel des Wohnorts auf der Suche nach neuen Beschützern oder Alliierten; erzwungen wird der Wechsel durch Ver-

---

43 Die hoch emotionale Rede der Frau, die auch ihre Enttäuschung über die versprochenen, jedoch unterbliebenen Hilfeleistungen der „Patrons“ an der Spitze der Klientel nicht verhehlt (Versetzen des Silbergeschirrs zu ihrer materiellen Unterstützung, Erziehung ihres Knaben), wird von einem Bekannten vor Gericht referiert, der als Augen- und Ohrenzeuge ihr Gespräch mit einer vertrauten Verwandten mitbekommen hatte, Simon-Muscheid, Die Dinge (wie Anm. 23), 310-315.

44 Die Demütigung wurde von Frauen aus Adel und Patriziat als besonders schwer empfunden, wenn sie vor einem städtischen, mit Bürgern und Handwerkern besetzten Gericht eine Niederlage erlitten hatten.

bannung, Flucht vor Feinden oder einem drohenden Prozess. Auf der Ebene der Zeichen wird der soziale Abstieg sichtbar durch nicht mehr standesgemäße Kleidung, Nahrung und Lebensweise allgemein sowie das Fehlen standesgemäßer Objekte. Das obrigkeitlich erzwungene Tragen bestimmter Kleidungsstücke und Abzeichen machen im Fall der privilegierten Armen wie der Leprösen den neuen Status gegen außen sichtbar.

Sozialer Abstieg bedeutet nicht nur ein vertikales Absinken in der Hierarchie, sondern kann mitunter das Abdriften in Randbereiche der Gesellschaft nach sich ziehen. Obgleich Armut und Randständigkeit nicht deckungsgleich sind, überschneiden sie sich doch zu einem Teil.

Maria Bendinelli Predelli

Dame Poverty among Saints, Poets, and Humanists: Italian Intellectuals Confronted with the Question of Poverty

Introduction

The theme of poverty is prominent in Italian literature, and recurs frequently in both lyrical poetry and didactic prose from the thirteenth century to the dawn of the Renaissance. Poverty is, however, a multifaceted concept, which underwent important transformations over the course of the centuries, at the same time as medieval society evolved from the essentially rural setting of the higher Middle Ages to the urban landscape of the thirteenth and fourteenth centuries. My presentation will concentrate on some texts of the fourteenth century, which I believe will provide a fair picture of the diverse positions vis-à-vis the question of poverty in a century especially representative of Italian history and culture. This essay is divided into three parts: in the first one I examine two Italian re-elaborations of some famous passages on poverty found in Pope Innocent III's *De contemptu mundi*; in the second part I shall focus on the literary expressions of the Franciscan exaltation of poverty and the reactions to it in lay society; in the third one I point to a different way of considering the same question, greatly influenced by the humanist movement.

1. Re-elaborations of De contemptu mundi

In his work *De miseria condicionis humane*, also known as *De contemptu mundi*, Lotario de' Segni (later to become Pope Innocent III) has a passage on "the miseries of the poor" which was repeated in several Italian writings. We are concerned here with the re-elaborations by Bono Giamboni (c. 1240-1292) and Antonio Pucci (c. 1310-1388). Bono Giamboni, a writer known for his vernacular translations of Latin historical works and his moral treatises, was a judge in Florence from 1261 to 1291. He re-elaborated

Lotario's work in his *Della miseria dell'uomo,* a book which was in turn the source of Antonio Pucci's passage.[1] Antonio Pucci, who also lived in Florence, was an employee of the Commune and a prolific author of gnomic, historical and romantic poems.[2] His *Libro di varie storie* is a personal book of notes, a "Zibaldone", where he recorded information and ideas from the books he was reading. It is most interesting to compare how the three texts deal with the same subject, poverty, and note how different the spirit of the three passages is, in spite of the fact that the authors drew upon each others' ideas.

Ch. 14: Pauperes enim premuntur inedia, cruciantur erumpna, fame, siti, frigore, nuditate; vilescunt et contabescunt, spernuntur et confunduntur. O miserabilis condicio mendicantis!

Et si petit, pudore confunditur, et si non petit, egestate consumitur, set ut mendicet necessitate compellitur. Deum causatur iniquum quod non recte dividat; proximum criminatur malignum quod non plene subveniat; in-

Some say that [...] those who are poor in terms of material possessions, in terms of food, drink, dress, and footwear, are shabby, that they are scorned and sneered at, and others whisper behind their backs so that they become timid, and faint-hearted, and are afraid to request that other people assist in meeting their needs. Therefore, poverty has a significant hold on them. Many services are requested of them and they are weighed

Poverty, some say, is far worse than wealth, because the poor are not only poor in terms of money, but also in terms of food, drink, dress, and footwear. They are shabby; they are scorned, sneered at, and mocked. Others whisper behind their backs, so that they become timid, faint-hearted, and afraid to request anything from other people. Meanwhile, they become servants to the rich, who shout out commands such as "Go

[1] Cf. Santorre Debenedetti, 'Bono Giamboni,' *Studi medievali* 4 (1913), 271-277; Cesare Segre, Introductions to his editions of *Volgarizzamenti del Due e Trecento* (Torino, 1964), 317-18 and Bono Giamboni, *Libro de' vizi e delle virtù e il Trattato di virtù e di vizi*, ed. Cesare Segre (Torino, 1968), XIII-XXIX. Among Giamboni's translations are *Le Storie contra i Pagani di Paolo Orosio*, ed. Francesco Tassi (Firenze, 1849); *Dell'arte della guerra di Vegezio Flavio*, ed. Francesco Fontani (Firenze, 1815); *Fiore di Rettorica,* ed. Gianbattista Speroni (Pavia, 1994); and *Libro de' vizi e delle virtù.*

[2] Cf. Natalino Sapegno, "Antonio Pucci" in *Pagine di storia letteraria* (Firenze, 1986), 87-114 (1st ed. Palermo, 1960, 135-81); *Firenze alla vigilia del Rinascimento. Antonio Pucci e i suoi contemporanei*, ed. Maria Bendinelli Predelli (Fiesole, 2006). A selection of texts may be found in *Rimatori del Trecento*, ed. Giuseppe Corsi (Torino, 1969), 778-900.

dignatur, murmurat (*sic*), imprecatur.	down with duties.	here, go there! Do this, do that!", and they, for whom even the smallest burden is already too onerous, become weighed down with duties.
[Ch. 15 ... Quod si non habet, habere compellitur, et si habet, cogitur non habere.	And yet if they have some money, they are compelled not to have it, and if they do not have it, they are able to think only of getting it; and they are abused and beaten, and no one has any sympathy for them. If a rich man is injured by others, he gains from it;	If they do not have money, they are compelled to have it, and if they have it, they are constrained not to have it. If a man cannot have money, he is humiliated, abused, and beaten; and if he abuses others, a double punishment is inflicted upon him, and the rich are the only ones to gain anything from it.
Culpa domini, servi pena; culpa servi, domini preda.	and if a rich man commits a crime, the poor man will bear the punishment.	It often happens that a crime is committed against a poor man, and he is condemned as if he were the perpetrator and not the victim. Furthermore, if a rich man commits a sin, the poor man bears the punishment. The poor become thieves out of necessity,[3] and even if they do not become thieves, they are believed to be so by oth-

[3] G. Chaucer translated the same passage in his Prologue of the *Man of Law's Tale*. Vv. 104-105 read: "thou most for indigence / or stele, or begge, or borwe thy despence."

"Quicquid delirant reges, plectuntur Achivi."]

Adverte super hoc sentenciam sapienties: "Melius est mori quam indigere." "Eciam proximo suo pauper odiosus eris." "Omnes dies pauperis mali." « Fratres hominis pauperis oderunt eum, insuper et amici procul recessereunt ab eo. » "Cum fueris felix, multos numerabis amicos. Tempora si fuerint nubila, solus eris."

Lotario de'Segni, *De miseria condicionis humane* (1195)[4]

Horace says that when the aristocrats fight, the poor folk and the servants are the ones who suffer. Because of this, and many other things that could be added, one can agree with Solomon's view of the poor man: "It is better to die than to be poor, because a poor man's days are all unhappy, and his brothers hate him."

(Translation: Amanda Glover)

Bono Giamboni (1240-c. 1292), *Della miseria dell'uomo*[5]

ers and are trusted by no one. They are considered bad and wicked; rude comments are directed at them and they do not dare respond. Their wisdom is worthless and is reputed to be madness. Their strength is said to be laziness, their bravery is thought to be cowardice, and if one turns to religion others say "he was not brave enough to endure the hardships of secular life." Hence why Solomon's remark is so a propos, "'Tis better to die than to live a life of poverty, a life in which all of one's days are unhappy."

(Translation: Amanda Glover)

Antonio Pucci (c. 1310 -1388), *Libro di varie storie*[6]

---

[4] Lotario dei Segni (Pope Innocent III), *De miseria condicionis humane*, ed. Robert E. Lewis (Athens, 1978), 114-119.

[5] "Furono certi, che dissono ... coloro, che sono poveri d'avere, di manicare, e di bere, e di vestire, e di calzare, sono male in arnese, e sono spregiati e scherniti, *e mormorato è loro dietro,* e però diventano tipidi e vili e temono di richiedere altrui in su i bisogni, laonde la povertà maggiormente li distrigne. *E sono molti di servigi richiesti e di fazioni gravati,* e però se hanno alcuna cosa, sono costretti di non ne avere, e se non ne hanno, fa loro bi-

Lotario (1160-1215) was a nobleman (the son of a count), a monk who studied theology in Paris, and the nephew of pope Clement III, who made him cardinal. His book *De miseria condicionis humane*, written in 1195, enjoyed immense popularity and was translated into all the major European languages. Among others, Chaucer also provided a partial translation of it. The chapter on poverty is part of the first book, where Lotario deals with *de miserabili humane conditionis ingressu,* all the sufferings which affect human life from the moment of conception until old age, without any distinction of condition, social status or age.[7]

Chapter 14 of the first book, appropriately titled *De miseria pauperis et divitis*, offers within the same chapter reasons to pity the poor and reasons to

---

sogno di pensare pur d'averne*; e sì ne sono straziati e sono ingiuriati e battuti, e niuno se ne duole.* Se gli è ingiuriato il ricco da altrui, ne guadagna; e se il ricco commette il peccato, il povero ne porta la pena; onde dice Orazio: Di ciò che tencionano i grandi, i minori e soggetti lo comperano. Per queste e altre molte miserie, che dell'uomo povero si potrebbero dire, disse Salamone: Meglio è a morire, che esser povero, però che i dì suoi sono tutti rei, e i fratelli lo hanno in odio." Bono Giamboni, *Della miseria dell'uomo*, ed. Francesco Tassi (Firenze, 1836), ch. 11. Italics show Giamboni's additions.

[6] "Povertà, disse alcuno, è molto peggio che ricchezza, però che i poveri son poveri non solamente di danari, ma di mangiare, di bere, di vestire e di calzare, vanno male in arnesi, sono spregiati, ischerniti e uccellati ed è mormorato lor dietro, onde diventano timidi e vili e temorosi de richiedere altrui e sono richiesti da' più ricchi di servigi *con atto comandativo: 'Vammi qua e vammi là, fammi questo e fammi quello'*, e sono gravati di fazioni, *che non hanno sì picciola soma che non sia loro troppo grande.* E se hanno alcuna cosa sono costretti di non avere e se non hanno conviene loro procacciare d'avere *e se non ne possono avere* sono straziati e ingiuriati e battuti; e se ingiuriano altrui portano la pena doppia e 'l ricco ne guadagna, *e molte volte sono ingiuriati e condannati come s'egli avesser dato, e hanno ricevuto.* Ancora, se il ricco commette il peccato, il povero porta la pena; *diventano per bisogno ladri, e se non diventano, sì sono tenuti e niuno si fida di loro, sono tenuti cattivi e tristi, odono villania e non osano rispondere, il loro senno niente vale ed è riputato mattezza, loro fortezza è detta poltroneria, loro prodezza è tenuta viltà, se diventa religioso si dice: 'No gli dava il cuore di vivere'.* E però disse bene Salamone: 'Meglio è morire che viver sempre povero, però che i dì suoi son tutti rei'." Antonio Pucci, *Libro di varie storie,* ed. Alberto Varvaro, Atti della Accademia di Scienze Lettere e Arti di Palermo, s. IV, vol. 16, Parte seconda, fasc. 2 (Palermo, 1957), 100-101. Italics show Pucci's additions.

[7] The second book deals with the desires of man and shows how seeking for riches, pleasures and honours leads to sin and guilt (*de culpabili humane conditionis progressu*); the third book insists on the moments of death and decay, the punishments of hell and the terrible awe of the Last Judgment (*de dampnabili humane conditionis egressu*).

pity the rich.[8] If we analyze the passage we realize that the style is very detached. *Pauperes* are indicated as a collective entity, with a plural noun, which is the subject of verbs conjugated in the passive form. The distance between the narrator's voice and the object of discussion is even more apparent in the sentences that follow, where the impersonal form is used: *Deum causatur iniquum, proximum criminatur malignum*: 'the situation is such that God is being accused of being unjust, the neighbor is being accused of being evil...' The poor are never a "subject": they don't *do* anything. They only function as grammatical subjects of a passive or an intransitive verb or they are vaguely referred to by an impersonal form. The few introductory statements on the conditions of the poor are immediately followed by quotations from the Bible. The critique of how judgments are formulated according to the fortunes of a person (always in the passive form) serves as a transition to statements on the misery of the rich. Although fewer reasons are found to pity the "misery" of the rich, it is clear that the author intends to keep an equally distant and superior point of view vis-a-vis both conditions. The rhetorical figures he uses, especially the many parallelisms, reveal not only the "characteristics of the medieval classroom"[9] but also the attitude of an author for whom the poor existed in an entirely alien and distant universe.

Turning our attention to Bono Giamboni's text, I shall first point out that, in spite of it being a fairly faithful translation of the passage from the *Contemptu mundi*, its inspiration stems from very different concerns. In fact, Bono Giamboni borrows the description of poverty from Lotario only to refute the thesis that the connotations of poverty are exclusively negative. The approach of the Florentine judge is that of an educator whose primary intent is to give good moral advice to his readers. The negative statements on poverty are presented as the opinions of someone else,[10] and the judge refutes them in the following chapter, maintaining that poverty may be an asset, especially from a moral point of view, provided that certain conditions

---

[8] It is one of a group of chapters where the author exposes the miseries of the different conditions: 14. *De miseria pauperis et divitis*, 15. *De miseria servorum et dominorum*, 16. *De miseria continentis et coniugati*, 17. *De miseria bonorum et malorum*.

[9] Robert E. Lewis, Introduction to Lotario dei Segni (Pope Innocent III), *De miseria condicionis humane* (*op. cit. supra*, n. 3), 3.

[10] "Furono certi, che dissono: Pogniamo che le ricchezze siano ree; io ti vo' mostrare che la povertà è vie peggiore, però voglio fuggire povertade e abbracciare ricchezze, perché coloro, che sono poveri d'avere, di manicare, e di bere, ecc." (ch. 11). (Some authorities state the following: Let's admit that riches are morally reprehensible; yet, I want to show you that poverty is far worse, and therefore I want to avoid poverty and embrace riches because those who are poor in terms of material possessions, in terms of food, drink, etc.)

are respected. To paraphrase the author: responding to what has been said, the sages state that poverty may be good or evil. I will show you the qualities a poor person must have in order to make his poverty a good thing ... and I will show you that a life of poverty is better than a life of wealth because it leads to salvation with lesser risks and obstacles.[11] The rhetorical device whereby the writer directly addresses the reader and the use of the first person plural already indicates a more cordial and participatory approach as well as a didactic attitude. The general intent of the passage (and in fact of the whole book) also demonstrates a more optimistic outlook on life. The writer addresses himself to ordinary lay people; he does not advocate the flight from this world in order to attain holiness, but maintains that people may attain 'buono fine' (eternal salvation), regardless of the socio-economic condition in which they find themselves in this world.

The statements on poverty lend themselves to further observations. Interestingly, Bono merges two consecutive chapters of Lotario's work into one chapter, those on the misery of poor and rich and the misery of servants and masters (*De miseria servorum et dominorum*). What Lotario had in mind in the second of these two chapters was probably the relationship between feudal lords and their serfs, within the context of a (rural) castle or borough. In Bono's culture, however, *servi* are immediately identified with the poor, and the masters are identified with the rich. Therefore Lotario's concise expression "Culpa domini, servi pena", translated as "se il ricco commette il peccato, il povero ne porta la pena" appears somewhat imprecise and of uncertain interpretation. Note that Bono translates the classical quotation "Quicquid delirant reges, plectuntur Achivi" with words that correspond exactly to those used by his contemporaries to describe the social classes of an Italian Commune: 'grandi', versus 'minori' e 'soggetti'. Bono also adds certain details that portray the unjust treatment of the poor in more concrete terms than does Lotario's text: "E sono molti di servigi richiesti e di fazioni gravati... e sì ne sono straziati e sono ingiuriati e battuti, e niuno se ne duole." (Many services are requested of them and they are weighed down with du-

[11] Chapter 12 begins: "A rispondere alle cose, che sono dette di sopra , e acciò che possiamo vedere certi ammonimenti, che pongono i Savi sopra la povertade, ... perché la povertade e la ricchezza può essere buona e rea, sì ti voglio in prima mostrare, che cose debbono essere nel povero, acciò che sia buona la sua povertade; appresso che cose debbono essere nel ricco, acciò che sia buona la sua ricchezza. Appresso ti mostrerrò come la vita povera è migliore che la ricca, perché ne mena al buono fine con minore rischio, e per più piana via."

ties ... and they are abused and beaten, and no one has any sympathy for them.)

When reading Pucci's notes, which obviously derive from Bono's text, one finds several additions that result in a remarkable transformation of the source. Some of the additions simply clarify the meaning of the original sentences, but others vividly emphasize the subordinate role of the poor with a more intense sentiment of human participation. Notice the abrupt transition to direct discourse "Vammi qua, e vammi là! Fammi questo, e fammi quello!" ("Go here, go there! Do this, do that!") that illustrates the arrogant attitude of the rich toward the poor; the unjust treatment in the courts of law ("It often happens that a crime is committed against a poor man, and he is condemned as if he were the perpetrator and not the victim."); the remarks about the tricks played on the poor for pure amusement and especially the observations on the bad opinion one forms of the poor against evidence to the contrary. A sentence found a few lines after the end of the quotation clarifies the matter even further:

> e se sarai malvestito ti diranno dietro che tu sia un tristo e che non vuogli lavorare a otta che tu non cercherai d'altro e se tu sarai ben vestito diranno: "Di che fa egli tali spese?" e questo sarà un farti ladro con sue parole.[12]
>
> (If you are poorly dressed, people will say that you are a bad character and that you don't want to work, meanwhile you do nothing but search for work, and if you are well dressed people will say "Where did he get the money for those clothes?", and you will be made a thief by the words of those people. [Translation: Amanda Glover])

It almost seems as if Antonio Pucci has had some direct experience of the arrogant treatment reserved for the poor. One might bear in mind that while Bono Giamboni belonged to the upper class, Pucci was a relatively modest employee of the municipal administration. The phrase "Their wisdom is worthless and is reputed to be madness," is reminiscent of a sonnet that begins *Signor priori, i' sono una cicala*, (*Lord governors, I am a cicada*)[13] in which the same author, Antonio Pucci, laments that he is not allowed to appear before the governors of the city to express his opinion – presumably on the way certain affairs of the city were conducted. Most of all, one hears in

---

[12] A. Pucci, *Libro di varie storie* (*op. cit. supra*, n. 5), 102.

[13] 'Cicada' means here 'a voice to which nobody pays attention'.

Pucci's words a firm denunciation of the infringement of the dignity of the poor.

Antonio Pucci appears to be the fittest representative of people of median status and culture living in an Italian medieval Commune. His office as town-crier put him in contact with the offices of the governors on one hand, and the common people to whom he announced the decisions of the government on the other. He was open to the responses of the crowd and the comments of city folk about the various political and social events that marked the history of the Commune. He also left a picturesque description of the crowd of "little people" that congregated every day in the market square in Florence, in a poem titled *Le proprietà di Mercato Vecchio*, which is one of the rare medieval texts that describe the poor with realism yet without disdain.

2. Religious and Lay Responses to the Question of Poverty

Although they describe poverty from an external point of view, Giamboni and Pucci's texts reflect well, in my view, the social conditions of an Italian Commune with regard to the distribution of wealth. We know that money more than nobility had become the driving force behind the power-relations in the cities.[14] The old polarity between *potens* and *pauper* had transformed itself into the polarity between rich and poor; the activities of certain merchants had created immense private wealths. The newly rich emulated the old nobility in behavior and possessions, and although the laws of 1292, which appeared revolutionary at the time, had excluded the families of old nobility from public offices,[15] the distance between noblemen and those who came to be called the "fat people" quickly faded away, with the help of intermarriage. The distance, however, between the well to do on one hand and the small artisans, the subordinate trade workers, the servants, the peasants, and those who owned no property, on the other, grew exponentially. With it grew the arrogance in human relations as represented by Pucci's passage in his *Zibaldone*. In the city rich and poor lived side by side and the disparity became obvious; the sumptuary laws attempted without success to restrain

[14] Several poems since the end of the 13th century denounce how riches are supplanting old values. Examples may be found in sonnets by Niccolò del Rosso, *Denari fanno l'uomo comparére* and Pieraccio Tedaldi, *Il mondo vile è oggi a tal condotto*, in *Poeti giocosi del tempo di Dante*, ed. Mario Marti (Milano, 1956), 491, 732.

[15] Ordinamenti di Giano della Bella, whereby only members of a trade corporation could be appointed to public offices.

the vainglorious display of jewels and precious garments paraded by the ladies.

It is precisely against the background of such arrogance (Dante would say "pride, envy, avarice")[16] that the example of poverty given by St. Francis (1182-1226) and his companions appeared. Like the monastic movement of earlier centuries, St. Francis' message challenged the established order of the world and called for a return to the purity and poverty of early Christianity. But, instead of fleeing the world like the anchorites had done, or creating a separate society like the Benedictine monks were still doing, St. Francis realized a radical form of poverty in the world; he mingled with the destitute, and preached in the squares and the churches.

It is well known that the Franciscan movement was not only extremely successful but also inspired a great number of literary writings. Of these, the highest example is probably Dante's *Divine Comedy, Paradise* XI, appropriately known as the canto of St. Francis. Here, Dante concentrates the saint's life and its significance in a few powerful images, the principal of them being the love story between Francis and Lady Poverty which culminates in their wedding. The creation of this image is not entirely new. An allegorical description of poverty as a woman living on top of a mountain, isolated and abandoned by everyone, had already appeared in the well known Latin pamphlet *Sacrum Commercium sancti Francisci cum domina Paupertate*, and occasional allusions to the saint's love of poverty as similar to a relationship between two lovers are already in some of the biographies of St. Francis.[17]

---

[16] When Dante meets Ciacco in *Inferno* VI, the compatriot identifies the sources of Florence's decline in three vices: "superbia, invidia, avarizia, sono / le tre faville c'hanno i cuori accesi" (vv. 74-75). These vices seem to correspond to the attitudes of the three main components of the city population: the Pride of the nobility, the Envy of the lower classes, and the Avarice of the mercantile middle class.

[17] See, for example, *Sacrum Commercium* (c. 1227), 3: "Mirabilis est, fratres, desponsatio paupertatis, sed facile poterimus ipsius frui amplexibus, quia facta est quasi vidua domina gentium, vilis et contemptibilis omnibus regina virtutum"; Thomas a Celano, *Vita prima sancti Francisci* (1228), *Opusculum primum*, 5-7: "Putabant homines quod uxorem ducere vellet, ipsumque interrogantes dicebant: - Uxoremne ducere vis, Francisce? - Qui respondens eis aiebat: - Nobiliorem et pulchriorem sponsam quam unquam videritis ducam, quae ceteris forma praemineat et sapientia cunctas excellat. – Et equidem immaculata Dei sponsa est vera religio..."; Thomas of Celano, *Vita secunda sancti Francisci* (1246-47), *Opus secundum*, XXV 3-5: "Amator igitur factus formae illius, ut uxori fortius inhaereret, ac duo essent in uno spiritu, non solum patrem matremque reliquit, verum etiam universa submovit. Proinde castis eam stringit amplexibus, nec ad horam patitur non esse maritum." Source: http://www.paxetbonum.net/biographies. The allegory of poverty as a wo-

Dante brings novelty to this theme by emphasizing the image of a wedding between lovers. He fuses into one event the successful wooing of an extraordinary woman and the biographical information on the strained relations between Francis and his father, thus the wedding coincides with the episode of the restitution to the father of all his belongings ("*et coram patre* le si fece unito," v. 62 – *et coram patre* he wed her). The communion between Francis and his ladylove appears then to be the cause for other people to become followers of St. Francis:

La lor concordia e i lor lieti sembianti,
amore e maraviglia e dolce sguardo
facieno esser cagion di pensier santi;
tanto che 'l venerabile Bernardo
si scalzò prima, e dietro a tanta pace
corse e, correndo, li parve esser tardo.
Oh ignota ricchezza! Oh ben ferace!
Scalzasi Egidio, scalzasi Silvestro
dietro allo sposo, sì la sposa piace. (*Par.* XI, vv. 76-84)[18]

(Their harmony and their glad looks, their love / And wonder and their gentle contemplation, / Served others as a source of holy thoughts; / So much so, that the venerable Bernard / Went barefoot first; he hurried toward such peace; / And though he ran, he thought his pace too slow. / O wealth unknown! O good that is so fruitful! / Egidius goes barefoot, and Sylvester, / Behind the groom – the bride delights them so. [Translation: *The Divine Comedy of Dante Alighieri. Paradiso.* A Verse Translation by Allen Mandelbaum. New York, 1986])

The accent is on the mystical fervor of such love, which is rendered by the accelerated rythm of the style: note, in the Italian version, the accumulation of nouns, (concordia, lieti sembianti, amore, maraviglia, dolce sguardo), the parallelisms, the exclamation marks, the use of the term 'scalzarsi' as a metaphor for 'embracing a life of poverty', the conclusion of the clause on the repetition of 'sposo', 'sposa'.

Other writers focus on Franciscan poverty in a direct way, without the intermediary of the allegory. The theme is recurrent in Franciscan literature. An example can be found in the anonymous *canzone O povertà gioiosa*, a

---

man appeared of course also in Jean de Meung's *Roman de la* Rose : "Povreté siet a l'autre chief / Plaine de honte et de meschief..." Jean de Meung, *Roman de la Rose,* ed. Silvio F. Baridon (Milano, 1954), vv. 8091-8323.

[18] Dante Alighieri, *La Divina Commedia. Paradiso*, ed. Natalino Sapegno (Firenze, 1968).

joyous exaltation of poverty which aptly represents the point of view of the Spiritual Franciscans:

Povertà sant'è di cotal natura,
che nulla cosa tien né vuole avere;
di ricchezze, d'onor nïente cura;
per ogni cosa in tutto possedere
ogni mondan piacere
tien più che loto e più che paglia vile.
Tant'è di cuor gentile
Che sol d'amar Iesù se pasce e posa.
...
Povertà è contenta d'un vil tetto,
e panno tanto aver che cuopra 'l dosso:
massarizie non vuol, botte né letto,
sarco né zucca, per andare scosso;
vuol pane e cibo grosso...
...
Povertà vuol co' suoi, per istar gaia,
fervor con pianto e sospir per sollazzo:
stride mugghiando, come can ch'abbaia,
sì che tenuto sia da ciascun pazzo.
Non trova albergo o stazzo
Ove mangiar abbia, tovagli' o desco;
ché tanto dorme al fresco,
seguendo [lui] la povertà amorosa.

(*O povertà gioiosa*, vv. 5-12; 85-89; 181-188)[19]

(Holy poverty is of such a nature / that it allows you to value and desire nothing; / to riches, to honour, it pays no mind; / in order to possess everything / it holds every worldly pleasure no dearer than mud or straw. / It is of such a gentle heart / that it is nourished by the love of Christ / and finds peace in his love alone. / ... / Poverty is content with a shabby roof, / and enough clothes to cover the back: / it does not want possessions, nor barrels nor a bed, /nor a bag nor a canteen, / because in this way it can walk about free of a heavy load; / it wants brown bread and simple food / ... / Poverty wants as company, in order to be gay, / fervour with tears and sighs as solace: / the poor man screeches and howls like a barking dog, / so that others assume he is mad. / He does not find an inn or a pen, / where

[19] *Miscellanea di prose e rime spirituali*, ed. Francesco Zambrini (Imola, 1879), 162-167. Also published in *Florilegio francescano*, ed. Guido Battelli (Torino, 1923), 222-226.

he can eat on a dinner table with a cloth, / for he often sleeps outside, / accompanied by lovely poverty. [Translation: Amanda Glover])

The reasons that justify such exaltation of poverty are that it intimately unites the faithful with an absolutely poor Christ, teaches humility, is a source of love, peace, and tranquility, and guarantees entry into heaven. The rhetorical use of the language renders the tone of mystical rapture that is typical of this kind of literature.[20] Jacopone da Todi, a major Franciscan poet, insists and expands on similar notions. Poverty removes any fear of loss or anxiety for litigations; poverty provides full control of oneself; better yet, on account of its union with God the poor faithful do possess everything.[21] Most of all, poverty is a sign of the full control that man's will has over his desires. We may read a passage from one of Jacopone's *laude*:

Chi descidra è posseduto,
a cquel c'ama s'è venduto;
se ll'om pensa que n'à auto,
ànne aute rei derrate.
Troppo so' de vil coraio
ad entrar en vassallaio,
simiglianza de Deo c'aio

[20] See for example a passage from *I fioretti di San Francesco* (composed perhaps between 1370 and 1390), ch. 13: "[la povertà] è tesoro sì degnissimo e sì divino, che noi non siamo degni di possederlo nelli nostri vasi vilissimi, con ciò sia cosa che questa virtù sia quella virtù celestiale, per la quale tutte le cose terrene e transitorie si calcano, e per la quale ogni impaccio si toglie dinanzi all'anima, acciò ch'ella si possa liberamente congiungere con Dio eterno. Questa è quella virtù la quale fa l'anima, ancor posta in terra, conversare in cielo con gli Agnoli. Questa è quella ch'accompagnò Cristo in sulla croce; con Cristo fu soppellita, con Cristo resuscitò, con Cristo salì in cielo; la quale eziandio in questa vita concede all'anime, che di lei innamorano, agevolezza di volare in cielo; con ciò sia cosa ch'ella guardi l'armi della vera umiltà e carità." ("For it is a treasure so great and so divine, that we are not worthy to possess it in these vile bodies of ours. It is this celestial virtue which teaches us to despise all earthly and transitory things, and through it every hindrance is removed from the soul, so that it can freely commune with God. Through this virtue it is that the soul, while still on earth, is able to converse with the angels in heaven. This virtue it is which remained with Christ upon the Cross, was buried with Christ, rose again with Christ, and with Christ went up into the heaven. This virtue it is which even in this world enables the souls who are inflamed with love of him to fly up to heaven; it is also the guardian of true charity and humility." (Text and Translation: http: //www.paxetbonum.net)

[21] Jacopone da Todi, *Laude*, ed. Franco Mancini (Bari, 1974), *laude* 36, 47.

detorpirla en vanitate! (*O amor de povertate*, vv. 23-30)[22]

(He who desires, belongs, because he sold himself, to what he desires; if he thinks of it, he will realize that he got a bad deal. Too cowardly is my heart if I make myself a servant, if for the sake of vanities I degrade the part of me that resembles God)[23]

But poverty is nothing but the first step on the way to perfection. In the Franciscan ethos poverty is part of a larger project of self-denial, penance, and humiliation.[24] This is why it is not enough to get rid of one's possessions - one must also renounce any kind of honours, including knowledge and fame. It is interesting to note how aware the Franciscans are that their choice may be construed as "pazzia", madness. They even strive to be judged as fools by ordinary folks. The point is that their madness imitates the folly of Christ who, for love of man, did not cling to his prerogatives as God's equal, but "emptied himself and took the form of a slave, being born in the likeness of man."[25] God's attitude towards his creatures shows such an incredible love that it elicits a reciprocal love from man's soul in response. And as God's "irrational" gesture towards the soul is dictated by love, so it is for the sake of and on account of his burning love for God that the poet engages in a systematic "lowering" of oneself. It is the habit of what he calls "self-hatred" that allows Jacopone to use humor and irony when he describes the horrors of his life in prison: his underground cell, his latrine full of flies, the chains that hamper him even in his sleep, his food kept in a hanging basket to protect it from rats, the bitter cold:

O amirabele odio meo
D'onne pena à' signorìo,
non recipi nullo eniurio,
vergogna t'è essaltazione.
[...]

---

[22] Jacopone da Todi, *lauda 36*.

[23] Translations are mine unless otherwise indicated.

[24] Cf. *The Little Flowers of Saint Francis,* ch. 7: "Above all graces and gifts of the Holy Spirit that Christ gives to His friends is the grace to conquer self, and willingly to bear any pain, injury, insult, and hardship for love of Christ. For we cannot glory in any other gifts of God except these, because they are not ours, but God's [...] But in the cross of suffering and affliction we may glory, because this is our own. So the Apostle says : «I will not glory except in the Cross of our Lord Jesus Christ»." *The Little Flowers of Saint Francis*, transl. Leo Sherley-Price (Harmondsworth, 1959).

[25] St. Paul, *Letter to the Philippians*, 2: 2-7.

Questa pena che·mm'è data,
trent'agn'à ch'e' l'aio amata;
or è ionta la iornata'
d'esta consolazione. (*Que farai, fra' Iacovone?*, vv. 115-126)[26]

(O admirable self-hatred / That masters all suffering, / Nothing can injure you, / For to shame you is to exalt you. [...] The suffering they've inflicted on me, / For thirty years I have loved it, / For thirty years longed for it / And now the day of my consolation is here. [Translation: Serge and Elizabeth Hughes, *Jacopone da Todi. The Lauds*, New York, 1982])

Most of these arguments in favor of poverty appear understandable only in the context of a state of psychological exaltation that only religious fervor could sustain. It is true that laymen close to the Franciscan movement also wrote in praise of poverty (one of whom was Antonio Pucci); but their voices sound much less passionate and far less convincing.[27] In fact, lay writers did not fail to express their responses to the Franciscan positions, opposing and rebuking the praises of poverty. Their responses essentially take two forms: they are either statements that oppose the Franciscan positions on moral grounds or parodies of the celebrated *topos* of the wedding with Dame Poverty.

Interestingly, most of the poems that tackle the theme on moral grounds, although attributed to certain prestigious figures, in fact remain anonymous. Their date is also uncertain, though it is safe to assume that they were written within the first half of the fourteenth century. The most important poem is perhaps the *canzone Molti son quei che lodan povertate*, attributed by the two manuscripts that preserved it, probably erroneously, to the painter Giotto. The approach in this poem is rational and didactic, not dogmatic. It may have been composed at the beginning of the fourteenth century, at a time when the discussions between the Franciscan Spirituals and the Conventuals were being brought before the tribunals of the Popes, and Pope John XXII definitely disavowed the thesis of the absolute poverty of Christ (1323). The author seems aware of the different positions put forward by the various representatives of the Franciscan Order but he opposes the very

---

[26] Jacopone da Todi, *lauda* 53.

[27] See, for example, Pucci's canzone *O gloriosa e santa povertate* in *Rimatori del Trecento*, ed. Giuseppe Corsi (*op. cit. supra*, n. 2), 893-897. The arguments to which lay writers seem to have been more responsive are 1. that poverty allows people to be free from anxiety (Pucci), and 2. that poverty diminishes temptations (Bono Giamboni, *Della miseria dell'umana condizione,* cap. XVIII).

statement that is at the heart of the Franciscan movement that poverty leads to a state of perfection. At the beginning he states that a literal observation of the rule of poverty would be, in his opinion, an "extreme" and for this reason it is not to be praised: in accordance with the widely known Aristotelian axiom, in fact, it rarely occurs that "something extreme is without a fault," and the Gospel warns that it is not advisable to set the foundations of one's life on something that is not solid enough. The author then distinguishes between voluntary and involuntary poverty. The latter is without a doubt 'tutta ria' (absolutely evil), because it leads to sin:

> ché di peccare è via
> faccendo spesso a' giudici far fallo,
> e d'onor donne e damigelle spoglia,
> e fa far furto, forza e villania,
> e spesso usar bugia
> e ciascun priva d'onorato stallo... (vv. 18-23)[28]
>
> (it corrupts judges, deprives women and girls of their honour, causes theft, rape and injury. It often turns people into liars and robs them of honour and reputation).

As far as voluntary poverty is concerned, the author insists that apart from the discrepancies that exist even among those who claim to embrace poverty, poverty is not praiseworthy because "discrezion né provedenza / o alcuna valenza / di costumi o virtute le s'affronta. / Certo parmi grand'onta / chiamar virtute quel che spegne el bene..." vv. 36-40 - "it allows no discretion, foresight, noble habits or virtue. It surely seems a great shame to call virtue what smothers all good things"). The *canzone* then confronts one of the most important points of the Franciscan position, that of the evangelical counsel of poverty ("Il Signor nostro molto la commenda," v. 47 - Our Lord praises it constantly). First of all, the author responds, Christ as God could have anything he wanted. Secondly, if he was content with little, it was to induce us to avoid greed, certainly not to encourage us to take a road that leads to sin. Finally, the author attacks the hypocrisy of those who, while proclaiming the praises of poverty, seize the first opportunity to occupy positions of honour and power.

In essence, the author rejects poverty because it contradicts other virtues: discretion, prudence, worthiness of habits, magnanimity; all virtues that the

---

[28] *Molti son quei che lodan povertate* in *Rimatori del Trecento*, ed. Giuseppe Corsi (*op. cit. supra*, n. 2), 918-922.

Italian urban society of the fourteenth century had learned to appreciate and that, in my opinion, were associated with the lay upper-class rather than with a religious walk of life.

Other poems, in particular two anonymous *canzoni*, elaborate similar themes, although at a lower level of conceptual sophistication. The most interesting remarks are once again those that contrast poverty with a sense of honour and worthiness:

Ai lasso! Quanti e qua' sarebon quelli
che spanderien la lor bontà sovrana
infra la gente humana,
se ttu no·lli spogliassi di baldança;
ma ttu occupi lor costumi belli
e fa' tener lor contenença vana...
[...]
Canzona, vanne per ciascun paese
[...]
dicendo che già mai
la sozza povertà non farà onore
ad uom ch'ami valore
E brami al [...] di virtù salire.
(*O povertà che tti distrugga Iddio*, vv. 31-36; 76-81)[29]

(Alas! How many and how good are they / who would spread their sovereign kindness among the human race, / if you didn't deprive them of their self-confidence; but you infiltrate their customs, / enabling them to behave vainly. [...] My song, travel to every country [...] saying that never / will despicable poverty honour a man who loves value and wishes to attain virtue. [Translation: Amanda Glover])

In the second *canzone*, *O povertà come tu sei un manto* (probably later than, and indebted to *O povertà che tti distrugga Iddio*), the honour that poverty negates had acquired a clearly humanistic connotation, as witnessed by the importance attributed to fame after death:

La morte può ben l'uom privar di vita,
ma non di fama e di virtute altera:
anco felice e vera
riman perpetual nel mondo e viva.

---

[29] Santorre Debenedetti, 'Una canzone contro la povertà citata dal Barbieri,' *Bullettino della Società di Filologia Romana*, N.S. III (1912). I quote from the excerpt, pp. 1-5.

Ma chi a tua foce sconsolata arriva,
sia quanto vuol magnanimo e gentile,
ch'e' pur tenuto è a vile;
e perciò chi nel tuo abisso cala
non speri in alcun pregio spander l'ala. (vv.18-26)[30]

(Death can well deprive man of life, / but not of fame and proud virtue: / still happy and true, / They remain forever living in the world. / But he who arrives, disconsolate, at your door, / as magnanimous and noble as he may be, / he is rendered small and powerless; / and for this reason he who falls into your abyss / cannot hope to ever be praised. [Translation: Amanda Glover])

In sum, in response to the notion of poverty as the source of all virtues, lay circles affirm a definition of virtue as something inseparable from social prestige, magnanimity, self-confidence, and *courtoisie*. In contrast, if not synonymous with vice, poverty is portrayed as akin to vice, or at least to unworthiness, cowardice, baseness. It is interesting to recognize that the morals alluded to in these *canzoni* coincide with those found, for example, in Boccaccio's *Decameron*. In one of his *novelle*, Boccaccio explicitly indicates the opinion that the Florentine upper class held of the religious:

Essi, il più stoltissimi ed uomini di nuove maniere e costumi, si credono più che gli altri in ogni cosa valere e sapere, dove essi di gran lunga sono da molto meno, sì come quegli che per viltà d'animo non avendo argomento, come gli altri uomini, di civanzarsi, si rifuggono dove aver possono da mangiar, come il porco. (*Decameron*, III 3)[31]

(These religious, being, for the most part, great blockheads and men of odd manners and habits, do nevertheless credit themselves with more ability and knowledge in all kinds that fall to the lot of the rest of the world; whereas, in truth, they are far inferior, and so, not being able, like others, to provide their own sustenance, are prompted by sheer baseness to fly thither for refuge where they may find provender, like pigs. [Translation: The Decameron Web])

It is therefore not surprising that the highly poetic image of St. Francis' choice of lifestyle as a mystical wedding with Dame Poverty soon became an object of mockery or, at least, of parody. The earliest of such parodies is the *Canzone del fi' Aldobrandino*. Likely composed in the middle of the

---

30 *Liriche edite ed inedite di Fazio degli Uberti*, ed. Rodolfo Renier (Firenze, 1883), 177-180.

31 For more accusations against false claims of poverty and hypocrisy of the Franciscans, see *Il Fiore* (an Italian re-elaboration of *Roman de La Rose*), esp. sonnets 89-90, 120 and passim, in *Il Fiore e il Detto d'amore*, ed. Gianfranco Contini (Milano, 1984).

fourteenth century, the canzone is again the only one attributed to an otherwise unknown historical figure, indicated rather mysteriously as "the son of Aldobrandino".[32] In it, the narrator pretends to invite a friend to his wedding and describes the fiancée, her house, her relatives, her dowry, and her love. The fiancée is, of course, Dame Poverty. It may be worth noting that the physical appearance of the allegory of poverty is never described in Franciscan literature. The *Canzone del fi' Aldobrandino* on the contrary describes the figure of the fiancée, drawing on details from earlier representations of poverty: thus the woman

> non mostra altro che l'ossa, tanto è magra,
> e 'l mal della podagra
> par ch'aggia in sé; più negra è che la notte.
> Ahi, quanto orribil cosa pare e agra
> la fronte sua vestita de capello
> e collo enfiato ciglio!
> Piangoli li occhi e 'l capo sì li gotte,
> e poi, apresso le dolenti grotte
> de l'ampio naso, mostra pur le fossie
> coi denti radi e lunghi;
> i labri ha curti: par che se raggiunghi,
> sì l'una gota co l'altra se cossie. (vv. 17-28)[33]

> (She is so skinny that all her bones stick out: it looks as if she is suffering from gout. Her skin is darker than night. How bitter and awful her forehead looks, with hair growing all over and its thick eyebrows! Tears fall from her eyes, her whole head is wet. Next to the awful cavities of her large nose her mouth shows long and sparse teeth; her lips are thin, her cheeks seem to touch one another)

In Poverty's house rain seeps through the roof, there is no furniture, not even a chair; ten hungry daughters ask for bread (notice that young girls were deemed less apt to earn money and therefore more of a burden than young boys); Dame Poverty wears a short, dilapidated and sleeveless tunic. The perfect love that Dame Poverty expressed to Christ and Francis in Dante's

---

[32] Claudio Giunta has identified the author of the *canzone* as a Buccio d'Aldobrandino from Orvieto. In his opinion, the *canzone* dates of the latter part of the 14th century. Cfr. Claudio Giunta, 'Chi era il fi' Aldobrandino,' *Nuova rivista di letteratura italiana* 2, n° 1 (1999), 27-151.

[33] *Canzone del fi' Aldobrandino* in *Poeti del Duecento*, ed. Gianfranco Contini (Milano-Napoli, 1960), 435-440.

poem has now become an object of derision. The fiancée is so attached to the narrator that

tutto giorno m'ha le braccia al collo
sì che tutto mi mollo
del pianto ch'ella fa per drudaria.
[...]
Leccami tutto il volto
e non mi lassa star notte né dia;
tanto ell'ha preso di me gelosia
ch'ella s'uccide s'um ricco m'apressa.. (vv. 62-70)

(She keeps her arms around me all the time, / so that I am soaked / with her tears of love [...] She licks my face / and never lets me be night or day; / she is so consumed with jealousy that she would kill herself / if a rich man were to approach me.)

In the conclusion, the poet emphasizes another poignant motif associated with poverty, the fact that the poor are abandoned by all their friends:

Ché mille volte chiamo
'nanti che l'uom mi voglia pur rispondere.
Sí malamente a tutti sono in camo,
che fugge ogni uom da me più pauroso
che non dal can rabbioso
e là onde io passo veggio onne uom nascondere:
nessun m'aspetta, nessun mi vuol giongere;
solo mi trovo là dovonque io vada... (vv. 93-100).

(Even if I call out a thousand times / not a single man will answer me. / I annoy others so much / that every man flees from me, more frightened / than if he had seen a rabid dog / and every man who sees me approaching tries to hide: / no one waits for me and no one walks with me; / I find myself alone wherever I go)

In subsequent decades, the mock wedding or betrothal to Dame Poverty became a *topos* of popular literature, and later still, one of folk literature. The process is exemplified in a *frottola* written towards the end of the fourteenth century by the jongleur Zaffarino Povaro.[34] By then, however, the impact of the Franciscan movement had considerably faded, and the *topos* was exploited merely for entertainment purposes.

---

[34] Tito Saffioti, *I giullari in Italia. Lo spettacolo, il pubblico, i testi* (Milano, 1990), 458-462.

3. A humanist approach

Perhaps the most interesting result of the passionate debate surrounding poverty is the newfound moral ideal which surfaced in the realm of literature, the ideal of relative poverty, or should we say austerity, whereby a man earns his living by his work and shares with the poor any surplus he attains. It presumably took form in Franciscan preaching, for example in the sermons by friar Servasanto from Faenza (who preached in Florence in the years 1244-60) which were incorporated by Bono Giamboni in his *Della misera dell'umana condizione*. As we have already noted, Giamboni redresses and corrects the common opinion that poverty is entirely negative. Followed by Pucci and others, he recommends that the poor work with their hands so as not to fall into beggary, even if this meant neglecting the pursuit of learning. Poverty has a positive value in that it allows people to be free from anxiety and diminishes temptations: it is therefore the way to a happier and temperate life in this world, and to salvation in the next. But by the end of the fourteenth century the influence of Petrarch and Boccaccio was providing new and powerful models. The once religious ideal of a modest life merged with the historical accounts of the spurn of riches attributed to ancient Romans, thus acquiring new prestige. The ancient anecdotes of Valerius Maximus and Vergil which had until then been confined to the roles of occasional *exempla*, took on a new life harking back to a previous age which, although not touched by the revelation of Christ, represented an alternative - and a positive one - to the decline of contemporary mores.

The best example of a humanist treatment of the theme of poverty is to be found in a passage of Boccaccio's late work *Genealogie deorum gentilium* (which is roughly contemporary to the passage we have read from Antonio Pucci's *Zibaldone*). In the last two chapters of his extensive research into the mythology of classical antiquity, Boccaccio defends his choice to devote his life to poetry and literature, responding to the argument that such studies do not bring him any riches. He promptly admits that poetry is not a lucrative business, but he adds that this is not a reason to spurn the poets because, in fact, they tend to much higher tasks.

Once the section on defense of poetry is concluded, Boccaccio adds a few eloquent considerations that directly address the question of poverty:

> Nunc autem post hec libet paululum exire limen, si forte queam abloquentium in paupertatem frenare impetus. Est igitur paupertas, quam multi fugiunt tanquam importabile malum, ut vulgo placet, caducorum bonorum paucitas, esto ego existimem eam animi egritudinem fore, qua etiam abundantes persepe laborant. Prima quippe, si desiderio careat

augendi, placida atque optabilis est, et eius infinita sunt comoda; secunda vero pacis et quietis hostis est, misere crucians mentes, quibus inhabitat. Prima poetarum fuit, quos isti pauperes volunt; eis quippe, dum modo esset quod vite sufficeret, satis erat. Hac enim duce libertatem volentes consequimus, animi tranquillitatem et cum eis laudabile ocium, quibus mediis viventes in terris gustamus celestia. Hec in solido sita est, nec Fortune, mundana versantis, minas aut iacula timet: fulminet ether desuper, concutiat ventorum impetuosa rabies orbem, inundent campos ymbres assidui, diluant flumina, sonet classicum, tumultuosa oriantur bella, discurrant predones undique; hec, ruinas ridens et incendia, dulci securitati letatur. (*Genealogie deorum gentilium*, XIV.IV.20-21)[35]

(At this point let me turn a little aside in hope of curbing the violence of those who inveigh against poverty. This poverty, then, which most people flee as an intolerable ill, is really a mere paucity of perishable goods. Yet I should call poverty also a mental disease that often afflicts even the rich. The first kind – mere paucity of perishable goods – where one cares naught for increase, is highly desirable as a bringer of tranquillity and infinite comforts. The second – a mental illness – is the enemy of peace and quiet, and cruelly tortures the mind it possesses. The first has been the lot of the poets whom my opponents call poor, but who were satisfied with enough to live on. For, with such poverty as our leader, we by choice attain to liberty and peace of mind, and thereby to honorable ease; whereby, while we dwell in the midst of earth, we taste the delights of heaven. Such poverty is founded upon a rock, fearing neither threat nor thrust of Fortune, who confounds this world. Let thunders fall and mad winds smite the earth; incessant rain submerge the fields, rivers wash them away; let trumpets sound the battle and tumultuous wars arise, and plunder rage on every hand. Amid all, Poverty smiles at fire and ruin, and rejoices in sweet security. [*Boccaccio on Poetry*, trans. Charles G. Osgood, New York: The Liberal Arts Press, 1956])

A series of *exempla* from Antiquity follows and demonstrates how secure and happy, even in the midst of turmoil, was the condition of Aglaus Sofidius, Diogenis, Democritus, Anaxagoras, Amiclates and Aronta. The last sentence in the passage I just quoted may sound somewhat rhetorical and exaggerated, but then Boccaccio pushes his argument further with sarcastic questions:

Dicant, oro, si oportuisset Homerum de re agraria cum villico litigare, aut de domestica a curatore domus rationem exigere quando Yliacum ex-

---

[35] Giovanni Boccaccio, *Genealogie deorum gentilium*, ed. Vittorio Zaccaria. *Tutte le opere di Giovanni Boccaccio*, dir. Vittore Branca, VII-VIII (Milano, 1998).

cogitasse carmen et nomen suum claritate syderea floridum in hodiernum usque protendere potuisset? Quando Virgilius, quando reliqui poeticam cum paupertate sectantes?
(Genealogie deorum gentilium, XIV.IV.24)

(Pray, let them say whether it was incumbent upon Homer to go to law with his overseer about the management of his farm, or exact an account of household affairs from his housekeeper, as long as he could produce the *Iliad*, and hand down his name bright in starry splendor even unto this day. I might ask the same regarding Vergil or the others who have cultivated the art of poetry in poverty. [*Boccaccio on Poetry*, trans. Charles G. Osgood, New York: The Liberal Arts Press, 1956])

In my view, the author's tone shows that his statements about a dignified poverty are not remote to his own experience and express a heartfelt conviction. Boccaccio thus lays the ground for an appreciation of poverty based on human values, without a necessarily religious motivation. This attitude will have long lasting repercussions. It will, for example, be emphasized in the late sixteenth century epic poem *Jerusalem Delivered* and the play *Aminta* by Tasso. Yet, it appears that even when grounded in a humanist attitude, poverty has enormous difficulties in becoming a dominant discourse, even more so in the Renaissance than in the Middle Ages.

A good example of such ambiguity in the humanist view of poverty can be found in the short *Liber De Paupertate* composed by the little known humanist Antonio da Romagno towards the end of his life, around 1405 (he died in 1409). The *Liber de Paupertate* is essentially a dialogue between a pious person ("faithful") and his spiritual father St. Francis on poverty. The "faithful" gathers all his reasons for rebelling against poverty, St. Francis rebukes his arguments. Both sides of the discussion appear thoughtful and fresh and are interestingly representative of a humanistic point of view. However, in my opinion, the arguments against poverty are more cogent than the ones in praise of it. An attention to the importance of the well being of the body as a prerequisite for the well being of the mind, or soul (*animus*) is reminiscent of the famous classical motto *mens sana in corpore sano* which was reflected in the way in which the great school masters Vittorino da Feltre and Guarino Veronese organized the life of their pupils. A new thought about the nature of man and his place in this earthly world is reflected in the question "What's the difference between the human and the animal species, if not that men have more than the bare necessities of life, which birds and quadrupeds normally enjoy?" The contributions of man to his society are stressed in a typically humanistic attitude: without an abundance of goods, man can neither be generous with his friends, nor contribute anything honorable to his homeland. Great artists need colours to realize their paintings, bronze to cast their statues. Some of the old arguments against poverty are repeated: it is the source of all sorts of crimes, it eradicates piety, loyalty and charity from the society of men; it elicits "insolentium contemptus, delicatorum nausea, derisorum iocus"(spurn from the insolents, disdain from the sophisticated, mockery from the jokers). It represents a distortion of the original equal distribution of all the worldly wealth that nature had intended. What is worse is that, by reducing some free men into servitude, poverty forces people who were made for lordship to become servants. The emphasis is on characteristically humanist values: honorable reputation in one's society, an ardent desire to learn, fame after death. Like dense smoke the shadow of poverty obscures any merit, be it personal or ancestral:

> Nil maiorum tituli, nil propria gesta proficiunt, nec ulla nobilitatis aut generis tanta lux est que perrumpat paupertatis fumum: umbra hec omnibus immo noctem velut imo emissa Herebo furva Proserpina rebus obicit. An administrandas ad res occupandosque illum suscipi magistratus credas qui nec a lege dicendis admittitur testimoniis?[36]
>
> (Neither merits of ancestors nor personal worthy deeds are of any avail; no splendor of title or family ties will suffice to dispel the shadows of poverty. As if it were dark Proserpina herself emerging from the depths of Hell, the night of poverty hides everything in its shadows. Or do you think that he will be appointed to public office and key positions who is not even admitted as witness in a court of law?)

The author himself has often wept bitter tears because poverty prevented him from acquiring learning, "qua beatius homini nil contingit in terris" (the happiest experience that man can enjoy in this world):

> Ego, mehercule, paupertatis onera, que fere nulla non videor expertus, cum omnia tolleratu gravia tum hoc unum sentio gravissimum, quod a studiis avocat sapientie measque hinc ortas potuisti de celo videre sepius, pater, lacrimas lugentis hunc paupertatis culpa prereptum michi pastum ... suavissimum animorum.[37]
>
> (I myself, by Jove, who have escaped almost none of poverty's burdens, although I perceive all of them as heavy, this alone I perceive as the heaviest, that I

[36] Maria Chiara Ganguzza Billanovich, *L'umanista feltrino Antonio da Romagno e il suo "Liber de Paupertate"* (Firenze, 1980), 72.

[37] *Ibid.*, 73.

am prevented from the pursuit of learning. In fact, from heaven you yourself, o father, could often see me crying because, on account of poverty, the pursuit of learning, that sweetest nourishment of the soul, was denied to me.)

Finally, poverty even deprives the dead of their memory:

> Quid, quod non tantum crudelis in vivos, etiam mortuos infesta persequitur? Nonnullos partim accepi, partim, ut videor, memini hac urgente expertes, ut dicam, pompa funeris aut titulo inscripti lapidis caruisse, imo proiectos et inhumatos, inhumatos, inquam, o rem detestandam, feras volucres pavisse![38]

> (What else besides poverty would not only torment the living but also persecute the dead? Some I have seen, of some I have heard who, under the curse, so to speak, of poverty, have lacked a proper funeral and an inscription engraved on a stone; so that having been thrown in a shallow grave and buried –buried, I say – still they were in danger of being devoured – o abomination! - by beasts or birds of prey.)

St. Francis' reply rebukes the arguments that poverty prevents noble and honorable contributions to one's family or society or the acquisition of learning by proposing the examples of famous Romans (Publicola, Agrippa, Quinzio, Curione, Fabrizio) and Greek philosophers (Anaxagoras, Anacharsis, Xenocrates, Diogenes):

> Quem horum igitur [...] quem, inquam, horum quicquam cum et in alios et in se tum et in patriam et in suos non liberaliter, non amice, non iuste, non pie, non continenter, non pudice coegit facere paupertas? Cuius aut honores obscuravit aut gloriam calligavit aut fidem depuravit aut gravitatem movim aut magnitudinem minuit? Cuius denique fame nocuit, libertati obstitit, venerationi maiestatique detraxit ?[39]

> (Which one of these was forced by poverty to act in a way that was not generous, or friendly, or just, or pious, or moderate, or chaste, either towards his neighbors or himself, or towards his country and his people? Of which one of the above poverty obscured the merits, or trampled the glory under foot or betrayed the loyalty, or removed the authority or diminished the magnanimity? And finally, whose fame did poverty damage, whose freedom did poverty obstruct, whom did poverty deprive of dignity and prestige?)

His arguments appear rather un-Franciscan in that the Saint appears to adhere to the "faithful"'s humanist scale of values, and simply denies that pov-

---

[38] *Ibid.*, 73.
[39] *Ibid.*, 76.

erty is an obstacle to attaining them, without bringing forward any specific positive connotation of poverty. In fact, the main thrust of Francis' reply is the lament about the degeneration and avarice of the Church, religious orders, and lay people. As I said, the booklet was left unfinished, which may be indicative of the difficulty the author had in elaborating a coherent plan to illustrate the positive aspects of poverty. The reader is thus left with a sense of unresolved contradictions. It is as if, in spite of the author's intentions, a credible defense of the state of poverty grounded in the new appreciation for classical models and stoic literature could not really be carried out.

Before leaving this text, however, I should like to return to the conclusion of the "faithful"'s speech against poverty. At this point, the "faithful" directly addresses his protector Saint Francis, casting doubts about the famous legend of his mystical marriage:

> Cuius olim tue, pater, quod cum tua bona, queso, dicatur venia, insuavissime coniugis michi fit impossibile pene creditu mores te asperimos tristissimumque convictum, tranquillo tulisse animo.[40]

> (If you please pardon my saying so, it seems to me almost impossible to believe that you would peacefully bear the most unpleasant habits and the saddest company of this the least gentle of wives.)

This rhetorical figure of a direct challenge issued to the authority which recommends the appreciation of poverty is reminiscent of another text, a *canzone* recently published by Claudio Giunta, presumably composed in the first half of the fifteenth century.[41]

The lyrical voice directly addresses Jesus Christ, the authority who obviously had the most power in recommending poverty. The *canzone* does not have a mocking attitude, but objects to the recommendation of poverty with an unconstrained attitude that would have appeared blasphemous a few decades earlier. The lyrical voice does not refer to the views held by a group, be it a social or scholarly one, but it dares to confront and discuss the question with Jesus Christ person to person. The speaker's arguments are drawn from the appreciation of natural human instincts, just as the arguments found in a famous dialogue by Poggio Bracciolini, where Antonio Loschi is introduced to justify the pursuit of wealth.[42] The results generate a smile, and are cer-

---

40 *Ibid.*, 73.

41 Claudio Giunta, "Chi era il fi'Aldobrandino," (*op. cit. supra*, n. 32), 123.

42 Poggio Bracciolini, *De avaritia. Dialogus contra avaritiam*, ed. Giuseppe Germano (Livorno, 1994). The dialogue was, composed in 1428-29.

tainly indicative of a new vision of man and God. Take for example the following stanza:

> Ma responde arragion, dì, como posso
> voler la povertà? Non ò io bocca?
> La rabbia non me tocca
> s'io non ò da mangiare e bere spesso?
> Deh, prego, dì, quando la neve fiocca,
> s'io non mi calzo e non mi copro el dosso,
> non rinfreddo e non tosso?
> Sì faccio certo e ben lo sai tu stesso.
> Dell'arosto e del lesso
> m'ài fatto vago: ordunque, Gesù Cristo,
> puoi che tu sai che del cappone io godo,
> ben di' saper s'io rodo
> quando ò del pan secco, e s'io me ne ratristo.
> Però in ciò non sarò mentecatto,
> ché esser voglio tal qual tu m'ài fatto.
> (*Deh, dimmi,Cristo, quando fuste al mondo*, vv. 31-45)[43]

(Tell me, and think about it, how can I / desire poverty? Do I not have a mouth? / Does rage not consume me / if I fail to eat and drink regularly? / Alas, I beg of you, *tell me*, when the snow falls in large flakes / and I have no socks and no clothes, / do I not shiver and cough? / Of course I do, and you know it. / You have made me such that I desire / roast beef and boiled meat: therefore, Jesus Christ, / because you know that I enjoy goose, /you must be well aware that when I gnaw / on dry bread, I become depressed. / For this reason I won't be deceived, / and I want to be as you have made me. [Translation: Amanda Glover])

When we see how natural human instincts are now considered and appreciated, rather than voluntarily and systematically repressed as was the case with the religious preaching of earlier centuries, we realize that the age of penance is definitely over. We also see that, in spite of Boccaccio's idealized statements, the examples of the Ancients did not foster a more favorable attitude towards poverty. On the contrary: the question of poverty was as controversial in the Middle Ages and in the Renaissance as it is today.

---

[43] Claudio Giunta, "Chi era il fi'Aldobrandino" (*op. cit. supra*, n. 32), 123.

APPENDIX

From Antonio Pucci, *The Properties of the Old Market / Le proprietà di Mercato vecchio*, vv. 85-111.[44]

Gentili uomini e donne v'ha da lato,
che spesso veggion venire a le mani
le trecche e' barattier c'hanno giucato.

Noble men and women stand aside, observing the hubbub as peddlers and swindlers get up from the game table.

E meretrici v'usano e ruffiani,
battifancelli, zanaiuoli e gaglioffi
e i tignosi, scabbiosi e cattani.

Prostitutes are there, and pimps pederasts, errand boys, and ne'er-do-wells, people ridden with skin diseases like ringworm and scabies, and bullies.

E vedesi chi perde con gran soffi
biastimar con la mano a la mascella
e ricever e dar dimolti ingoffi.

You see a man losing at dicing, he is cursing in frustration, and receiving and giving many blows.

E talor vi si fa con le coltella
e uccide l'un l'altro, e tutta quanta
allor si turba quella piazza bella.

And now and then these fights occur with knives, and the two men kill each other, and all of this disturbs that beautiful square.

E spesso ancor vi si trastulla e canta,
però che d'ogni parte arriva quivi
chi è vagabondo e di poco s'ammanta.

Often people trifle and sing here, because arriving from all parts of the world are vagabonds who carry little with them.

E per lo freddo v'ha di sì cattivi
che nudi stan con le calcagna al culo
perché si son di vestimenti privi,

And because of the cold there are some poor devils that sit naked with their heels underneath their rumps because they have no clothes.

e mostran spesso quel che mostra il mulo;
pescano spesso a riposata lenza
perch'è ciascun di danar netto e pulo.

And they show parts of the body that it is only proper for mules to show; often quietly looking for an opportunity to steal from others (?), because none of them has a cent.

Quando fa oste il Comun di Firenza,
quinci vi vanno guastatori assai
per ardere e guastare ogni semenza;

When Florence goes to war, they recruit these men as spoilers who will burn and destroy every enemy crop.

esconne manigoldi e picconai,
di cui la gente molto si rammarca

From their ranks come executioners and taskmasters: people look down on them,

[44] *Rimatori del Trecento*, ed. Giuseppe Corsi (*op. cit. supra*, n. 2), 870-880.

perché guadagnan pur de gli altru' guai.

because they gain from someone else's griefs.

(Translation: Amanda Glover and George Predelli)

Anonymous, *Molti son quei che lodan povertate* (Many are those who praise poverty).[45]

Molti son quei che lodan povertate
e ta' dicon che fa stato perfetto
s'egli è provato e eletto,
quello osservando nulla cosa avendo:
a ciò inducon certa autoritate,
che l'osservar sarebbe troppo stretto.
E pigliando quel detto,
duro estremo mi par, s'io ben comprendo:
e però nol commendo
ché rade volte estremo è sanza vizio,
e a ben far difizio
si vuol sì proveder dal fondamento,
che per crollar di vento
e d'altra cosa così ben si regga,
che non convegna poi si ricorregga.
Di quella povertà ch'è contro a voglia,
non è da dubitar ch'è tutta ria,
ché di peccare è via
faccendo spesso a' giudici far fallo,
e d'onor donne e damigelle spoglia,
e fa far furto, forza e villania,
e spesso usar bugia
e ciascun priva d'onorato stallo,
en piccolo intervallo,
mancando roba, par che manchi senno,
s'avesse retto renno,
o qual vuol sia che povertà tal giunga.
Però ciascun fa punga
di non voler che incontro gli si faccia,
ché, pur pensando, già si turba in faccia.

De l'altra povertà, che eletta pare,
si può veder per chiara esperienza
che sanza usar fallenza
s'osserva o no, non sì come si conta.
E l'osservanza non è da lodare,

Many are those who praise poverty;
some even say that it leads to perfection,
if a person is chosen and perseveres
in observing the rule of not possessing
anything: but some authorities that they
invoke are too strict to be followed.
That pronouncement
appears to me to be extreme, if I am not
mistaken; that's why I do not approve of it
because too rarely extremes are faultless.
If we want to build well, in fact,
we must lay so solid a foundation
that in spite of winds
or other mishaps, our building will stand
and not be in need of repairs.
Unwanted poverty
is obviously an evil thing
because it induces to sin:
it corrupts judges,
deprives women and girls of their honour,
causes theft, violence and injury.
It often turns people into liars
and robs them of honour and reputation.
Lack of earthly goods, in no time
will look as lack of judgment,
even if you had governed a kingdom,
before becoming poor.
For this reason people strive
not to fall into poverty;
the very thought of poverty is enough to
upset them.
About voluntary poverty,
It is clear that both observing it and not
observing it may be without fault,
that is not how it is told.
To observe poverty is not praiseworthy

---

[45] *Ibidem*, 918-922.

perché discrezion né provedenza
o alcuna valenza
di costumi o virtute le s'affronta.
Certo parmi grand'onta
chiamar virtute quel che spegne el bene,
e molto mal s'avene
cosa bestial preporre a le virtute
le qual donan salute
a ogni savio intendimento accetta,
e chi più vale in ciò più si diletta.
Tu potresti qui fare un argomento:
– Il Signor nostro molto la commenda. –
Guarda che ben l'intenda,
ché sue parole son molto profonde
ed in loro hanno doppio intendimento
e vuol che 'l salutifero si prenda.
Però 'l tuo viso sbenda
e guarda 'l ver che dentro vi s'asconde.
Tu vedrai che risponde
le sue parole a la sua santa vita,
ché podestà compita
ebbe di soddisfare a tempo e loco:
e però 'l suo aver poco
fu per noi iscampar da l'avarizia
e non per darci via d'usar malizia.
Noi veggiàn pur col senso molto spesso
chi più tal vita loda manco in pace
e sempre studia e face
come da essa si possa partire;
s'onore o grande stato gli è commesso,
forte l'afferra qual lupo rapace
e ben si contrafface
pur ched e' possa suo voler compire
e sassi sì coprire,
che'l peggior lupo par migliore agnello
sotto falso mantello:
onde per tale ingegno è guasto il mondo
se tosto non va in fondo
questa ipocresia, ch'alcuna parte
non lascia al mondo sanza usar su'arte.
Canzon, va e se truovi de' giurguffi,
mostrati loro sì che gli converti;
se pure stesson erti,
sia sì gagliarda che sotto gli attuffi.

because it allows no discretion, foresight,
noble habits or virtue.
It surely seems a great shame
to call virtue what smothers all good things,
and it is bad judgment to prefer
a beastly habit to the virtues
that lead to proper behavior,
which pleases all wise persons.
The better someone is the more he will
delight in those virtues.
Here you might object:
"Our Lord praises it constantly."
I answer: "Make sure you get Him right,
because His words are very deep
and may be understood in more than one way.
We have to grasp the true meaning of His
words. Therefore, open your eyes
and understand the hidden truth.
You will then realize that His words
correspond to His saintly life,
during which he was able to provide fully for
his needs according to circumstance:
therefore his possessing little
meant to dissuade us from greed,
not to induce us to embrace vice."
Furthermore, we often see that those who
praise poverty are not at peace with
themselves; but, on the contrary, strive
to find ways to depart from it.
Should an honorific office be proposed to
them, they will jump at it, as if they were
rabid wolves. They can disguise themselves
in order to attain what they want.
They are so good at hiding their true desires
that the worse wolf among them looks like
a lamb properly disguised.
Because of this trickery the world is
corrupted unless an end is put to this
hypocrisy which extends to every corner of
this world.
Go now, my song, and if you find people who
are still mistaken show them your wisdom,
so that they may be converted; but if they
remain obstinate, don't hesitate to give them
a lesson they will never forget.

(Translation: Amanda Glover and George Predelli)

MARIA DOBOZY

The Wayfaring Singer's Penury: Use of a Literary Commonplace

Mir ist der wint gevere,
daz hemd er mir zuo den oren weut,
sne und regen dar under streut.

(Johann von Nürnberg)

One criterion for estimating the value of art to society is the wealth of its artists. With rare exceptions, poverty is the case everywhere in the Middle Ages for poets and singer-performers. Their lives were characterized by economic and social deficiency. Most poets from 1150 to 1400 followed or at least sang of the same life spent in constant wandering without adequate clothing, food or shelter, while offering people music and song. In Germany, France, Provence and Spain, the itinerant poet-singers often protested their inadequate remuneration and in the process styled themselves in their poems as penurious. Whether the complaints are true or merely literary topoi, the interesting question is how the poets tied the topic of penury to social and aesthetic issues. Some poet-singers framed their complaints to highlight what they saw as an ironic contradiction in society: The very people capable of enriching the lives of the wealthy were left to live in poverty.

It is instructive to begin with Johann von Nürnberg (c. 1300–1340) because he stands identifiably in the poetic tradition of the complaint song. His single extant poem has been given the title *De vita vagorum* or *Von einem fahrenden Schüler*.[1] Although he is the most recent of the poets under discussion, we know almost nothing about him. Like the wandering singer-

[1] The German title was given by Wilhelm Grimm in his edition of the text in *Altdeutsche Wälder* 2 (1815), 49-59. I cite from the edition in *Lyrik des späten Mittelalters*, ed. Hermann Maschek (Darmstadt. 1964), 194-202.

scholars of earlier centuries, he relates stereotyped experiences that may also reflect his own life. By the time he writes, he is able to parody the wayfaring singer-scholar's life in lengthy detail because descriptions of their privation and poverty have become fixed commonplaces. Already well-known in the Latin goliardic poetry of the twelfth century from poet-singers like the Arch-poet, these commonplaces were adopted and elaborated in the thirteenth and fourteenth centuries by the vernacular German didactic-political poets (*Sangspruchdichter*).

Johann's poverty is voluntary because he has chosen the activities and itinerancy of a student and performer. Unlike his earlier counterparts, however, Johann parodies the typical sufferings and hardships by means of an extended metaphor of the large monastic order of "fear and cares" he has joined. It is far more stringent than all others, one whose monastery extends from sea to sea. When he praises his order for providing a completely free life (p.196, 4), he evokes an ironic reminder of denigrating Latin phrases calling these scholar-poets *gyrovagi* or free and unrestrained vagabonds.[2] He is also free of gold, pennies, food, even straw for a bed. The commonplaces he uses thus recapitulate those of earlier poets and address two essential needs: The bare necessities of food and shelter, and the protection of one's person.

The metaphoric frame of the "religious house" allows the poet to express his privation and suffering in even more extreme terms than his predecessors by setting up a comparison on two levels. The ensuing description of conditions, because they are so extreme, can be readily understood first as parody of the complaint genre and secondly as a criticism of the elective poverty of monastic orders, especially of the mendicants. Monks, he tells us, shave their heads, but he and his comrades constantly tear their hair not knowing where to find their next meal. And if the Franciscan, having taken a vow of poverty, knows where he can turn in each night, Johann's living conditions exemplify the genuine experience of poverty: His neighbors are hunger, thirst, and frost, and his housekeeper is scarcity. The students' house is the wide forest where not even a mouse has found any pleasure in a thousand years: *So hant schuler ein hus, / zuo tusent jar wurd ein mus / dar inne nicht gefrawet* (p.196, 24-26). The mouse as image of extreme privation clearly be-

---

[2] Johann's comment on freedom, meaning free from responsibility, is also reminiscent of phrases like *solutos et errantes* that are traceable to Isidore of Seville. See Helen Waddell, *The Wandering Scholars. The Life and Art of the Lyric Poets of the Latin Middle Ages* (Garden City, NY, 1961), 179.

longs to the rhetorical repertory defining poverty. Instead of sheltering him, his house exposes him to cold, wind, snow, rain and danger. The frame thus defines Johann's privation as permanent rather than temporary. The regular monastic houses are thus discovered to be places of well-being.[3]

Wayfaring scholar-poets were marginalized and, therefore, poor (*pauper*) also in the sense that they lacked the stable social connections that would protect and support them. Moreover the profession of performing arts was dishonorable and curtailed a poet-singer's legal rights.[4] In literary depictions, penury as a sign of outsider status needs to be immediately and highly visible. For this reason clothing has become one obvious and favored sign of poverty. Complaints of thin, tattered clothing are invoked like a refrain by poet-singers. A particularly apt commonplace is Johann's scarecrow simile for expressing his marginality. Johann also uses ever more extreme images to describe the effects of his unpresentable, threadbare rags that cause children to flee him. In a second comparison with mendicant friars who have knots in their cord belts, his shirt has more knots than the year has days so that the wind blows in and out at will. Worse yet, when he sits down by the fire everything is on view and his back freezes (p.195, 11-14). Johann also plays on the appellation of *varender* as the scholars and singers are normally called saying it's a misnomer because he rides (*fahren*) far more rarely than he walks.

Marginality is also accompanied by physical and emotional abuse since Johann's right to protection of his person is seldom respected. Nor could

---

3 Hannes Kästner has shown that mendicants were frequently in serious competition with poet-minstrels for the attention of audiences in homes of burghers and nobility. See his '"Sermo Vulgaris" oder "Hövischer Sanc". Der Wettstreit zwischen Mendikantenpredigern und Wanderdichtern um die Gunst des Laienpublikums und seine Folgen für die mittelhochdeutsche Sangspruchdichtung des 13. Jahrhunderts (am Beispiel Bertholds von Regensburg und Friedrichs von Sonnenburg)', in *Wechselspiele. Kommunikationsformen und Gattungsinterferenzen mittelhochdeutscher Lyrik*, ed. Michael Schilling and Peter Strohschneider, GRM Beiheft 13 (Heidelberg, 1996), 209-243.

4 The *Sachsenspiegel* defines minstrels as having forfeited freeman status and placed themselves in bondage. Less than freemen, they are not definitively bondmen either, so that they find themselves between two distinct legal categories: "Minstrels and all those who have given themselves into bondage are awarded the shadow of a man." *The Saxon Mirror. A Sachsenspiegel of the Fourteenth Century*, tr. Maria Dobozy (Philadelphia, 1999), Bk III, 46. For a more detailed discussion of minstrel rights see Maria Dobozy, *Re-Membering the Present: The Medieval German Minstrel in Cultural Context* (Turnhout, 2005), ch.2.

such people be protected by the law.[5] One person gives Johann clothing, another food, a third his fist, the fourth a lashing, the fifth a lump, and the sixth a kick (p. 200, 29-31) proving that rough treatment is far more frequent than kindness. Like the Archpoet, he trudges on all day and yet does not always find shelter or a host when he is tired and hungry in the evening (p. 201, 1-2).

His dire condition he characterizes right at the beginning as the type of life only a wicked parent who wants to kill his son would choose (p. 194, 10–11). This perspective is reiterated at the end of the piece to ensure that the danger and severe misery are understood by the audience:

Welch man sim sun nicht guotes gan, /
den sol er gerne spilen lan, /
tribt ers ein wil on grozzen schaden, /
ez kumt dar nach mit leid geladen.

(If a man wishes his son misfortune, he should encourage him to perform, and if he carries on a while without serious detriment, it will eventually cause him severe suffering, p. 202, 3-6.)

The rule of hospitality Johann depends on customarily allows a person shelter and food for a maximum of three days. Yet it is not always forthcoming. People frequently cast him out or turn him away. In a cloaked reference to hospitality, he tells of his forest dwelling: Once a person is in, he can never be driven out but must flee on his own if he is to avoid starvation (p. 196, 31-33). Johann is willing to do almost anything to survive. He certainly cannot be considered a beggar because he seeks to give something, namely songs, in return for food and shelter. With humorous self-mockery he describes his additional survival tactics of trickery typically attributed to traveling scholars. For example, he describes how he gives a maid a recipe for enlisting the service of a gremlin and mixes love and healing potions for servant women who give him food and drink (p.198, 35-p.199, 21).

Johann is not shy about pointing out the hypocrisy of clergy who turn him away with lame excuses such as “my master just finished eating” or *min herr der pharrer an der stunt/ heizzet mir tun mit wortten kunt,/ er sie geritten uber velt* (my master the priest just now told me to say he has ridden

[5] “People with diminished legal capacity have no wergeld. However, if anyone robs, injures, or slays one of these people, or if someone rapes a woman with reduced legal capacity and violates the peace against her, he shall be judged according to the peace law.” *Saxon Mirror* (*op. Cit. supra*, n. 4, Bk III, 47).

away. (p. 197, 16-20). Such callous treatment causes him to respond with a bitter lament of suffering: *So sing ich hoch clagende leit,/ wenn mir die rede kumet fur,/ dennoch so ist mir die tur /vil vaste vor beschlozzen* (I sing a bitter lament when I encounter such talk, but they still shut the door tightly in my face, p. 197, 23-26). In contrast when he finds a pious host, he bows as a suppliant demonstrating how anxious he is to please. He excitedly sings his entire repertory for him in exchange for supper because his singing and his relationship to his host constitute the basis for his survival:

ich han gelaufen allen tak,
daz ich vor muode nicz enmak,
so such ich einen frummen man,
dem sing ich allez, daz ich kan,
ich nig im nider uff den fuz,
daz er mich behalten mus. (p. 201, 1-6)

(I have walked the entire day so that I cannot go on from exhaustion. I seek out a pious man and to him I sing everything I know and bow down before his feet so that he will have to retain me.)

His excitement in singing all the songs he knows signals his gratitude for the hospitality. Johann's reception and his response to it are essential for his continued survival, because all singers are to some extent suppliants. Establishing the correct working relations between host and guest, patron and artist is essential for making a living and also for creating aesthetically pleasing songs. Consequently, these rather unreliable relations exemplify medieval social-cultural values.

Without the singer's customary right to hospitality and remuneration, a wayfaring life would not have been possible. Since the guest-host relation can be either adverse or salutary, the singer has two different ways of reacting: Johann is capable of both caustic criticism and joyful songs. The different songs thus reflect two different aesthetic responses: When the singer is turned away, the song is full of bitterness and when he is welcomed, the songs are full of joy and as a result bring pleasure to the listener. We may thus conclude that the type of reception a singer receives directly inhibits or supports the production of gratifying and eloquent poetry. Johann informs us that he often sings for supper and shelter, but the poem also gives broad validity to the denigration he experiences. The humorous veneer with scattered notes of self-irony lightens up the bitter complaints describing the typical itinerant lifestyle of the "adventuresome scholar" (*wilder schuler*, p. 194, 2) as he calls himself. Even within the context of this poem, Middle High German *wild* most likely means restless, unbridled behavior, and possibly imagination and a fascination with that which is out of the ordinary.[6] At the end of the poem he also makes light of his hardships juxtaposing the Latin cliché, *non est ordo, sed sempiternus horror* to his indomitable disposition that carries him onward: *min wild gemuot treit mich enbor* (p. 201, 35-36).

Johann's parody is directed against the social situation of poet-singers and the poetic conventions of the complaint song. Of course, such a parody demonstrates the poet's mastery of the genre. More importantly, however, by virtue of the fact that Johann sings about his penury, he is also informing his audience about the sad condition of the performing arts in general. Admittedly Johann's poem lacks the complexity and sophistication of the better known *Spruchdichter*. Still, in this poem he outdoes his predecessors in his use of imagery and metaphor associated with these commonplaces, and by these means places his own poetic abilities on display. At the same time, he does not appear to have high aspirations because he does not discuss explicitly the value of his songs, whereas the *Sangspruchdichter* reflect upon and praise their own songs, claiming that their songs enrich people's lives. In spite of this reservation concerning his artistic intentions, Johann's song teaches the same poignant lesson: Those who are best capable of producing excellent, serious art songs are left impoverished. Thus his description of penury suggests a contradiction between the necessities for sustenance and the singer's offering of aesthetic pleasure. Sadly, medieval society in general rarely considered these offerings a necessity, and Johann suggests no remedy. We shall see that other poet-singers do.

Since Johann von Nürnberg draws on a long tradition, it is necessary to examine two earlier poet–singers who were already using these same complaints sometimes for similar and sometimes for different purposes. They too publicize their penury and need of a supportive patron. The major difference is that these thirteenth century poet–singers treat the subject seriously and do not parody either the genre or the wayfaring lifestyle. For this very reason the gestures, behaviors, and signs of poverty intentionally appropriated by these poet-singers is vexing. What could they hope to achieve artistically and socially by fashioning themselves as unsavory figures, especially since they repeatedly stress that they are not asking for alms? To what purpose do the poet-singers adopt a pose or even a genuine complaint of penury? In answer,

---

[6] See Wolfgang Monecke's study of the word, *Studien zur epischen Technik Konrads von Würzburg. Das Erzählprinzip der Wildekeit* (Stuttgart, 1968), 2-12.

I examine selected poems by two more poet-singers, Walther von der Vogelweide and Konrad von Würzburg, who had already employed all the commonplaces of poverty before Johann.[7] I submit that these singers used their self-stereotyping to discuss the value society places on art to convey that remuneration is intimately connected with the audience's enjoyment of a performance. Consequently the complaint song within the performance context came to be used as a tool to inculcate an appreciation of art, to teach audiences to discriminate between good poetic artistry and doggerel, and to accept a moral imperative to support the arts.

Many complaint songs in Germany and elsewhere center around the argument that good art is not valued by society, and artists of merit deserve much greater compensation. One may trivialize the claims and say that each poet values his own work more than that of others, but the complaint must at least in some cases have been genuine. Moreover, penury need not be understood as a subjective concern. The poet is not necessarily seeking greater rewards for himself only, but may well be concerned with an audience that cannot discern genuinely serious artistic productions from hackneyed, superficial ones. Consequently the greater issue for some poet-singers is not the singer's poverty, but the concomitant poverty of art.

Turning to Walther von der Vogelweide (c.1170–1230), arguably the best and most famous German wayfaring poet-singer, we see that even he was not immune to poverty although he sang at the highest and wealthiest courts. He composed a song of supplication to King Frederick before his imperial coronation in 1220. It is a plea for shelter, for a permanent roof over his head that he expresses with the familiar topoi. Yet more significantly, he turns our attention to poetic creativity as he warns that the poverty of the singer produces impoverished and unappealing songs. His complaint that a man with such rich art is left to be so poor has been repeated by many including, as we have seen, by Johann von Nürnberg.[8] Because Walther can no longer sing

---

[7] Just about all the didactic poets or *Sangspruchdichter* could be used as examples. See my *Re-Membering the Present* (*op. cit. supra*, n. 4) for a discussion of several complaint songs, ch. 6.

[8] Meissner (c. 1250–1300) offers the same, typical complaint, actually a rewording of Walther's own complaint a half century earlier: *Min kumber weret mir ze lange; / daz ist mir schedelich unde ist mir swaere, / sol ich sus bi richer kunst verarmen unt verderben.* (My worries continue too long; it is painful and pernicious if I must fall into penury and die when my art is so rich.) Cited according to *Minnesänger. Deutsche Liederdichter des zwölften, dreizehnten und vierzehnten Jahrunderts*, ed. Friedrich H. von der Hagen (Aalen, 1962), vol. III, p. 104, tone XVI, strophe 4.

about the beauty of nature (birds, flowers), he implies that poverty is antithetical to beauty.

Von Rôme voget, von Pülle künec, lât iuch erbarmen
daz man mich bî sô rîcher kunst lât alsus armen.
gerne wolde ich, möhte ez sîn, bi eigenem viure erwarmen.
Zahî wie ich danne sunge von den vogelînen,
von der heide und von den bluomen, als ich wîlent sanc!
swelch schoene wîp mir denne gaebe ir habedanc,
der lieze ich liljen unde rôsen ûz ir wengel schînen.
Sus kum ich spate und rite vruo, 'gast, wê dir, wê!'
sô mac der wirt baz singen von dem grüenen klê.
die nôt bedenket, milter künec, daz iuwer nôt zergê. (L 28, 1)[9]

(Defender of Rome, King of Apulia, take pity on me, that I, a man with such rich art, am left so needy. I would gladly warm myself at my fireplace, if that could only be. Oh my, how I would then sing about those lovely little birds, the meadow, and the flowers, as I sang before. Any lovely woman who might thank me then – I would let roses and lilies bloom from her cheeks. As it is, I arrive late and ride out early: "Alas guest, alas for you." It's true, a master of his own house could sing much better about green clover. Consider my distress, generous king, that your own may soon be over.)[10]

Soon afterwards, Walther sang the joyful news of his grant. This second song tells us his wish has been fufilled so that what was desire earlier and conveyed by the subjunctive is now fulfilled and can be expressed by present indicative. The severe hardships of the first song are now relegated to memory recalled by means of the past tense. The two songs scan the same because they are composed to the melodic frame of the König Friedrichston. Yet the small differences between the two songs create strong contrasts in emotional content for the attentive listener:

Ich hân mîn lêhen, al diu werlt, ich hân mîn lêhen.
nû envürhte ich niht den hornunc an die zêhen,

---

[9] These two strophes, *Von Rome voget, von Pülle künec, lât iuch erbarmen* and *Ich hân mîn lêhen, al diu werlt ich hân mîn lehen*, are numbers 58 and 59 respectively in Walther von der Vogelweide, *Gedichte*, ed. Hermann Paul and Hugo Kuhn, ATB 1 (Tübingen, 1965), 98, I have also given Lachmann's numbering.

[10] Translations of the two Walther poems are my adaptations of those by Frederick Goldin, *German and Italian Lyrics of the Middle Ages* (Garden City. 1973), 108.

und wil alle boese herren dester minre vlêhen.
Der edel künec, der milte künec hât mich berâten,
daz ich den sumer luft und in dem winter hitze hân.
mîn nâchgebûren dunke ich verre baz getân:
si sehent mich niht mêr an in butzen wîs als si wîlent tâten.
Ich bin ze lange arm gewesen âne mînen danc.
ich was sô voller scheltens daz mîn âtem stanc:
daz hât der künec gemachet reine, und dar zuo mînen sanc. (L 28, 31)

(I've got my fief, listen everybody, I've got my fief! Now I don't have to fear the frost on my toes, I will be a far less frequent suppliant at stingy masters' doors. The noble king, the munificent king, has outfitted me, for in the summer I have a breeze and in winter my fire roars. My neighbors find me a much more respectable man. No more do they look at me as though I were a scarecrow. I hated being poor, and I was poor too long – my mouth was so full of reproaches, my breath stank. Now the king has purified my breath and my song.)

Walther's elation is unmistakable. With its faster cadence and immediacy of images this second song stands in marked contrast to the longing in the supplication song. A stable home now makes him socially presentable; he's no longer a scarecrow and can tend his frostbitten feet. But more importantly, Walther explicitly links food, a fire in the hearth, and Frederick's gift with artistic creativity, claiming that poverty thwarts beauty and artistry. While he was impoverished, his breath stank but now his pure, sweet voice sings joyfully. Consequently, if the poet is poor, audiences are not treated to artistically sophisticated songs. Walther states adamantly that beauty is incompatible with the poverty of the singer–composer. This implies, as he says, that art itself is not valued. And if art is not valued, it is because audiences and patrons are not discerning. They do not always recognize "rich art." With his song, Walther thus proves by example that release from 'fear and care' produces better aesthetic quality. Therefore, the important point here is that Walther illustrates by means of his "before" and "after" songs just how much a song increases in aesthetic appeal when the singer is no longer poor. Teaching by example, Walther avoids presenting his lesson on artistic appreciation through precept. These two songs lend themselves to being performed together as an example of what excellent songs result from generosity. As the audience listen and compare the "before" and "after" situations, they experience heightened pleasure. Thus each song derives a deeper, more poignant message by means of contrast created in performance rather than from the words alone.

Konrad von Würzburg (c.1220–1287) took this complaint of poverty and the problem of reception one step farther. Seeking to discover the reason for the singer's penury, he found that audiences lacked critical understanding. If audiences were responsible for the singer's penurious condition, then he needed to explore ways of educating them.[11] He began trying various rhetorical strategies to distinguish between different types and levels of performative offerings in order to provide instruction by example. I intend to show that Konrad von Würzburg's "Klage der Kunst" ("Complaint of Art") reveals a complex strategy designed to assess the performative situation and educate his audience. In this text Konrad's major concern is the lack of recognition and appreciation for artistry and virtuosity, and the resulting impoverishment of the singer. When he asks, "who is responsible for serious art?" his rhetorical strategy becomes critical to the answer. Like Walther, he cannot simply place all blame on the audiences. If he emphasizes audience support too strongly as the determining factor in the aesthetic process, then he undermines the singer's own role in that process.

Evidence suggests that Konrad was a professional wayfaring poet-minstrel early in his career because he is listed as a *vagus*.[12] Later he was able to make enough of a living from commissions to settle in Basel. Some scholars read the "Complaint" as a straightforward request for remuneration which leads them to conclude that it was composed during Konrad's itinerant years. Such general internal evidence cannot be definitively connected with any part of Konrad's personal life even though this poem is reminiscent of other *Sangpruchdichter* songs.[13] Although Hartmut Kokott accepts that the song is not about personal, material gain but rather about the artist's creative ability, he dates the work as part of Konrad's early, itinerant period because it sounds to him like a piece composed by someone whose name is not yet established.[14] Nevertheless, it must be stressed that in this song Konrad goes

---

[11] Walther Haug was the first to recognize that Konrad's poetic program stresses virtuosity and education of audiences, see his *Literaturtheorie im deutschen Mittelalter von den Anfängen bis zum Ende des 13. Jahrhunderts* (Darmstadt, 1992), 360.

[12] For documentation see Rüdiger Brandt, *Konrad von Würzburg* (Darmstadt, 1987), 65.

[13] Konrad's *Klage* has been accused of being an indirect demand for higher remuneration. I agree with Rüdiger Brandt's review of the research where he disputes this as being too narrow a reading in 'Ein Kunstplädoyer als "Botenbericht". Allegorie, Kunst und milte-Thematik in Konrads von Würzburg "Die Klage der Kunst",' *Jahrbuch der Oswald von Wolkenstein Gesellschaft* 5 (1988/89), 154.

[14] See Hartmut Kokott, *Konrad von Würzburg Ein Autor zwischen Auftrag und Autonomie* (Stuttgart, 1989), 85.

far beyond the usual supplication theme and does not take a personal moral stance as *Sangspruchdichter* do. In addition, Konrad has created in form and style a new type of song that displays his virtuosity. Furthermore, Konrad's case for supporting serious art includes an aesthetic component that is far broader in scope than simply a request for compensation for himself: The main theme is the poverty of art itself.[15] If the value of art is indeed the lesson presented by the poverty topos, and if it is sung by someone without a reputation, then it may imply the singer lacks skill and seeks more praise and remuneration than is his due. However, an established, renowned poet-singer can present a more convincing argument for the value of art and the need to bring audiences up to his aesthetic level. For this reason I suggest it was composed during his settled period.

In this complaint song Konrad accepts a Platonic aesthetics that assumes the unity of ideal beauty and goodness which implies that art elevates the soul. But he also knows that the social value of art develops out of actual daily interaction of performers with patrons, audiences, and other performers. He is aware that artistic standards and fashions are formed by the training and apprenticeship of performers, and yet the interaction with audiences was far more influential throughout the entire career of a poet-singer.[16] Hence the missing element here, as the poet points out, is the discriminating audience which means that monetary support does not reach the right, that is, the best artists. To produce a change, poets must make the listeners themselves more aware of their role. To do this Konrad resorts to a higher authority in order to lend his claims greater validity and, more importantly, to achieve a greater voice in an early attempt to distinguish what we may call serious and popular art.[17]

Konrad's poem "The Complaint of Art" (c.1270–1280) is an allegory of the dream-vision type. German vernacular poetry contains visions of heaven

---

[15] As pointed out by Brandt, *Konrad von Würzburg* (*op. cit. supra*, n. 12), 96-97.

[16] The usual definition of Konrad's aesthetics is based on the well-known statement that he would pursue his art even if no one listened, like the nightingale. For background on the nightingale interpretation, see Trude Ehlert, 'Zu Konrads von Würzburg Auffassung vom Wert der Kunst und von der Rolle des Künstlers,' *Jahrbuch der Oswald von Wolkenstein Gesellschaft* 5 (1988/89), 79-94. This does not, however, apply to the "Complaint". Since medieval artists live from their audiences and patrons, Konrad can be seen as very much wanting to appeal to audiences as Haug, *Literaturtheorie* (*op. cit. supra*, n. 11), 361 has made clear.

[17] Only gradually did the distinction between learned and popular art emerge after the thirteenth century. See my *Re-Membering the Present* (*op. cit. supra*, n. 4), 13-16.

in the hagiographic mode, (like *Annolied*) but here for the first time in secular German literature and earlier than any other literature, we have a paradise vision in a consistent allegory. In the court trial, Art sues Largess for driving her to poverty. The court's solution is to give the narrator-observer a public mission to warn patrons of their responsibility to recognize serious art. Konrad fuses lyric imagery, strophic form and narrative elements with masterly skill giving his listeners an opportunity to hear and recognize the artistry involved. Because of its strophic form we should imagine that this was performed before audiences. The poem's uniqueness, however, lies in the way Konrad defines art as the interconnection between the human temporal reality and the ideal realm of the Virtues, for he shows the Virtues injecting their influence into human affairs.[18]

Konrad's poem begins as the narrator is led into a *locus amoenus* by his companion Lady Wildekeit where amidst the beauty of nature he comes upon thirteen Virtues, all crowned, labeled and richly attired. Using the nature introduction of minnesong, Konrad sets up audience expectations of a love song, and then he cleverly interweaves lyric and narrative elements as he unfolds the story. The identification labels on the crowns of the Virtues indicate that the written or spoken word is required to make them tangible and comprehensible (as in a manuscript illumination). The ladies are Justice, Mercy, Loyalty, Constancy, Modesty, Kindness (*guete*), Prestige or Honor (*êre*), Largess, Shame, Moderation, Good Breeding (*zuht*), Truth, and Love (*minne*). Next Art enters bringing a suit against Largess for being false. Emaciated and dressed in tatters and rags, she stands like a scarecrow in shocking contrast to the Virtues; Art literally embodies the neglect, scorn and poverty of her suit. After the formal accusation has been presented and the defense has summed up its case, the court finds against Largess determining that she has indeed been misdirected.

The case against Largess raises several questions. Has she herself been false and deliberately misled patrons to give gifts to artless fiddle scrapers and singers of doggerel? According to Art, she has. She makes all the artless wealthy while allowing serious art to waste away in poverty:

si wil daz manec süezer list

---

[18] Wolfgang Achnitz notes the correspondance of the allegory to actual court procedure that provides the link between the two levels of the poem; see 'Die schlafende Minne. Die Rezeption der Kunstauffassung Konrads von Würzburg bei Peter Suchenwirt,' *Euphorion* 96 (2002), 349-368, here 361.

in armekeit nu valle,
und machet rîche in kurzer frist
die künstelôsen alle. (16, 5-8).

(She wants many a lovely artistic skill to fall into penury now and speedily makes all the artless rich.)[19]

But is Largess alone the guilty party? She indeed urges her admirers, her ministerials (*dienestman*) to be generous, but it seems they are even more to blame than she for their lack of discrimination in rewarding performers. These lords, knights and pages disdain serious art because they cultivate less virtuous, far less skilled composer-performers (21, 5-6). Thus their generosity is indeed falsely placed for they reward cheap entertainers instead of serious artists. Justice takes this into account and chastizes the guilty in her verdict:

swer rehte kunst niht minne
und doch hie milten namen truoc,
den lânt mit ungewinne
hie leben durch den ungefuoc
den er hât an dem sinne. (30, 4-8)

(Whosoever fails to love true art and yet has been called generous, shall live to his own detriment because of the fatuous intentions in his mind.)

This means that the blame for the singer-poet's penury and lack of support for art is placed on the (paying) audience. Without remuneration and support, Art cannot flourish. Sadly enough, misplaced or false generosity means that these listeners and spectators fail to recognize quality performances deserving their support.[20]

Our narrator has been observing the trial passively; he is not personally involved in order to avoid the complaint of penury becoming a trivial request for remuneration and thus hiding the broader issue. Before all disperse from the court space however, Justice appoints him court herald. She gives him the task of making public the endangered status of Art and the judgment of the court that those who do not love and cultivate Art will be abandoned by

[19] I cite from the edition by Edward Schröder, *Kleinere Dichtungen Konrads von Würzburg*, (Zurich and Dublin, 1967), 1-7. The translations are mine.

[20] R. Brandt has also noted that Konrad speaks of "quality" and thereby intimates a distinction between serious and popular art anticipating what is commonly understood today, 'Ein Kunstplädoyer' (*op. cit. supra,* n. 13), 155.

the Virtues. At this point our first person narrator is revealed to be the poetic persona of the author-singer himself, referred to here as Cuonz.

The poet-singer does not find the *locus amoenus* by himself; his guide and muse, Lady *Wildekeit*, leads him there. Her importance, as her name implies, is "creative ability or virtuosity" or perhaps "narrative imagination" that probably only a master poet–singer might have.[21] In this instance, by leading the poet-singer to the *locus amoenus* she enables the singer encounter new opportunity for artistic production, and new poetic material. Presumably her guidance places him in this special, select position first of observer, and later as court herald, that, as we shall see, only a poet-singer can fulfill. She has led the poet to the Virtues to underscore the fact that he has been chosen to serve them because of his poetic artistry.

Konrad's placement of the court suit into a *locus amoenus* defines Art as an ideal to be found in the company of the Virtues and not deriving from human experience, but influencing it instead. Art is not a Virtue herself, but is shown through her companions and supporters, Truth and Constancy, to be a complement to them and is later defined implicitly as the essential mediator between the human and ideal worlds. Art's follower and representative is the first person narrator, our poet-singer. This self-definition makes the poet-singer Konrad the privileged partner of the Virtues who is capable of mediating between them and humankind.[22]

As Konrad records and describes the trial of Largess and the consequences of neglecting Art, he defines Art as the mediator between human action and the Virtues. Once appointed court herald, the poet-singer is free to define his own role by implication. He is officially the spokesman of the Virtues because of his skill in producing serious art. By means of his eloquent metaphors and turns of phrase, he guides his audiences to an increasingly sophisticated understanding of Art. She in turn enriches their lives and leads them to Virtue. Why are audiences in need of such aesthetic education? To learn to discriminate between serious art and simplistic, shallow entertainment. Only from experiencing examples of beautiful, true art in performance can one learn to distinguish the good from bad and cultivate it. Konrad's project of aesthetic education can only be successful if the audience assumes

[21] See Achnitz, 'Die schlafende Minne' (*op. cit. supra*, n. 18), 361 and Kokott, *Konrad von Würzburg* (*op. cit. supra*, n. 14), 91 on the meaning of *wildekeit*. They understand Lady Wildekeit as the personification of poetic imagination that enables the poet-singer to bring insight to others.

[22] Achnitz, 'Die schlafende Minne', (*op. cit. supra*, n. 21), 363.

responsibility for distinguishing quality art. Art is thus shown to enrich the aesthetic and moral life of individuals.

In other words, Konrad claims that the audience is in need of education in the performing arts. How is this to occur? Konrad's song itself is an example of artistic virtuosity and offers the remedy. Remaining consistent with contemporary aesthetics, Konrad maintains a congruence of content and form to make clear that the listeners can only learn to appreciate art by learning to understand it's intricacies. The logic of the argument may at this point appear circular: One can recognize and cultivate good art only when one appreciates it but one learns to enjoy it only by cultivating it. On the aesthetic level, however, the process is actually open-ended because each subsequent experience brings increased pleasure and discernment. The poet receives his instructions from Justice, but does not know how Art will fare in the future; and neither do we. Thus there is no closure, only a coda where the identity of the narrator is revealed to be our poet.

Once the audience realize that the poet and narrator are one and the same, this revelation sends them back to the beginning to contemplate the song anew. Only then does the composition fully reveal its function at the level of allegory because the song itself serves as the example of what constitutes excellent poetry. The strategy of skillfully placing his "essay" on art within the context of the vision allows Konrad the narrator-singer to claim the authority to define the poet-singer's function as teacher and creator of works of high artistic merit, and he does so without praising himself. Konrad's association with Virtues within the vision ennobles him and his aesthetic enterprise. The entire allegory, therefore, becomes an aesthetic means not merely of defining but also demonstrating by example, the function of art and artist in society, which is to contribute to the aesthetic and moral life of the audience.

The ties are formally strengthened when he is named court herald. With his selection to this role, a new definition of art is implied. Konrad himself has created a new form with a new type of allegory as example of his creative artistry. At the same time, by placing the onus on the audience, by expecting them to learn to distinguish trivial entertainment from serious art, he has established a distinction that to my knowledge has not been made before: He lays out the earliest suggestion of the concept of high versus popular art that is so prevalent today.

Konrad had no single court or patron to cater to, no ruler's aegis to stand under as others like Walther occasionally did, because he was centered in the city of Basel and received commissions from wealthy urban nobles and burghers alike. Therefore, creating a vision was perhaps the best way to enhance his own reputation. But as a poet-singer who was asked to produce a large variety of genres for his many patrons, he was in an excellent position to use allegory constructed as a unique generic amalgam of lyric and narrative elements to illustrate clearly the issues involved in aesthetic reception that leads to cultural and moral enrichment.

The commonplaces traced here are framed in the familiar complaint song. Examples of the genre are easily found in the repertory of all poets who attempted to make a living from their songs and performances from the eleventh to the end of the fifteenth century. What distinguishes each song is the use to which the topoi were put. Any song could easily be understood as a request for remuneration although I have attempted to show that many poets were concerned with broader issues of societal support for performance art. I began with a song that parodies the itinerant poet-singer's lifestyle in order to outdo previous complaints. It may also reflect the continuing competition between itinerant singers and the mendicants. The poet uses self-mockery to produce a humorous complaint with an exaggerated elaboration of the commonplaces. In my next example the topoi were used for a ploy that allowed the singer to illustrate by example the impact of remuneration on the quality of his artistic productivity. And finally some of the same commonplaces were used in an allegory to put forth a project to educate audiences to appreciate masterful and rich artistic songs. The singer's alliance with the Virtues justifies his own role in the process of aesthetic education. We may thus conclude that all the poet-singers discussed here were aware of the aesthetic component of their output. They each took different approaches to addressing the societal causes of the poverty of art and artist which are reflected in the way the singers elaborated on the topoi. The singers all implied the same underlying contradiction that those who produce cultural wealth must live in poverty.

AXEL BOLVIG

What Does Poverty Look Like? Its Notion in Late Medieval Danish Wall Paintings

How did late medieval painters delineate poverty in wall paintings? Did they really do it? If they did are we able to recognise depicted poverty?

Before trying to answer these questions it is necessary to underline the individual character of the different medieval means of visual communication: wall painting, oil painting, woodcut, etc. The same subject depicted in each of these media will be presented in quite different ways caused by their specific structures. Expression and contents are united in the image by the sign so you cannot separate the two. Consequently we must accept that the media determines – part of – the contents.

In his stimulating book based on his TV-presentations 'Ways of Seeing' John Berger writes that oil paintings often depict things, things that can be bought and possessed. If you buy an oil painting you buy the sight of the depicted things too.[1] Berger's remarks deal with the post-medieval period. Oil painting can also depict other subjects related to people's social conditions among these the poor. If you buy or commission an oil painting according to Berger's point of view you shall get a closer and more intimate relation to the depicted contents. Oil paintings, drawings and woodcuts have their individual existence being (in principle) portable. They can be placed or stored everywhere. On the contrary wall paintings are connected with the building. Architecture and picture constitute a unity. Depicted things or persons in murals do not have the same textural effect. They are not experienced as physical objects with the same intensity as their oil-painted sisters. I am tempted to write that you cannot own a wall painting even if it is not just right. The topic of this paper is to analyze the relationship between representations of poor people and of poverty? The latter is an abstract notion,

[1] John Berger, *Ways of Seeing* (Harmondsworth, 1972).

which is based on our interpretation of concrete accurate depictions and accuracy is a rare guest in Danish wall paintings.

In a way Keith Moxey in his article 'Reading the "Reality Effect"' is transferring Berger's considerations to the late Middle Ages but on late medieval conditions.[2] Moxey argues 'that the "realism" attributed to late medieval images is the product of cultural forces rather than inherent characteristics of the art of the period'.[3] Moxey is in my opinion not quite right if you take the different visual media into consideration. The inherent characteristics of wall paintings do not and cannot deal with 'the reality effect' in the same way as oil paintings. They do not and cannot depict realistic details. Referring to Campin's Merode Annunciation Moxey asks, 'what is the purpose of representing the Annunciation in an everyday domestic interior?'[4] At least Danish wall painters often depicted the Annunciation but never in a domestic interior.

This lack of realistic details might make it difficult in the wall paintings to find physical appearances of people and material things of daily life including poverty and its victims.

Maybe the difference between wall painting and oil painting is not that big. Moxey concludes 'that images are not reducible to the world they represent'.[5] But what about images, that omit 'domestic and similar details'? Both kinds of images cannot be conceived in similar ways. My topic, poverty, cannot be understood in the same way presented in respectively oil painting and wall painting. The visual expression of wall paintings does on the contrary fit into the view expressed by Gerhard Jaritz when writing 'dabei ist jedoch zu berücksichtigen, dass es dort in der Darstellung meist nicht um ein "authentisches Portrait" im weiteren Sinne geht, sondern um das "Typische"...'[6]

Because of the lack of realistic details wall paintings almost only present 'das Typische'. It means that it is very difficult for an (art) historian to find factual information of the poor and of all other social groups and matters.

---

[2] Keith Moxey, ‚Reading the "Reality Effect"', in *Pictura quasi fictura. Die Rolle des Bildes in der Erforschung von Alltag und Sachkultur des Mittelalters und der frühen Neuzeit*, ed. Gerhard Jaritz (Vienna, 1996), 15-21.

[3] *Ibid.*, 15.

[4] *Ibid.*, 17.

[5] *Ibid.*, 21.

[6] Gerhard Jaritz, "‚Et est ymago ficta non veritas'", in *Pictura quasi fictura* (*op. cit. supra*, n. 2), 10.

The denotative aspect of wall paintings is subordinated the connotative aspect. The iconographical reference to Luke 1:28-38 is the same in respectively the Merode Annunciation and a wall painting of the same subject but on the denotative or pre-iconographical level you cannot compare the two kinds of depictions. The oil painting is laid for the eye's delightful stroll among material things whereas in the wall painting there is only little to divert the beholder's attention from the iconographical subject. Of course this reflection also applies to images of poverty.

As long as we rely on iconography it is rather easy to classify poverty. Depictions of 'The Rich and Poor Man's Prayer', 'Saint Martin Offering his Cloak to a Beggar', 'Saint Laurence and the Poor', the story of Lazarus have poverty as a subject.

But do such iconographical subjects refer to poverty of real life or just its notion? And furthermore did the painters and the commissioners have an interest in depicting real poor men and women? It is an anachronism to expect social realism.

Saint Martin and the Poor

'Das Typische', which in my optic means the conventional strictly coded image of the poor we find in depictions of St Martin cutting his cloak into two halves in front of 'a poor man, almost naked'.[7] According to the typical iconographical convention the poor man has lost his feet and consequently is using a kind of footstool (fig. 1).[8]

Does such a depiction of a poor man tell anything about the living and survival conditions of the poor? It might be as far off from any analogy to real life as are the signs in our modern society indicating say roadmaking. There is almost no analogy to the surrounding life in such signs/pictograms. According to iconography, which has the same function as captions the image does not tell more than: poor half-naked man. But the visual sign referring to the lack of the feet is not unambiguous and does not exclusively signify poverty. In Ottestrup church we find a man linked to footstools but in violent motion and blowing a horn. Actually he is heading the procession around Jesus bearing his cross, which in fact is an impossible physical action, his handicap taken into consideration (fig. 2).

---

[7] Jacobus de Voragine, *The Golden Legend*, tr. William Granger Ryan (Princeton, 1995), vol.2, 292.

[8] Elmelunde church, Lynge church, Vigersted church, Vrangstrup church.

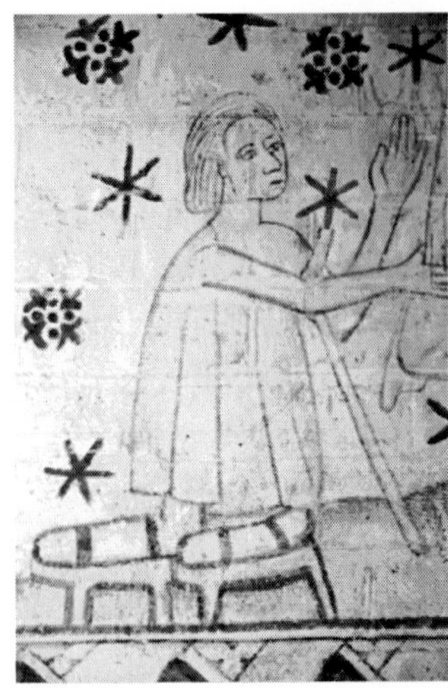

Fig. 1: Saint Martin and the Poor Man, detail. Vigersted church, 1450-60

This figure represents an evil person and has nothing to do with poverty. In the same image another ugly figure dragging and beating Jesus Christ has attached a stick to his left knee because he has lost one of his feet (fig. 3). The two figures in the Bearing of the Cross are not depicted as poor men but as grotesque and brutal tormentors.

Fig. 2: The Bearing of the Cross, detail. Ottestrup church, c. 1500

Fig. 3: The Bearing of the Cross, detail. Ottestrup church, c. 1500

A footstool and a wooden leg are loaded with negative connotations. One should think that the poor in depictions of 'St Martin and the Poor' represent the social group, which can be labelled the deserving poor contrary to the huge group of scroungers. But there is no definite answer to this.

Fig. 4: Saint Martin and the Poor Man, detail. Tuse church, 1460-80

An exception from the (negative?) iconographical convention attached to the loss of feet one finds in Tuse church. The man receiving the cloak has no physical defects. But it is difficult to interpret this figure as a visual sign denoting a poor man deserving alms because he looks like being able to work (fig. 4). The connotation attached to a visual sign is framed by the context. Consequently it might explain the different connotations attached to the figures of the different representations. But do coded connotations from one image disappear in other images for that reason?

Lazarus

Depictions of Lazarus are as conventional and deficient in details as 'the poor man, almost naked' receiving a piece of St Martin's cloak. At the rich man's gate 'lay a poor man named Lazarus whose body was covered with sores'[9].

Fig. 5: Lazarus. Saint Mary's church, Elsinore, 1475-1500

[9] Luke 16:20.

The few existing depictions of this scene focus on the rich man and his conduct of life. Luke does not describe the poor Lazarus except for his sores, which we may presume were the inevitable complications of poverty. But the two existing depictions of Lazarus do not focus on sores. On the contrary Lazarus' face and hands look well groomed in both depictions (fig. 5). It is tempting to ask, were dirty stinking handicapped outcasts full of sores allowed at a rich man's gate and even at his table? At least in wall paintings they are absent.

Saint Laurence and the Poor

Even if wall paintings do not present domestic interiors they bring interesting information of poverty. In Over Dråby church we find a series depicting the story of St Laurence. Two of the many sub-subjects present the poor more or less in agreement with the Golden Legend. One image refers to Laurence distributing the treasure of the church to the poor. The other image refers to Laurence presenting to the emperor the treasure of the church, which is constituted by the 'poor, the lame and the blind'.[10]

Fig. 6: St Laurence distributing the treasure of the church to the poor, detail. Over Dråby church, 1460-80

[10] Jacobus de Voragine, *The Golden Legend* (*op. cit. supra*, n. 7), vol. 2, 65.

One would think that the poor in both images were depicted in similar ways but this is not the fact. The poor receiving the treasure are in a rather bad condition. One, linked to a footstool, has lost his legs, some hold a beggars bowl in their hands, most of the others are using a beggars staff and wallet and another figure is scantily dressed (fig. 6). On the contrary the poor standing in front of the emperor still wear a beggars wallet but now they are nicely dressed happily looking men and women except for one man. They look well groomed and their physical handicaps have disappeared. They behave well in front of influential officials. The iconographical reference to the text is telling us that these people are poor; the image itself presents another version brought about by social conventions of good manners (fig. 7).

Fig. 7: St Laurence presenting the treasure of the church to the emperor, detail. Over Dråby church, 1460-80

It is tempting to put in: when presented to a prince even the poor took care of looking nice and decent and even St Laurence purged those with physical handicaps.

The Rich and the Poor Man's Prayer

Images of 'The Rich and the Poor Man's Prayer' are interesting because of their attitude towards the two social groups. The former isn't really wealthy and the latter looks like a rather well to do peasant. The lack of iconographical textual references and of visual conventions seems to give the artists and the commissioners free hands to work out the subject.

All the depictions follow the same standard. The rich man is thinking of certain material objects first of all clothes, wine and a horse whereas the poor man is thinking of the wounds of Jesus Christ.

In this connection the poor man is the important one. His appearance is far away from the appearance of St Martin's poor and from Lazarus. The only things to indicate his poor condition are the wholes in his dress on the elbows and the heels. Maybe the poor of 'The Rich and the Poor Man's Prayer' shall not be classified as the poor on social and economic terms but in a strictly religious connection representing a religious ideal. Indeed in one image he looks like a pilgrim (fig. 8).

Fig. 8: The Rich and the Poor man's prayer, detail. Tingsted church, c. 1500

It is tempting to put in: The painter is underlining the pious aspect of the poor praying man more than his social condition. In another connexion I have tried to link the poor man in this subject together with the peasants of the local parish who most often were the commissioners of the decorations.

They may have had an interest in connecting themselves to the pious praying man in opposition to the local lord.[11]

Heading towards poverty?

In the wall paintings one can find some other depictions of persons who might be labelled undeserving poor. Apparently these figures have no physical handicaps and no sores. One cannot say they are badly dressed. What they have in common are the tankards with beer or wine they hold in their hands (fig. 9). It does not signify poverty and not even the deadly sin 'gluttony'. But maybe these figures are heading towards poverty and perdition?

Fig. 9: A drunkard. Undløse church, 1425-50

[11] Axel Bolvig, 'Images of Late Medieval 'Daily Life': A History of Mentalities', *Medium Aevum Quotidianum* 39 (1998), 94-111.

Adam and Eve

One could argue that Adam and Eve after the Expulsion were forced to a life in poverty. The only initial capital they got were some garments from skin[12.] They had to start from scratch on harsh conditions. The first human beings on earth were poor. In a Romanesque painting from twelfth century the couple is depicted with no mitigating circumstances bare of a possibility of making a living and without children (fig. 10). But in the late Middle Ages Adam and Eve do not accept God's punishment. She is a nicely dressed married woman sitting in a comfortable chair spinning. He is not depicted as a worn-out labourer. On the contrary he is also well dressed. Between the two is a small child in a cradle. They form a well to do nuclear family far way from the poor living condition, which should be the consequence of the Fall and the Expulsion (fig. 11)[13].

Fig. 10: Adam and Eve. Todbjerg church, 1225-50

[12] Genesis 3: 21.
[13] Bolvig, 'Images of Late Medieval 'Daily Life'' (*op. cit. supra*, n. 11), 107.

Fig. 11: Adam and Eve. Hjembæk church, c. 1500

Nancy B. Black

Medieval Depictions of "Poor Queens" in Art and Text

In the Prologue to "The Man of Law's Tale," Geoffrey Chaucer's story of the falsely accused queen Custance, the narrator castigates poverty: "O hateful harm, condicion of poverte!/ With thurst, with coold, with hunger so confoundid!" After deploring the extremes to which indigence can lead – stealing, begging, or borrowing – he warns his readers against falling into poverty: "Alle the dayes of povre men been wikke./ Be war, therfore, er thou come to that prikke!"[1] This passage has been a puzzle to Chaucer scholars because it seems to contradict the message of the tale of Custance that follows. That tale extols the fortitude and spiritual wealth of a heroine subjected to extreme poverty: she is twice deprived of all material possessions and social status by being exiled and set adrift on the sea in a rudderless ship. Rather than, as some scholars have done, read this seeming contradiction between the Prologue and the Tale as a sign of the unfinished nature of Chaucer's *Canterbury Tales*,[2] I use it to begin a discussion of poverty as seen through the lens of medieval narratives of "poor queens." In short, "The Man of Law's Tale" provides us with two definitions of poverty: the negative view of the Man of Law, who equates it with hunger, thirst, and cold; and a positive view provided by the story itself, which equates poverty with spiritual fortitude and constancy. The disparity of attitudes toward poverty

---

1 *The Riverside Chaucer*, ed. Larry D. Benson. 3rd ed. (Boston, 1987), 88-89. Hereafter all quotations from Chaucer will be from this text and cited in the essay by the abbreviation for the work: *The Canterbury Tales* (*CT*) or *Troilus and Criseyde* (*TC*). The parenthetical reference to *CT* will be followed by fragment number and lines as here: II. 99-100 and 118-119. The parenthetical reference to *TC* will be followed by the number of the book and the line numbers.

2 Patricia J. Eberle's explanatory notes to *The Riverside Chaucer* (*op. cit. supra*, n. 1), 856, summarize the scholarly commentary on the problematical connections of the Prologue to the Tale.

found at the start of the tale reflects larger cultural anxieties and philosophical debates about poverty and wealth in the fourteenth century in France and England.

Evidence of contradictions in medieval attitudes toward poverty can also be found in the preceding century and in other source materials. In her recent book, *Surviving Poverty in Medieval Paris: Gender, Ideology, and the Daily Lives of the Poor,* Sharon Farmer analyzes not only traditional historical documents, such as wills and tax assessments, but also sermons and sixty-five posthumous miracles of St. Louis for what they reveal about the condition of the poor in thirteenth-century France.[3] I am particularly interested in the larger attitudes toward the poor that emerge from her study. The elite discourse about the poor, particularly about the disabled or begging poor, is largely negative. Although Farmer acknowledges that alternative views of the poor existed and mentions a few,[4] my essay follows up on her brief discussion and explores the works of several authors in the next century, authors close to or working for royal patrons in Paris and London between 1314 and 1400. Study of these works reinforces the view that positive notions toward the poor indeed existed. I shall demonstrate that stories of "poor queens" were an important part of that discourse; that during this period attitudes toward wealth and poverty were complex; and that this discourse is inseparable from contemporary critiques of justice and power.

The "poor queens" of my title is shorthand for all fictional noblewomen—whether queens or countesses or marquises—who experience an abrupt change in social status. These include "falsely accused" noblewomen, the subject of my prior research,[5] as well as the narrative of one who might more accurately be called "abused": Griselda, the wife of Walter, Marquis of Saluzzo, the subject of Chaucer's "Clerk's Tale." While the "falsely accused" women, of which Custance is a notable example, experience a sudden removal from court into the extreme poverty of exile, the "abused" Griselda moves abruptly in the reverse direction. When Walter stops by her hut one day and asks her father for her hand in marriage, she moves suddenly from the life of a shepherdess to that of a marquise, a surprising elevation in social status. Whether these heroines move abruptly down or up the social ladder, their stories relate closely to one another, as a comment from Christine de Pizan indicates. She speaks both of an accused queen (the empress of Rome,

[3] Ithaca, 2002.

[4] *Ibid.*, 70-73.

[5] See Nancy B. Black, *Medieval Narratives of Accused Queens* (Gainesville, 2003).

whom she calls Florence) and Griselda when she writes in *The Book of the City of Ladies* that they "both endured great adversity with amazing patience."[6] And Chaucer himself introduces the stories of both Custance and Griselda into his *Canterbury Tales* in such a way that they become important, parallel examples of virtuous women, the heroines of two key stories: "The Man of Law's Tale" and "The Clerk's Tale," respectively.

This study examines both accused and abused fictional noblewomen to see what their stories can tell us about medieval depictions of and attitudes toward poverty. My starting point is not the modern editions of the tales but rather the manuscripts themselves. Analysis of the manuscript as cultural artifact enables us to understand both the language of text and the language of art, different types of signifiers used to evoke poverty to audiences in the Middle Ages. Two illustrated manuscripts provide evidence of visual depictions of poverty in fourteenth-century France. The first is the only illustrated manuscript of the *Roman du Comte d'Anjou* by Jehan Maillart, secretary to the king of France, Philip IV, BNF n.a.fr. 4531, dated 1316.[7] The second is an illustrated dramatized version of the story of Griselda, *L'Estoire de Griseldis*, based on a work by Philippe de Mézières, tutor to the French dauphin, BNF fr. 2203, dated 1395.[8] After analyzing the relationship of art and text in these manuscripts, I then move to the larger issue of attitudes toward poverty, placing these documents into the context of debates about poverty in Paris. Finally, I will show how Chaucer incorporated these ideas into his *Canterbury Tales*, thus transferring those debates across the Channel to London.

Jehan Maillart's story is typical of narratives of accused queens in that it follows a four-part structure: the heroine falls twice from a position of high status and then twice recovers that status, a cyclical movement that echoes the turnings of the wheel of fortune. The heroine, who is the daughter of the count of Anjou, flees from the court with her governess in order to escape her father's incestuous desires. Her life in exile is one of poverty, which the author frequently compares to the life of luxury she has left. Taken in by a poor woman in Orleans, the count's daughter and her governess begin to embroider for a living. The heroine is eventually rescued by the count of Bourges, who marries her and restores her to a life of luxury. During the count's absence on a military expedition, she gives birth to a beautiful boy.

---

[6] Tr. Earl Jeffrey Richards (New York, 1982), 176.

[7] Ed. Mario Roques (1931; reprint Paris, 1974).

[8] Ed. Barbara M. Craig, Humanistic Studies 31 (Lawrence, 1954).

However, letters announcing the birth are altered by a jealous aunt, the countess of Chartres, and the result is a death sentence for mother and child. Just before they are about to be murdered, the henchmen take pity and allow mother and child to flee on foot. The mayoress of Etampes rescues them and sends them to the bishop at Orleans, who has a reputation for helping the poor. Meanwhile, the count of Bourges returns home, learns what has happened, and pledges a life of poverty and fasting until he finds his wife and son. Eventually the family is reunited in Orleans in the presence of the bishop, who turns out to be the heroine's uncle. The happy couple returns to Bourges, and the count appeals to the king of France to punish the falsely accusing aunt, the countess of Chartres. With the king's approval, the count launches an attack on his aunt, who is finally called to justice and burned at the stake. The happy couple returns to Anjou to claim the lands as part of their inheritance.

The sudden removal of this aristocratic woman from her luxurious, courtly surroundings plunges her into a hard-scrabble world where she needs to find shelter, and the artist of BNF n.q.fr. 4531 depicts both her involuntary poverty as well as the voluntary poverty of her husband when he leaves the court to search for her. Within the program of twenty-seven illustrations that originally accompanied the text (one miniature has been cut out and lost), two miniatures depict the poverty of the heroine and one the poverty of her husband. In these three illustrations, clothing is the principal signifier.[9] The first image of the heroine and her governess in exile (Fig. 1) depicts them dressed simply in dresses and tunics barely distinguishable from those of the poor, old woman who offers them some of her bread. Later, after the falsification of letters, the heroine is depicted in much more dire straits (Fig. 2). In this scene, mother and child wait to be murdered and thrown into the large pit shown in the center of the illustration: the countess wears only her undergarment, indicating that she has been nearly stripped naked of all her material possessions and, needless to say, her social status.

---

[9] For a more general discussion of the use of clothing by medieval artists, see Françoise Piponnier and Perrine Mane, *Dress in the Middle Ages*, tr. Caroline Beamish (New Haven and London, 1997); originally published as *Se vêtir au Moyen Âge* (Paris, 1995). For the relationship between sumptuary laws and social status, see *Showing Status: Representation of Social Positions in the Late Middle Ages*, ed. Wim Blockmans and Antheun Janse (Turnhout, 1999).

Fig. 1: Paris, BNF n.a.fr. 4531, fol. 12r;
reproduced by permission of the Bibliothèque Nationale de France

It is interesting to contrast the artist's rendering of the involuntary poverty of the countess to that of the voluntary poverty of the count (Fig. 3). After learning that his wife had been falsely accused, he decides to embark on a pilgrimage: his garments consist of a flimsy tunic, reflecting his rejection of the clothing of wealth.[10] The text just below the picture explains that he has given away his good robe and quite deliberately assumed the tunic, shoes, and hat of a poor servant.[11] How different is the status of the count, countess, and their son at the happy ending of the tale when they make their entrance into Anjou. Now they can travel in comfort in a closed carriage instead of wandering on foot like poor people, begging bread as they journey along (Fig. 4).

[10] The green leaf-like marks on his garment are a puzzle; perhaps they suggest a spiritual renewal similar to that referred to by Chaucer at the start of the *Canterbury Tales*.

[11] "Lors a sa bonne robe ostee,/ Celle a un serf a endossee;/ D'uns soulers a lïenz se chauce,/ Si ne mist dessouz nulle chauce;/ Un chaperon ot deschiré;/ Con povres s'est bien atiré,/ Et en sa main prist un baston"(5293-5299).

Fig. 2: Paris, BNF n.a.fr. 4531, fol. 34r;
reproduced by permission of the Bibliothèque Nationale de France

Fig. 3: Paris, BNF n.a.fr. 4531, fol. 43r;
reproduced by permission of the Bibliothèque Nationale de France

Fig. 4: Paris, BNF n.a.fr. 4531, fol. 61v;
reproduced by permission of the Bibliothèque Nationale de France

The emphasis on poverty in this manuscript is not merely the whim of the *artist*, for Jehan Maillart's *text* also frequently contrasts the world of poverty experienced by the heroine to the life of luxury she has left behind. In addition to using clothing as a signifier, however, the poet also employs food as a key signifier.[12] Maillart's principal flight of rhetorical fancy occurs in a passage found just after the image above in which the daughter of the count of Anjou and her governess beg bread from a poor, old woman. The fifty-three-line passage is notable for its length and the details of fine meats, fish, pastries, and wines enjoyed at the court. It begins with the heroine's memory of "Mes viandes chieres et fines,/ Chapons en rost, oisons, gelines,/ Cynnes, paons, perdris, fesanz,/ Herons, butors qui sont plesans" and ends with a list of fourteen outstanding wines (see the Appendix I for the entire passage).

It is significant that this passage, and others like it, were copied and incorporated into another important work from the same period, Chaillou de

[12] Alice Planche, 'Omnipresence, police et auto-censure de pauvres. Le témoignage *du Roman du Comte d'Anjou* (1316)', in *Littérature et société au moyen âge: actes du colloque des 5 et 6 mai 1978*, ed. Danielle Buschinger (Amiens, 1978), 263-283; 'La Table comme signe de la classe. Le témoignage du *Roman du Conte d'Anjou* (1316)', in *Manger et boire au moyen âge: actes du colloque de Nice (15-17 octobre 1982)*, 2 vols. (Nice, 1984), 1: 239-260.

Pestain's *Roman de Fauvel* (1316-18),[13] a remarkable critique of fourteenth-century Parisian abuses of wealth and power by means of an animal fable in which a horse named Fauvel is crowned king. According to the editors of the recent facsimile edition of BNF fr. 316, Chaillou and Maillart were part of the same circle of clerical writers who complained about abuses of power following the death of King Philip IV (d. 1314) and who campaigned to restore legitimate and effective royal leadership.[14] This close connection between the two texts suggests that the depiction of poverty in the *Roman* functions both to illustrate the inner virtues of the heroine – who can resist her father's incestuous advances and survive a life of poverty away from court – *and* to serve as a critique of the wealthy class, an "admonitio" to the ruling classes.

As former royal secretary to Philip IV, Jehan Maillart had a vested interest in presenting a view of the world in which virtue reigns in the affairs of government. In his fictional world, a powerful king and an effective, centralized royal administration maintain order and carry out justice. Rejecting the fanciful geography of earlier narratives of accused queens, the author writes "Une aventure veritable" and sets the events in towns and counties under the control of the French king. More important, he devotes over one thousand lines of his 8156-line narrative to describing in detail the elaborate process by which the count of Bourges accuses his aunt of treason in the royal court and obtains a judgment permitting him to make war on her and ultimately order her death by fire. Thus, the count of Bourges becomes an example of a virtuous, effective ruler in contrast to the bearer of the title of the work, the willful count of Anjou whose incestuous desires cloud his mind and make him an ineffective ruler. The rhetorical contrasts between poverty and luxury that occur throughout the text serve to underscore this admonitory message.

---

[13] For a complete list of passages from *Roman du Comte d'Anjou* used in *Roman de Fauvel*, see Roques' edition of *Roman* (*op. cit. supra*, n. 7), 256-258. In addition to the banquet scene printed here in Appendix A, the following passages have been borrowed: prayer to God (877-1008); more rich food (2353-2367, 2369-2370, 2371-2382, 2738, 2887-2888); richness of bed coverings (2896-2920, 3010); riches dispensed (6397-6402); lavish entry into Bourges (6507-6520).

[14] *Le Roman de Fauvel in the Edition of Mesire Chaillou de Pesstain. A Reproduction in Facsimile of the Complete Manuscript Paris, Bibliothèque Nationale, Fonds Français 146*, intr. Edward Roesner, François Avril, and Nancy Freeman Regalado (New York, 1990), 8.

In contrast to the *Roman du Comte d'Anjou*, the story of Griselda has a well-documented literary history and a broader audience. The story was first written by Boccaccio in the *Decameron* in 1353, the last of his stories in that collection. Petrarch retold the story in Latin and sent it in a letter to Boccaccio, first draft in 1373, revised in 1374, the year of Petrarch's death.[15] The letter was translated into French as *Le Livre Griseldis* by an anonymous translator and as *Le Miroir des Dames Mariées* by Philippe de Mézières (1385-89). In creating "The Clerk's Tale," Chaucer used both Petrarch's Latin version and the anonymous French prose version, perhaps with some consultation of Philippe's contemporary version.[16] Philippe used his version of the Griselda story as part of his *Le Livre de la Vertu du Sacrement de Mariage*,[17] but the story also circulated widely in France and was included in two fourteenth-century marriage manuals, *Le Menagier de Paris* and *Le Livre du Chevalier de la Tour Landry*.[18] It was also used for the only extant dramatized version of the story, *L'Estoire de Griseldis* (1395). The manuscript of this last work, BNF fr. 2203, includes nineteen illustrations and one historiated initial; it provides us with another source of information about visual representations of poverty at the end of the fourteenth century.

The story concerns the marquis of Saluzzo (a town in north-western Italy, near Turin), a man absorbed in his own pleasures, who declines to marry and produce an heir. His barons and knights select a "quint chevalier qui moult estoit ancien"[19] to plead with him to take a wife, and he agrees on the condition that he can make the choice without consultation with them. He chooses Griselda, a poor shepherdess, after she promises never to contradict him or express any displeasure about his behavior. She is a model wife and produces two children, first a girl and then a boy. After the birth of each child, the marquis decides to test his wife's fidelity by ordering her to let their child be taken away, presumably to be killed; he actually sends them off to his

---

[15] Judith Bronfman, *Chaucer's Clerk's Tale* (New York, 1994), 16.

[16] The Latin text of Petrarch's letter and the anonymous French translation (with translations into English) may be found in *Sources and Analogues of the Canterbury Tales*, ed. Robert M. Correale and Mary Hamel (Woodbridge, UK, 2002), 1: 101-167. See also the introductions to the editions of these two texts in the same volume by Thomas J. Farrell, 'The Griselda Story in Italy', 1: 103-106; and Amy W. Goodwin, 'The Griselda Story in France', 1: 130-139; Anne Middleton, 'The Clerk and His Tale: Some Literary Contexts', *Studies in the Age of Chaucer* 2 (1980), 121-150.

[17] Ed. Joan B. Williamson (Washington, D.C., 1993).

[18] Goodwin, 'The Griselda Story' (*op. cit. supra*, n. 16), 131.

[19] *L'Estoire de Griseldis*, p. 30.

sister, the countess of Panico (near Bologne), to be educated. A third test of his wife's fidelity occurs when he tells her that he wants to discard her as his wife and send her back home to her poor father so that he, the marquis, can remarry. Again, without a word of complaint, she leaves her rich clothes behind and returns to her father, dressed only in a simple shift. As a final test, the marquis calls her back to his home and asks her to prepare the house for his marriage to his new wife. After this last insult, she makes what may be read as one slight murmur of complaint, warning him that his new bride may not be tough enough to stand up to the same treatment she has received. And only then does the marquis reveal that their two children are alive and that the young woman he pretended to want to marry is actually their daughter. He takes Griselda back as his wife, and the family is reunited, presumably to live happily ever after.

An analysis of BNF fr. 2203 shows us that clothing is the principal signifier of poverty in both illustrations and text. In fact, the contrasts between wealth and poverty are more sharply accentuated in this program of illustration than in the *Roman du Comte d'Anjou*. At the start of the narrative, Griselda and her father are seen outside their "hut," which, admittedly, seems rather a substantial building in the depiction here (Fig. 5). Griselda's long, flowing hair, her simple dress, her shepherd's staff, and the sheep at her feet define her lowly status. Once married and in the marquis's home, with elaborately coifed hair, she wears an elegant gown with fashionable sleeves and long, dangling elbow pieces, clothing that *almost* matches that of the marquis in elegance (Fig. 6). I say "almost" because her dress lacks the embroidered "S" for Saluzzo that marks the marquis's garments, perhaps suggesting that her status as noblewoman has not yet been fully achieved or acknowledged. However, the most dramatic contrast in status, as depicted through displays of clothing in the illustrations, comes when the marquise is sent from the court to return to her father's hut (Fig. 7). The dress, marked this time (and the only time) with the "S," perhaps to indicate that it is the property of the marquis, is handed back to him; Griselda's hair is now covered by a simple, modest veil. Finally, at the end of the work, she has regained her aristocratic status and dress (Fig. 8).

Fig. 5: Paris, BNF fr. 2203, fol. 15[v];
reproduced by permission of the Bibliothèque Nationale de France

Fig. 6: Paris, BNF fr. 2203, fol. 33r;
reproduced by permission of the Bibliothèque Nationale de France

Fig. 7: Paris, BNF fr. 2203, fol. 46v;
reproduced by permission of the Bibliothèque Nationale de France

Fig. 8: Paris, BNF fr. 2203, fol. 52v;
reproduced by permission of the Bibliothèque Nationale de France

The attention to clothing in the illustrations is echoed by references to clothing within the text. For example, during Walter's third testing of Griselda, a chevalier comments on the action, noting the consistency of her deportment both when she was dressed poorly (as now) and when dressed richly (as she was before Walter rejected her).[20] When, toward the end of the work, Walter finally admits that he has tested Griselda enough and reveals that the woman he has pretended to marry is actually their daughter, she herself notes the need to have her mother reclothed: "Madame, il fault qu'on vous reveste,/ Car trop estes petitement."[21] In contrast to the distinction we saw in the *Roman du Comte d'Anjou* between the visual (clothing) and textual (food) signifiers, in this work clothing is the common signifier of social status, and hence the visual and textual signifiers merge. In fact, because this is a dramatic text destined for performance, it is the act itself of clothing/unclothing that becomes the focus of what is both seen and heard. Two dramatic scenes of undressing or dressing mark the performance and are noted in the rubrics. The first occurs just after Walter announces that he will take Griselda as his wife; a rubric not associated with a picture explains that "La premiere dame, faisant chamberiere et service a Griselda, la fait desvestir et parer richement."[22] The second occurs when Walter sends Griselda back to her father, a scene given prominence in the illustrations, as we saw above (Fig. 7). The illustration is followed by a rubric that makes the action on the stage clear: "La marquise sanz signe d'ire despoille son riche habit et reprent le viez qu'elle avoit laissie et se consent liement de retourner a son povre pere."[23] The dramatic representations of dressing and undressing Griselda reflect cultural anxieties about social status and its relationship to virtue.[24]

As in the *Roman du Comte d'Anjou*, the contrasts of rich and poor are used by the dramatist to critique the abuses of power. At the beginning of the narrative, Walter disregards the future of his realm, and he is arrogant in choosing a wife far beneath him in social status without consultation from

[20] "Ains est liee en dit et en fait,/ Et se porte en son povre habit,/ Combien qu'il soit simple et petit,/ Aussi bien et honnestement/ Comme s'elle feust richement/ De robes de soye paree" (2376-2381).

[21] *L'Estoire de Griseldis*: 2488-89.

[22] *L'Estoire de Griseldis*, p. 41.

[23] *L'Estoire de Griseldis*, p. 57.

[24] The role of "elite garments" in cultural discourse is explored by E. Jane Burns in *Courtly Love Undressed: Reading through Clothes in Medieval French Culture* (Philadelphia, 2002).

his advisors. His abuse of power continues with each new testing of Griselda, the worst being his scheme to employ her as a servant in the house in which she has previously reigned as marquise. The critique of aristocratic behavior suggests that the author, like Jehan Maillart, was also interested in providing advice to princes. Indeed, this hypothesis is borne out by what we know about the probable author of the play.

The dramatist of *L'Estoire de Griseldis* was most likely Philippe de Mézières, author of the prose version on which the play is based.[25] Like Jehan Maillart at the beginning of the century, Philippe was a significant presence in French royal circles from 1373 until his death in 1405: he was a counselor to Charles V and tutor of his son, the future Charles VI. Although the story of Griselda was, in some contexts, used to counsel proper female behavior in marriage, it is clear that Philippe's interest in the story was also due to its political value in providing advice to princes. Philippe was a strong proponent of peace between England and France and, in this connection, wrote a *Letter to King Richard II: A Plea Made in 1395 for Peace between England and France*.[26] In this work, he argues (not unlike the "quint chevalier" of the play) for a marriage, in this case the marriage of Richard II to the young Isabel of France. As part of his argument, he refers to the story of Griselda:

> May it please God, worthy Prince, for the furtherance of peace in Christendom and the comfort of your royal person, to grant you a wife such as Griselda, the wife of the Marquis of Saluzzo, who was but the daughter of a poor working man, yet, according to the authentic chronicle of the said Marquis of Saluzzo and Griselda his wife, written by that learned doctor and sovereign poet, Master Francis Petrarch, there is no record, from the beginning of the world until today, apart from the saints, of a woman of such great virtue, nor so loving towards her husband, nor of such marvellous patience, as this same Lady Griselda; and this you have read, or may come to read, in the said chronicle.[27]

If Richard II did indeed know the story of Griselda, he also knew that its meaning went beyond providing an example of female subservience in marriage; Walter, Marquis of Saluzzo, was an example of a willful and tyrrani-

---

[25] Barbara M. Craig, in the introduction to her critical edition of *L'Estoire de Griseldis* (*op. cit. supra*, n. 8), reviews the authorship evidence, pp. 4-6.

[26] Intr. and tr. G. W. Coopland (Liverpool, 1975).

[27] *Ibid*, 42.

cal ruler whose selfish desires were tamed through the judicious counsel of his advisors and the fortitude of his wife.

In addition to political ramifications, the stories of "poor queens" also have religious implications. Both Griselda and the daughter of the count of Anjou represent a type of patient suffering that is associated with the biblical story of Job and with a well-known passage from Isaiah 48:10: "See how I tested you, not as silver is tested, but in the furnace of affliction; there I purified you."[28] In the Vulgate text "furnace of affliction" is *camino paupertatis*, literally, the "furnace of poverty." The sufferings of the daughter of the count of Anjou in the French countryside and the multiple testings of Griselda by Walter represent experiences of poverty and affliction in this sense. *Paupertatis* carries positive religious connotations: women are tested and their ability to survive and recover their former social status illustrates their fortitude and the accompanying refinement of their souls. But the suffering of these "poor queens" is not gender-specific; it represents a type of religious fortitude available both to men and women, a type of suffering we also see in the experiences of Job.

Camino paupertatis, this quality of constancy in the face of adversity that leads to refinement of the soul, was well understood in the Middle Ages and originates in Boethian ideas current in fourteenth-century France and England. Keep your sight on God, Lady Philosophy tells Boethius in *The Consolation of Philosophy*.[29] The adversities of this world are but the twists and turns of fickle fortune. The constancy of your faith in God will be rewarded with eternal life. Or as Geoffrey Chaucer writes in *Troilus and Criseyde*, echoing Boethius:

> Repayreth hom from wordly vanyte,
> And of youre herte up casteth the visage
> To thilke God that after his ymage
> You made, and thynketh al nys but a faire,
> This world that passeth soone as floures faire.
>
> (*TC* V: 1837-41)

When Chaucer retells the story of Griselda in "The Clerk's Tale," he highlights both the political and religious messages inherent in the tale: the abuse of power and the virtues of constancy. He inserts explicit condemnations of

---

28 *The New English Bible with the Apocrypha*, Oxford Study Edition (New York, 1976), 782.

29 Tr. W. V. Cooper (New York, 1943), 120.

the behavior of the marquis and draws parallels between the sufferings of Griselda and those of Job. (For a sampling of additional passages, see Appendix II).[30] When handing her garments back to her husband, Griselda addresses her husband, echoing Job 1:21:

"Naked out of my fadres hous," quod she,
"I cam, and naked moot I turne again.
Al youre pleasance wol I folwen fayn;
But yet I hope it be nat youre entente
That I smoklees out of youre paleys wente.
....
Lat me nat lyk a worm go by the weye.
Remember yow, myn owene lord so deere,
I was youre wyf, though I unworthy were."
(*CT* IV. 871-75; 880-82)

Although Griselda's words echo those of Job, she manages to avoid the literal nakedness or state of undress that we find in artistic renderings of Job or in the personification of Poverty in the *Roman de la Rose*, two other popular texts that offer a view of poverty.[31] When she returns to her father's hut, she returns to a life of labor; her virtue was present before her rise in social status and will continue after her fall from power.

Like that of Philippe de Mézières, Chaucer's attitude toward the poverty of Griselda is a positive one, one that appears to reflect a growing criticism of the excesses of the aristocracy and an appreciation of the spiritual advantages of poverty.[32] Chaucer exposes the hypocrisy of many religious figures in *The Canterbury Tales* who have taken a vow of poverty but have been lured away by the attractions of wealth – such as the monk, the friar, and the prioress. However, through the stories of virtuous women – not only the patient Griselda in "The Clerk's Tale" but also the classic "accused queen," Custance in "The Man of Law's Tale" – Chaucer presents a positive model

---

[30] In her explanatory notes to 'The Clerk's Tale,' Patricia J. Eberle in *The Riverside Chaucer* (*op. cit. supra*, n. 1), 880-84, notes all Chaucer's additions to his sources.

[31] The nakedness or partial nudity of Job is a common theme; see, for example, New York, The Pierpont Morgan Library, G. 42, fol. 153[v]; H.8, fol. 127[v]; M. 1001, fol. 114[r]; M. 452, fol. 97[v]; M. 622, fol. 98[r]. The allegorical figure of Poverty in *The Romance of the Rose* is depicted with exposed breasts in BNF fr. 25526, fol. 5[r], and in tattered clothing in BNF fr. 19153, fol. 5[r].

[32] It is possible that Chaucer was familiar with the work of Philippe de Mézières; see Goodwin, 'The Griselda Story' (*op. cit.* supra, n. 16), 133-134.

for men and women alike who would follow the Boethian path to spiritual refinement and union with God.

If Chaucer's attitude toward poverty is so positive, why then does he place a speech castigating poverty – the one quoted at the start of this essay – into the mouth of the Man of Law? I suggest that he does so in order to undercut the authority of his own narrator and to present, without necessarily approving, multiple perspectives on poverty and wealth. The Man of Law is quoting a Latin source here, Lotario dei Segni's *De miseria condicionis humane*, a work Chaucer translated.[33] But the Man of Law quotes out of context, for *De miseria* castigates both poverty *and* wealth, viewing *both* as aspects of a transient earthly life, of little importance when viewed anagogically, or from the perspective of the Last Judgment. Thus, any reader who knows the source of the Man of Law's words also knows that the narrator misreads – or at least quotes selectively – perhaps to justify his own capitalist attitudes about the acquisition of wealth.[34]

Chaucer is notoriously difficult to pin down to a single point of view, particularly when it comes to a subject, such as this one, with political ramifications. Nowhere is the author's slipperiness more evident than in the speech on "gentilesse" that he imbeds into the tale of the Wife of Bath:

Looke who that is moost vertuous alway,
Pryvee and apert, and moost entendeth ay
To do the gentil dedes that he kan;
Taak hym for the grettest gentil man.
....
Poverte is hateful good and, as I gesse,
A ful greet bryngere out of bisynesse;
A greet amendere eek of sapience
To hym that taketh it in pacience.
Poverte is this, although it seme alenge:
Possessioun that no wight wol chalenge.
Poverte ful ofte, whan a man is lowe,

---

[33] Scholars have suggested that he was translating Lotario dei Segni (who became Pope Innocent III), around the same time that he was composing the "Man of Law's Tale"; see *The Riverside Chaucer* (*op. cit. supra*, n. 1), 856.

[34] See my discussion in *Medieval Narratives of Accused Queens* (*op. cit. supra*, n. 5), 134-36. In fact, it appears that Chaucer may have included Latin glosses to the text in order to highlight the narrator's "misreading." There are nine extant Latin glosses for this text, five of which are taken from *De miseria condicionis humane*.

Maketh his God and eek hymself to knowe.
Poverte a spectacle is, as thynketh me,
Thurgh which he may his verray freendes see.
And therfore, sire, syn that I noght yow greve,
Of my poverte namoore ye me repreve.
(*CT* III. 1113-16, 1195-1206)

The speaker here, a poor, old hag, argues that gentility is based not on inherited social standing or wealth but on good deeds. She quotes Dante, Valerius Maximus, Seneca, Juvenal, and Boethius to prove that aristocrats are not necessarily virtuous and that poor people are not necessarily thieves. But it would be facile to assume that the old hag serves as Chaucer's mouthpiece, for in many ways his characterization of the Wife of Bath and of the old hag of her tale mocks women, and he may even be questioning the ability of women to engage in intellectual discourse. Nonetheless, the words of the old hag and the examples of patience and constancy found in the Man of Law's and the Clerk's Tales remain an important part of broader discussions of poverty in fourteenth-century England and France.

Ultimately, a thorough understanding of Chaucer's treatment of poverty calls for a more extensive historical approach, placing his work in the midst of other important texts and events from the end of the fourteenth century in England, not merely in relationship to French texts. I think particularly of Langland's *Piers Plowman* and texts associated with the Lollard movement (with which Chaucer appears to have had some sympathy). In fact, recent Chaucerian scholarship depicts Chaucer as more intimately involved in the political upheavals of his day than previous scholars have thought.[35] However, such research clearly goes beyond the scope of this essay. It is my modest hope that the analysis of the two manuscripts I have presented, along with my discussion of related religious and political texts, will complicate and enrich future discussions of poverty in the Middle Ages.

---

[35] Paul Strohm, *Social Chaucer* (Cambridge, Ma., 1989) and *Hochon's Arrow: The Social Imagination of Fourteenth-Century Texts* (Princeton, 1992); Steven Justice, *Writing and Rebellion: England in 1381* (Berkeley, 1994); Terry Jones, Robert Yeager, Terry Dolan, Alan Fletcher, and Juliette Dor, *Who Murdered Chaucer? A Medieval Mystery* (New York, 2003).

Appendix I: Heroine's description of lavish feast she used to enjoy before her exile

Mes viandes chieres et fines,
Chapons en rost, oisons, gelines,
Cynnes, paons, perdris, fesanz,
Herons, butors qui sont plesans,
Et venoisons de maintes guisez
A chiens courans par force prises:
Cers, dains, connins, senglers sauvages,
Qui habitant en ces bocages,
Et toute bonne venoison;
Poissons ravoie j'a foison
Des meilleurs de tout le païs:
Esturjons, saumons et plaïs,
Congres, gournars et grans morues,
Tumbes, rougés et grans barbues,
Maqueriauz gras et gros mellens
Et harens fres et espellens,
Sartres graces, mullés et solles,
Bremes et bescües et molles;
J'avoie de maintes mennieres
Poissons d'estans et de rivieres
Atornéz chascun par grant cure,
Selonc son droit et sa nature,
A poivre, a sausse kameline;
J'avoie lus en galantine,
Grossez lemproiez a ce mesmes,
Bars et carpes, gardons et bresmes,
Appareilliéz en autre guisez;
Truttes ravoie en paste misez,
Lez dars, lez vendoisez rostiez,
En verjus de grain tooillies,
Et grosses anguilles em paste,
Autre foiz roustiez en haste
Et les gros bequés chaudumés,
Si com il sont acoustuméz
Des keus qui sevent lez sentances
De l'atorner; j'avoie tances

Que en appele renversees;
J'avoie gauffres et oubleez,
Gouieres, tartes, flaonciaus,
Pipes farses a grans monciaus,
Pommes d'espices, dirioles,
Crespines, bingnés et ruissoles;
Si bevoie vins precïeus,
Pyment, claré delicïeus,
Cythouandés, roséz, floréz,
Vins de Gascoingne colouréz,
De Mont Pellier et de Rochelle,
Vin de Garnace et de Castelle,
Vin de Biaune et de Saint Poursain
Que riche gent tiennent pour sain,
D'Auçuerre, d'Anjo, d'Orlenois,
De Gastinois, de Leonnois,
De Biauvoisin, de Saint Jouen....

(*Roman du Comte d'Anjou*, ll. 1107-59)

Appendix II: A sampling of Chaucer's additions to his source in "The Clerk's Tale."

A. On Griselda's virtues

Labor more virtuous than idleness:

Wel ofter of the welle than of the tonne
She drank, and for she wolde vertu plese,
She knew wel labour but noon ydel ese.

(*CT* IV. 215-17)

Griselda's actions as echo of Mary, Mother of Jesus:

And doun upon hir knes she gan to falle,
And with sad contenance kneleth stille,
Til she had herd what was the lordes wille.

(*CT* IV. 292-94)

Her religious faith when first child is taken from her:

And thus she seyde in hire benigne voyse,
"Fareweel my child! I shal thee nevere see.
But with I thee have marked with the croys
Of thilke Fader – lessed moote he be! –
That for us deyde upon a croys of tree,
Thy soule, litel child, I hym bitake,
For this nyght shaltow dyen for my sake."
(*CT* IV. 554-60 and 561-67)

Parallel to Job 42:6:

Men speke of Job, and moost for his humblesse,
As clerkes, whan hem list, konne wel endite,
Namely of men, but as in soothfastness,
Though clerkes preise women but a lite,
Ther kan no man in humblesse hym acquite
As womman kan, ne kan been half so trewe
As wommen been, but it be falle of newe.
(*CT* IV. 932-38)

B. Criticism of Marquis of Saluzzo:

On the need for the marquis to marry:

Wol nat oure lord yet leve his vantee?
Wol he nat wedde? Allas! Allas, the while!
Why wole he thus himself and us begile?
(*CT* IV. 250-52)

On marquis' first temptation of his wife:

…what neded it
Hire for to tempte, and alwey moore and moore,
Though som men preise it for a subtil wit?
But as for me, I seye that yvele it sit
To assaye a wyf whan that it is no nede,
And putten hire in angwyssh and in drede.
(*CT* IV. 457-62)

Faint regret of marquis after first temptation of wife:

> Somwhat this lord hadde routhe in his manere,
> But natheless his purpos heeld he stille,
> As lordes doon, whan they wol han hir wille.
>
> (*CT* IV. 579-81)

On marquis' second temptation of his wife:

> O nedelees was she tempted in assay!
> But wedded men ne knowe no mesure,
> Whan that they fynde a pacient creature.
>
> (*CT* IV. 621-23)

GÁBOR KLANICZAY

The Sign Language of the "Pauperes Christi"

> We, the Poor of Christ, who have no fixed abode and flee from city to city like sheep amidst wolves, are persecuted as were apostles and martyrs, despite the fact that we lead a most strict and holy life, persevering day and night in fasts and abstinence, in prayers, and in labor from which we seek only the necessities of life. We undergo this because we are not of this world. But you, lovers of the world, have peace with it because you are of the world.[1]

This quotation is from an appeal to St. Bernard of Clairvaux by Eberwin, Prior of the Premonstratensian abbey at Steinfeld, in 1143-44, telling him about the presence of "new heretics", and, after quoting their self-description, he is asking him advice, how to confront them.[2]

Eberwin seems to be quite anxious because of the strength of this religious rhetoric, and rightly so: the idea of voluntary poverty for Christ's sake became one of the most popular expression of a new spirituality in the twelfth century, first expressed by hermits and popular religious movements, on the margins of heresy,[3] then taken up and carried to success by Saint

---

[1] Walter Leggett Wakefield and Austin Patterson Evans, ed., *Heresies of the High Middle Ages* (New York, 1991), 129.

[2] For the context see, Arno Borst, *Die Katharer*, Schriften der Monumenta Germaniae Historica 12 (Stuttgart, 1953), 89-97. Now see the recent study by Uwe Brunn, *L'hérésie dans l'archevêché de Cologne (1100-1233)*, Études Augustiniennes, forthcoming in 2007. I thank Piroska Nagy for this reference.

[3] Herbert Grundmann, *Religiöse Bewegungen im Mittelalter* (Berlin, 1935, 2nd ed. Darmstadt, 1970); Tadeusz Manteuffel, *La naissance d'une hérésie. Les adeptes de la pauvreté volontaire au Moyen Âge* (Paris and La Haye, 1970); Gábor Klaniczay, 'Religious movements and Christian Culture,' in *The Uses of Supernatural Power. The Transformation of Popular Religion in Medieval and Early Modern Europe* (Cambridge, 1990), 28-50.

Francis of Assisi, Saint Dominic and their mendicant orders.[4] After decades of research on the religious uses of poverty in the surroundings of Michel Mollat,[5] and after the recent thorough examination of the theme in the volume edited by Gert Melville and Annette Kehnel[6] there seem to be rather few data in this field, which haven't been taken into consideration from the point of view of the history of spirituality. On the other hand, there has been less interest to evaluate, how voluntary poverty in dress and in other signs of distinction interacted and conflicted with the broader set of sign languages in those fields, regulated by custom, prestige and, increasingly, by fashion.

In a first round, let me list a number of cases between the eleventh and the thirteenth centuries, where the signs of the "Pauperes Christi" have been contrasted to the habits of different secular and ecclesiastic circles by hermits, monks, pilgrims, penitents, heretics, and then principally by the mendicant orders. I will situate the interpretation of these different (and concurrent) uses of the signs of voluntary poverty to the context of the historical anthropological enquiries in the 1970s – the times when my interest also turned to this subject.

Then, in a second part I will assess this medieval sign language of poverty by confronting them with some crucial passages from the Bible to which they frequently referred. I would also take in consideration the writings on Cynic philosophers and the work of the Church fathers, which resonated in medieval debates. The Cynic discourse and that of late antique Christianity will be characterized as a symbolic use of bodily and dress signs, as a sign language systematically different from the traditional or the fashion-related one, based on the true consistency of sign, identity and moral content.

In the third part of my study I will analyze how this sign language was interpreted and instrumentalized, how it lead to the subsequent emergence of various initiatives to discipline and regulate material culture in the courts and in the cities such as the establishment of sumptuary regulations, third orders, and the ample discussion of this theme in mendicant preaching.

I will conclude by referring to the resistance this ideological use of the sign language of poverty generated from the spheres upon which it was im-

---

4 Clifford Hugh Lawrence, *The Friars: the Impact of the Early Mendicant Movement on Western Society* (London, 1994).

5 Michel Mollat, ed., *Études sur l'histoire de la pauvreté (Moyen Age-XVIe siècle),* I-II (Paris, 1974).

6 Gert Melville and Annette Kehnel, ed., *In proposito paupertatis. Studien zur Armutverständnis bei den mittelalterlichen Bettelorden* (Münster, Hamburg and London, 2001).

posed as a regulating grid – these critics put in doubt and unmasked its claim for truthfulness and denounced it as hypocrisy, as yet another form of misleading disguise, the mendicant as "faux-semblant".

* * *

If there is one archetypical story to which the ascendancy of the *pauperes Christi* could be associated, it should be the legend of Saint Alexius, which, after remote Syriac and Byzantine origins, and its translation to Latin in the tenth century, became increasingly popular in Latin Christianity in the eleventh and twelfth century. "*Pauper sum et peregrinus*," as he describes himself in his Latin legend,[7] and the fascinating story of the *fuga mundi* by this Roman aristocratic youth became a powerful example for voluntary poverty, as practiced by the increased number of penitent pilgrims in these times. Another way for using poverty in dress for religious self-expression was offered by the eremitical movement of the turn of the millennium.[8]

These two religious categories were molded and given an increased visibility during the advent of the first crusade, with the increasing activity of itinerant preachers, such as Peter the Hermit, who "walked in his bare feet, over his naked body he wore a rough woolen tunic, which he covered with an ankle length cloak and a hood made of frieze."[9] Robert of Arbrissel also started his preaching as a crusade-preacher, in a similar habit: "having discarded his canonical dress, skin covered by a hairshirt and a worn-out cowl full of holes, his legs half-naked, his beard long and his hair trimmed at the brow, barefoot."[10] The signs of marginality became the distinguishing signs of *vita apostolica* among these itinerant preachers, who made this principle also a guiding line in organizing their new eremitic communities. Stephen of Muret, the founder of the community in Grandmont refused to chose other Rule than that of the Gospels (*non est alia Regula nisi evangelium Christi*) and provided his disciples around 1100 with a *propositum paupertatis,*

---

[7] Alexander Gieysztor, '*Pauper sum et peregrinus.* La légende de saint Alexis en Occident: un idéal de pauvreté,' in *Études sur l'histoire de la pauvreté*, ed. Mollat (*op. cit. supra,* n. 5), 125-40.

[8] André Vauchez, ed., *Ermites de France et d'Italie (XIe-XVe siècle)* (Rome, 2003).

[9] Guibert de Nogent, *Gesta Dei per Francos,* Patrologia Latina 156, col. 705.

[10] *Robert of Arbrissel. A Medieval Religious Life.* ed. Bruce L. Venarde (Washington D.C., 2003), 96; cf. Jacques Dalarun, *L'impossible sainteté. La Vie retrouvé de Robert d'Arbrissel (v. 1045-1116) fondateur de Fontevrault* (Paris, 1985).

which has been justly considered as one of the earliest forerunners of the lifestyle brought to triumph by Saint Francis.[11] Already Stephen of Muret referred to the important passages in Matthew: "*Si uis perfectus esse, uade, uende omnia quae habes, et da pauperibus, et habebis thesaurum in caelo; et ueni sequere me*", and "*Qui relinquerit domum, aut fratres, aut sorores, aut patrem, aut matrem, aut uxorem, aut filios, aut agros propter nomen meum, centuplum accipiet, et uitam aeternum possidebit*" (Mat, 19, 21, 29).

The sign language of poverty was apparently gaining popularity in the twelfth century unfolding of the second wave of monastic reform movement and the turmoil of itinerant preachers. These followers of the *vita apostolica* were gradually engaging into a more and more intensive critique of ecclesiastical richness, which provoked an intensifying controversy around the signs of poverty. Robert of Arbrissel was reprimanded by Marbod, Bishop of Rennes:

> ...reason is to be observed and moderation preserved in the mean and humble guise of common sense and with the authority of custom. ... Just as it is a sign of dissipation to desire finery, it is a sign of madness to shun what is ordinary and inexpensive to obtain. The toga should not dazzle but nor should it become filthy. It is far more praiseworthy to be humble in silk than to glory in rags.[12]

The successful popular preacher, Henry of Le Mans was labeled a heretic, and compared by a monk named William to a leper, on account of his "torn and filthy clothes".[13] A generation later, Otto of Freysing wrote sarcastically on Arnold of Brescia: "His clothes proclaim religion, but his doctrines do not serve it in any way".[14]

The controversy on poverty in dress and lifestyle takes a new turn when the spread of Catharist heresy lends a new potential to the confrontation of the richness of the Church with the poverty of the adepts of the heretical

---

[11] Gert Melville, 'In solitudine ac paupertate. Stephans von Muret Evangelium vor Franz von Assisi,' in *In proposito paupertatis*, ed. Melville and Kehnel (*op. cit. supra,* n. 6), 7-30).

[12] *Robert of Arbrissel* (*op. cit. supra,* n. 10), 96.

[13] The text of this debate is edited by Raoul Manselli, 'Il monaco Enrico e la sua eresia,' *Bolletino dell'Istituto storico italiano per il medio evo e Archivio Muratoriano* 65 (1953), 44-63, at 47.

[14] Otto von Freising, *Gesta Friderici imperatoris,* I, 28, Monumenta Germaniae Historica, Scriptores Rerum Germanicarum (Hannover, 1912), 47.

movement, who, as we have seen, labeled themselves simply *pauperes Cristi.* In 1165, in Lombers, south of Albi, at a public debate between some Catholic bishops and abbots and the *boni homines* of the Cathars, the latter called the representatives of the church "ravening wolves, hypocrites, and seducers, lovers of salutations at the marketplace, of the chief seats and the higher places at the table... wearers of albs and gleaming raiments, displaying bejewelled gold rings on their fingers".[15] Such debates, relying upon to the symbolic meaning and the message of the sign language of poverty are reflected in a later anecdote reported by Stephen of Bourbon on the confrontation of papal legate with the spokesmen of the Albigensians where the latter said:

> How can you believe these people who preach to you the word of our poor and humble Lord so arrogantly, from horseback, fitted out with such luxurious things? We, on the other hand, preach the word of Christ while living in poverty, humility and self-restraint. Everything we tell you is supported by our own actions and way of life.[16]

While voluntary poverty was just a tangential element in the complex set of dualistic teachings of the Cathars, it became central in the other large heretical movement of the age, the Waldensians. Around 1170, Valdesius, a rich merchant of Lyons converted to the lifestyle of poverty influenced by the commotion after hearing a recital of the *Chanson de Saint Alexis,* and having had translated several books of the Bible. Following the already mentioned call in Matthew 19:21 ("go sell your possessions and give to the poor...") he took them literally and, distributing his wealth, he started a life of voluntary poverty. His followers set off on their missionary tours in pairs, barefoot, wearing coarse woolen clothes, living on alms, modeling themselves on the Apostles.[17] Like the Cathars, they also referred to their own attire in their polemics: "The masters of the Roman Church are conceited

---

[15] *Acta concilii Lumbariensis,* Recueil des Historiens de Gaule et de la France XIV, 433, English tr. in Wakefield and Evans, *Heresies* (*op. cit. supra,* n. 1), 191.

[16] Albert Lecoy de la Marche, *Anecdotes historiques, légendes et apologues tirés du recueil inédit d'Étienne de Bourbon, dominicain du XIIIe siècle* (Paris, 1877), 127; this part is not yet published in the new edition: *Stephani de Borbone Tractatus de diversis materiis praedicabilibus: prologus, prima pars De dono timoris,* ed. Jacques Berlioz et Jean-Luc Eichenlaub (Turnhout, 2002).

[17] Giovanni Gonnet, *Enchiridion fontium valdensium* (Torre Pellice, 1958), 122-123: "hii certa nusquam habent domicilia, bini et bini circuerunt nudipedes, laneis induti, nihil habentes, omnia sibi communia tanquam apostoli, nudi nudum Christum sequentes."

both in their mode of dress and in their morals", this is what is reported from a Waldensian preacher at the beginning of the thirteenth century.[18]

There should come now an enumeration of how voluntary poverty became one of the most popular outward signs of several other religious movements, such as the *humiliati,*[19] the Beguines,[20] the *pauperes catholici* and the *pauperes reconciliati* (the two groups of reconciled Waldensians lead by Durandus de Huesca and Bernard Prim),[21] and, above all the followers of the most emblematic figure of this current, Saint Francis of Assisi, the *Poverello.* If we can believe the account of Thomas of Celano, for Francis the adoption of poor dress became a public drama, a *mutatio habitum* on the main square of Assisi, stripping naked in front of the crowd for restituting his shamefully rich attire to his father (*nudus nudum Christi sequere*), and being covered by the mantle of the bishop, or, according to more radical views, by putting on the rags of a leper.[22] Voluntary poverty was understood by Francis and his followers as the faithful imitation of the poverty of Christ. This is underlined in the *Regula prima* or *non bullata* of 1221, where the chapter on *de petenda elemosina* said: "And let them not be ashamed, but remember that our Lord Jesus Christ, the Son of the Living and omnipotent God... was not ashamed to be made a poor man and a stranger for us and lived on alms..."[23] The affection and sensibility of Saint Francis for the sign language of poverty was emblematized by a series of strong metaphors and exempla. Speaking of *Domina Pauertas* in his daily communication with his

---

18 Alexander Patschovsky and Kurt Viktor Selge, ed., *Quellen zur Geschichte der Waldenser* (Gütersloh, 1974), 75.

19 Maria Pia Alberzoni, 'Gli inizi degli Umiliati: una riconsiderazione,' in *La conversione alla povertà*, Atti dei convegni dell'Accademia tudertina e del Centro di studi sulla spiritualità medievale, n.s. 2 (Spoleto, 1991), 187-237; *eadem*, 'Die Humiliaten zwischen Legende und Wirklichkeit,' *Mitteilungen des Instituts für Österreichische Geschichtsforschung* 107 (1999), 324-353.

20 Walter Simons, *Cities of Ladies: Beguine Communities in the Medieval Low Countries, 1200-1565* (Philadelphia, 2001).

21 *Vaudois languedociens et pauvres catholiques,* Cahiers de Fanjeaux 2 (Toulouse, 1967).

22 Richard Trexler, *Naked before the Father: the Renunciation of Francis of Assisi* (New York, 1989).

23 *Regula non bullata* 9, in *Fontes franciscani*, ed. Enrico Mebestò and Stefano Brufani, (Assisi, 1995), 183-212; Malcolm Lambert, *Franciscan Poverty. The Doctrine of the Absolute Poverty of Christ and the Apostles in the Franciscan Order. 1210-1323* (St. Bonaventure, NY, 1998), 65.

companions and in his prayers[24] added another note to the voluntary poverty besides the ascetic and Christ centric aspect: that of the emotional dedication to the service to the admired lady in courtly love – a fascinating reversal and enrichment of perspectives; the compassion with the abject and the excluded turned into dedicated and respectful love. His care to impose a precise interpretation of the radical poverty he professed can be seen in the episode of *Legenda Antiqua* where Saint Francis reprimands and shames his companions for the too copious provisions of the Christmas table they prepared for themselves by disguising himself as a beggar and treating them as lords.[25] Among his other formulations of his faithfulness to the most radical state of poverty, which subsequently became an important reference point in the enduring debate around Franciscan poverty,[26] the anecdote on "True and perfect happiness" (*De vera and perfecta laetitia*) stands out.[27] Here we see him in the status of an outcast and beggar, in a ragged and drenched attire seeking refuge in a Franciscan house and being turned down by the guardian filled with self-importance because of the great successes of the new order in the royal courts and the universities of the age. His struggle with himself, whether he should confront this distortion of his original idea or just trust that his example, with the powerful moral message embedded in its sign language will do its effect by its own, will do the work, is a recurrent theme in his legends.[28]

Analyzing the impact of the ways Saint Francis gave a new vigor to the sign language of poverty, special attention should be paid to the influence of voluntary poverty upon female spirituality among religious women. The

---

[24] "Ave, regina sapientia, Dominus te salvet cum tua sorore sancta pura simplicitate. Domina sancta paupertas, Dominus te salvet cum tua sorore sancta humilitate..." *Salutatio virtutum*, 1-2, in *Fontes franciscani*, 223.

[25] *Legenda Antiqua,* c. 32; Rosalind B. Brooke, ed. and trans., *Scripta Leonis Rufini et Angeli sociorum S. Francisci: The Writings of Leo, Rufino, and Angelo Companions of St. Francis* (Oxford, 1970), 144-147. An insightful analysis how this story had been tamed and transformed by Thomas of Celano in his *Vita secunda Sancti Francisci* (2.31.61) and then by the *Legenda maior* written by Saint Bonaventure (7.9) is provided by Aviad Kleinberg, *Prophets in Their Own Country. Living Saints and the Making of Sainthood in the Later Middle Ages* (Chicago and London, 1992), 126-133.

[26] Kajetan Esser, 'Mysterium paupertatis. Die Armutsauffassung des hl. Franziskus von Assisi,' *Wissenschaft und Weisheit* 1951, 177-189; Lambert, *Franciscan Poverty* (*op. cit. supra,* n. 23), passim.

[27] Engelbert Grau, *Die Opuscula des hl. Franziskus von Assisi* (Grottaferrata, 1989).

[28] *Legenda Antiqua,* c. 75-76.

inclusion of Saint Clare and other female followers in 1212 to the community around Saint Francis, and their foundation of the order of the "poor sisters" in San Damiano,[29] was the first step in this direction. The attempt to convert a broader urban society in Italy to these same religious principles, the organization of penitent confraternities infusing with the principles of voluntary poverty the life of pious married couples,[30] the care of female religious recluses taking up the way of life of the *pinzochere*,[31] the tentative to develop the Franciscan "third order,"[32] indicate the further course of the spread of these ideas.

Beyond the Alps, Saint Elizabeth of Hungary, daughter of King Andrew II of Hungary and wife of Ludwig IV, Landgrave of Thuringia[33] was the key figure of the spread of the Franciscan ideas on poverty in another social and cultural context, in that of royal and princely courts. Under the influence of the preaching of the first Franciscans who arrived to Eisenach around 1221, and, subsequently, under the stern guidance of her spiritual director, Konrad of Marburg, she introduced the affection for voluntary poverty as a criticism of conspicuous courtly consumption of the Ludowing court and a confrontation with the ascendant principles of luxury, prestige and fashion. At the princely banquets, one of the main public events at court, the most Elizabeth was willing to do was to simulate partaking of the dishes served, for, as she said, there was no way of knowing whether the food was not from lands "unrightfully come by" and she was satisfied with only "coarse, hard, black bread" to eat, and water to drink.[34] The best visible refusal of royal luxury

---

[29] Maria Pia Alberzoni, *Clare of Assisi and the Poor Sisters in the Thirteenth Century* (St. Bonaventure NY, 2004).

[30] Gilles Gérard Meersseman, *Ordo fraternitatis. Confraternite e pietà dei laici nel medioevo,* in collaboration with Gian Piero Pacini, Italia Sacra 24-26 (Rome, 1977).

[31] Anna Benvenuti Papi, "*In castro poenitentiae": santità e società femminile nell'Italia medievale* (Rome, 1990).

[32] Gabriele Andreotti, 'Elisabetta e Lodovico. I santi patroni del Terzo Ordine di San Francesco,' *Analecta Tertii Ordinis regularis sancti Francisci* 26 (1995), 307-379.

[33] André Vauchez, 'Charité et pauvreté chez sainte Elisabeth de Thuringe,' in *Études sur l'histoire de la pauvreté*, ed. Mollat (*op. cit. supra,* n. 5), 163-175; *Sankt Elisabeth. Fürstin Dienerin Heilige* (Sigmaringen, 1981); Gábor Klaniczay, *Holy Rulers and Blessed Princesses. Dynastic Cults in Medieval Central Europe* (Cambridge 2002), 195-279.

[34] "grossum nigrum panem et durum," Albert Huyskens, ed., *Der sogenannte Libellus de dictis quatuor ancillarum s. Elisabeth confectus* (Munich and Kempten, 1911), 18-20; cf. Raoul Manselli, 'Santità principesca e vita quotidiana in Elisabetta d'Ungheria: La testimonianza delle ancelle,' *Analecta Tertii ordinis regularis sancti Francisci* 18 (1985), 23-45.

was that related to dress. "Setting aside her ornate attire, and putting on woollen and goat's hair garments instead of her dresses of purple and gold, she startled her ladies-in-waiting at the palace "by wrapping her body in a shabby cloak and her head in a tattered rag, and saying: 'This is the way I shall go about when I'll beg and suffer distress for God's sake'".[35] After the birth of her children, she went to her churching (*purificatio*) not, "like other women usually do... surrounded by a great company, and dressed in fine clothes", but "simply, in a woollen dress and barefoot."[36]

Elizabeth's model made a great impact among her relatives in other Central European courts, who started to emulate of her lifestyle. The first to follow her example was her cousin, Agnes of Bohemia (1205-1282), daughter of King Přemysl Ottocar I, who, "inebriated" by St. Elizabeth's example, founded a hospital and a convent for the Poor Clares in 1234 in Prague.[37] Agnes pledged her life to her "Heavenly Bridegroom" in a ceremony very similar to the one in which St. Clare had joined the community led by St. Francis some twenty years earlier. Like Clare, who had gone to take her vows on Palm Sunday looking her loveliest,[38] so Agnes appeared in church dressed--for the last time--in her most sumptuous attire. So much the greater was the contrast when she shed all this finery, and donned her coarse habit.[39] Her renunciation was much admired, even by Clare of Assisi herself, who

---

[35] "ornatu vestium depositisque, capitisque velamine mutato, vidualiter se gessit et religiose, laneis vel cilicio frequenter ad carnem induta, tunc etiam cum desuperaureatis vestibus aut purpura tegebantur...Et vestiens se in palatio coram eis vili pallio et vili panno caput suum operiens dixit: Sic incedam quando mendicabo et miseriam pro deo sustinebo..." Huyskens, *Der sogenannte Libellus* (*op. cit. supra,* n. 34), 22-23, 31.

[36] "Item in purificatione post partum singulorum puerorum suorum conpletis diebus consuetis, cum alie matrone in gloria multi comitatus et vestibus pretiosis ad ecclesiam venire consueverunt, ipsa in laneis et nudis pedibus familiariter ibat ad ecclesiam remotam." *Ibid.* 24-25.

[37] Maria Fassbinder, *Die selige Agnes von Prag. Eine königliche Klarissin* (Werl/Westf., 1957); Jaroslav Polc, *Agnes von Böhmen 1211-1282.* Lebensbilder zur Geschichte der böhmischen Länder, 6 (Munich, 1989); Franz Machilek, 'Die Přemysliden, Piasten und Arpaden und der Klarissenorden im 13. und frühen 14. Jahrhundert,' in *Westmitteleuropa, Ostmitteleuropa, Vergleiche und Beziehungen. Festschrift für Ferdinand Seibt zum 65. Geburtstag* (Munich, 1992), 293-306; Christian-Frederik Felskau, '*Vita religiosa* und *paupertas* der Přemyslidin Agnes von Prag. Zu Bezügen und Besonderheiten in Leben und Legende einer späten Heiligen,' *Collectanea Franciscana* 70 (2000), 413-484.

[38] Engelbert Grau, ed., *Leben und Schriften der heiligen Klara* (Werl/Westf., 1960), 40-41.

[39] Jan Kapistrán Vyskočil, ed., *Legenda blahoslavené Anežky a čtyri listy Sv. Kláry* (Prague, 1934), 107; cf. Fassbinder, *Die selige Agnes* (*op. cit. supra,* n. 37), 59-60.

wrote her four famous epistles, praising her vocation: "Though You, more than others, could have enjoyed the magnificence and honor and dignity of the world, and could have been married to the illustrious Caesar with splendor befitting You and His excellency, You have rejected all these things and have chosen with Your whole heart and soul a life of holy poverty and destitution." [40]

The row of saintly princesses rejecting courtly luxury and opting ostentatiously for holy poverty, in the footsteps of St. Elizabeth, multiplied spectacularly in thirteenth-century Central Europe: Elizabeth's maternal aunt, St. Hedwig of Silesia (1174/78-1243), canonized in 1265, as the second example after Elizabeth of female sainthood of a married laywomen, of highest rank, dedicated to the mendicant ideas of charity and self-abasement.[41] Hedwig's daughter-in-law, the sister of Agnes of Bohemia, Anne (1203-1265) finished her life as a Clariss nun.[42] St. Margaret of Hungary (1242-1270), daughter of Béla IV lived her life as a Dominican nun,[43] her sister-in-law, Salomea of Cracow (1211-1268), and the sister of Margaret, Saint Cunegond (Kynga) (1224-1292) entered the Clariss order after having become widows.[44]

The predilection of these princesses in refusing the signs of prestige and choosing poverty instead is well exemplified by the descriptions of Margaret's habits by her legend and by the testimonies her fellow nuns in her canonization process in 1272-1276:

---

[40] *Francis and Clare. The Complete Works.* tr. and intr. Regis J. Armstrong and Ignatius C. Brady (New York, Ramsey and Toronto, 1982), 190-191; cf. Grau, *Leben* (*op. cit. supra,* n. 38), 22-24.

[41] Joseph Gottschalk, *St. Hedwig Herzogin von Schlesien* (Cologne and Graz, 1964); Eckhard Grunewald and Nikolaus Gussone, ed., *Das Bild der Heiligen Hedwig in Mittelalter und Neuzeit* (Munich, 1996).

[42] Augustin Knoblich, *Herzogin Anna von Schlesien* (Breslau, 1865).

[43] Gábor Klaniczay, 'I modelli di santità femminile tra i secoli XIII e XV in Europa centrale e in Italia,' *Spiritualità e lettere nella cultura italiana e ungherese del basso medioevo,* ed. Sante Graciotti and Cesare Vasoli (Florence, 1995), 75-109; *idem, Holy Rulers and Blessed Princesses* (*op. cit. supra,* n. 33), 254-294.

[44] Halina Manikowska, 'Zwischen Askesis und Modestia. Buß- und Armutsideale in polnischen, böhmischen und ungarischen Hofkreisen im 13. Jahrhundert,' *Acta Poloniae Historica* 47 (1983), 33-53; Jerzy Wyrozumski, 'La sainteté des femmes dans le mariage en Pologne médiévale,' in *La femme au moyen âge,* ed. Georges Duby, Jean Heuclin and Michel Rouche (Maubeuge, 1990), 249-257.

> If her habit happened to be cut from cloth noticeably more expensive than those of the other sisters of her age, she would blush to wear them. Whenever she was forced to do so out of respect for her parents, she would hasten to blacken them with soot by washing up cooking pots and other dishes in the kitchen. She would scarcely ever take off a garment she had put on when it was new until it fell apart with age.[45]

Other accounts emphasize how Margaret would give her fellow nuns the "good clothes" and "delicate veils" that she received from her parents, and was content to wear "the shabbier and coarser ones" herself; "She refused to wear new clothes, and would only wear torn and patched ones".[46]

Further examples could follow, but my argument is already sufficiently illustrated. The sign language of the *pauperes Christi* which was adopted originally with purposes of penance by pilgrims, ascetic hermits, then, subsequently, becoming popular among itinerant preachers and representatives of a new type apostolic religious reform movements in the turmoil of the crusades, ended up as a complex symbolic system criticizing both the richness of the church and the ostentatious luxury of urban and courtly secular culture. This symbolic weapon was first used by the radical, heretic representatives of the religious reform movements, then carried to success and general acceptance by the mendicant orders and disseminated effectively precisely in those fields where its critical overtones could serve for infusing urban and courtly culture with a new religious spirituality.

* * *

Let me make a brief historiographic and autobiographic *excursus* at this point, recalling briefly, how this subject became interesting for me in the 1970s. Studying in Budapest between 1969 and 1974, my first encounter

---

45 "vestes habitus sui si de panno notabiliter precioso supra alias coevas suas fuissent erubescat portare et si quando cogebatur ob reverentiam parentum scaloribus coquine ablutionibus ollarum et ceterorum vasorum pulveribusque scopatorum denigrare festinabat et vestem quam induebat novam vix unquam mutabat donec vetustate esset laniata." '*Vita beate Margarite de Ungaria Ordinis Predicatorum*,' in Kornél Bőle, *Árpádházi Boldog Margit szenttéavatási ügye és a legősibb latin Margit-legenda* (Budapest, 1937), 18.

46 "et quando dabatur sibi velum subtile, dabat illud aliis sororibus, et grossum recipiebat, et portabat";"portabat malas vestes et petiatas, novas nolebat portare sine petiis." Vilmos Fraknói, ed., *Inquisitio super vita, conversatione et miraculis beatae Margarethae virginis*, in *Monumenta Romana episcopatus Vesprimiensis* (Budapest, 1896), t. I, 168, 227.

with this theme which became the subject of my M.A. and Ph.D. theses was in the sign of the struggle against what I perceived to be a simplistic Marxist interpretation of medieval heresy. The studies by Ernst Werner, while philologically accurate, saw the expression of early forms of "class struggle" and characterized the urban lower classes, especially weavers as the chief spokesmen of these heretic criticisms against the church under the emblem of the "*pauperes Christi.*"[47] I was more convinced, though, by the arguments advanced by Herbert Grundmann who interpreted the affinity of heretics to *textores* the other way round, pointing to the fact that they were called weavers *ab usu texendi,* adopting weaving rather as a part of spiritually motivated manual labour, like later the Beguines and the *humiliati.*[48]

While I did not refuse fully the social and contextual interpretation of these movements, represented, among others by the contributions of the important conference in Royaumont, organized by Jacques Le Goff,[49] I was looking rather for a more complex religious reaction to the emerging social problem of poverty and the ensuing symbolic reflection in late medieval Christianity. I could find ample support for these enquiries during a research scholarship in Paris in 1976 where I could frequent the seminars of Michel Mollat on poverty,[50] get acquainted with the related researches of Bronisław Geremek,[51] and also participate in the seminars on medieval "techniques of

---

[47] "Dabei sind die Träger dieser Lehren die unteren Schichten, Tagelöhner und vor allem die in den Quellen immer wieder auftauchenden Weber." Ernst Werner, *Pauperes Christi. Studien zu sozial-religiösen Bewegungen im Zeitalter des Reformpapsttums* (Leipzig, 1956), 188.

[48] Grundmann, *Religiöse Bewegungen* (*op. cit. supra*, n. 3); Gábor Klaniczay, 'Az eretnekség és a szövőipar kapcsolata a XII-XIII. századi eretnekmozgalmaknál,' (The relation of heresy and weaving in 12th- and 13th-century heretic movements), in *Dolgozatok a feudáliskori művelődés történetéből*, ed. Gábor Klaniczay, Gábor Pajkossy, and Éva Ring (Budapest, 1974, 9-46); for a recent critical discussion of Grundmann's theses, themselves not devoid of ideological overtones either, see Martina Wehrli-Johns, 'Voraussetzungen und Perspektiven mittelalterlicher Laienfrömmigkeit seit Innozenz III. Eine Auseinandersetzung mit Herbert Grundmanns "Religiösen Bewegungen"', *Mitteilungen des Instituts für Österreichische Geschichtsforschung* 104 (1996), 286-309.

[49] Jacques Le Goff, ed., *Hérésies et sociétés dans l'Europe pré-indurstrielle, XIe-XVIIIe siècle. Communications et débats du colloque de Royaumont* (Paris, 1968).

[50] Mollat, *Études sur l'histoire de la pauvreté* (*op. cit. supra*, n. 5); *idem, The Poor in the Middle Ages: an Essay in Social History* (New Haven and London, 1986).

[51] Bronisław Geremek, *Les marginaux parisiens aux XIVe et XVe siècles* (Paris, 1976); *idem, La potence ou la pitié. L'Europe et les pauvres du Moyen Age à nos jours* (Paris, 1987).

the body" and gestures directed by Jacques Le Goff and Jean-Claude Schmitt.[52]

My personal insights to the use of bodily symbols and express cultural criticism by the sign language of clothes were also influenced by the student movements and the youth counter-culture of those times, and I saw many similar features in the voluntary poverty of the medieval heretics and the signs of youth rebellion against the culture of their "affluent society", their long hair, blue jeans and shabby look.[53] This analogy was, among others, also recognized by some leading anthropological theorists of the age, such as Victor Turner in his memorable *The Ritual Process. Structure and Anti-Structure,* who likened the *communitas* represented by Saint Francis and his companion to the hippies of the age, and described the religious symbols of poverty as belonging to the broader system of *liminality,* a higher order of values regularly juxtaposed to those of *structure* in human societies by rites of passage and various religious actors.[54]

On the basis of these premises I tried to elaborate a historical interpretation of opposition of *liminal* and *structural* value-systems in medieval religious debates on beards, long hair, poverty and luxury in dress in a study entitled "Fashionable Beards and Heretic Rags", first published in 1978.[55] In my present study I am relying on the documentation assembled there and making a reassessment of those arguments in the light of more recent enquiries.

* * *

The opposition of luxury in attire and the bodily signs of poverty goes back to the Bible, to the invectives of Prophet Isaiah to the daughters of Zion:

> You have ravaged the vineyard, and the spoils of the poor are in you houses. Is it nothing to you that you crush my people and grind the faces of the poor? ... Then the Lord said: Because the women of Zion hold themselves high and walk with necks outstretched and wanton glances, moving with mincing gait and jingling feet, the Lord will give the women

[52] Jean-Claude Schmitt, *La raison des gestes dans l'Occident médiéval* (Paris, 1990).

[53] Charles A. Reich: *The Greening of America* (Harmondsworth, 1971), 198-202.

[54] Victor Turner, *The Ritual Process. Structure and Anti-Structure.* 2nd ed. (Ithaca and London, 1977).

[55] For the English version see Klaniczay, *The Uses of Supernatural Power* (*op. cit. supra*, n. 3), 51-78.

> of Zion bald heads, the Lord will strip their foreheads. In that day the Lord will take away all finery: anklets, necklaces, lockets, charms, signets, nose-rings, fine dresses, mantles, cloaks, flounced skirts, scarves of gauze, kerchiefs of linen, turbans, and flowing veils. So instead of perfume you shall have the stench of decay, and rope in place of a girdle, baldness instead of hair elegantly coiled, a loin-cloth of sacking instead of a mantle, and branding instead of beauty (Isaiah, 3, 14-24).

The dress of poverty, the sackcloth is evoked here as the dress penitence, but in other passages it quickly assumes the symbolic content of "anti-structure" in the sense of Victor Turner, and this humble attire became the preferred dress of the Prophets and the proselytizing Apostles. Isaiah himself "walked naked and barefoot for three years" (Isaiah, 20, 3), John the Baptist's clothing was "a rough coat of camel's hair with a leather belt round his waist" (Matthew, 3-4).

Judaism and early Christianity were not the only civilizations to give this interpretation to poverty in dress; remarkably similar principles can be discovered in the fourth century BC among the Cynic philosophers in Greece. These followers of Socrates (Antisthenes, Diogenes of Sinope, Krates of Thebe, etc,) got their name from the dog (kynos), and tried to put in practice the principle of *autarkia* (self-sufficience) they had learnt from their master, renouncing of superfluous riches.[56] Diogenes 'the dog' wrote allegedly: "I walk in double coat, with a beggar's sack on my shoulder, a walking stick in my hand..."[57] The Cynics were not only trying to scandalize their surroundings by adopting "this nomadic antisocial and bestial life," but they apparently added an articulate reasoning which opposed their own sign system with the values cherished by the society they intended to criticize. We learn from their writings, and especially from a long dialogue on them attributed to Lucian, that their outlook means more to them than a mere renunciation or refusal of affluence. It also serves their conscious self-expression, and the propagation through outward bodily signs of an elaborate philosophy:

> ...never may I reach out for more than my share, but be able to put up with less than my share. Such, you see, are our wishes, wishes assuredly far different from those of most men. Nor is it any wonder that we differ

---

[56] Georg Luck, *Die Weisheit der Hunde, Texte der antiken Kyniker* (Stuttgart, 1997).

[57] Rudolf Hercher, *Epistolographi Graeci,* Scriptorum Graecorum Bibliotheca 16 (Paris, 1873), 235. Though the letter is probably a forgery from the second or third century AD, from the revival of the Cynic movement, it certainly illustrates the movement's spirit.

> from them in dress when we differ so much from them in principles too... If good men need one particular dress of their own, what would be more suitable than this dress which seems quite shameless to the debauched men and which they would most deprecate for themselves?[58]

The principles one can recognize in the dress-style of the Cynics have two distinct features. The first is the ambition of consistency between internal philosophy of life and the external sign system of the outward appearance, in the line of the classical canon of *kalokagathia.* The second is more complex: for distinguishing themselves from the "debauched" and "effeminate" society, the Cynics adopt a sign language which is "deprecated" by this majority – this symbolic affiliation to a rejected, marginal minority out of moral and cultural protest will have a great future. Similar association of modern intellectuals to outcasts and subcultures have been described with the social-psychological interpretation of *stigma,* i.e. the proud and contentious putting on show of the bodily symbols which epitomize in the eyes of the majority the exclusion of the wearers.[59]

A similar attitude can be discovered in the early Christian use of the symbols of poverty in dress. This likeness was sometimes disturbing for the Christians who got sometimes mistaken for belonging to the "philosophers" wearing beard and the long coat called *pallium,* especially in the times when the Cynic movement got resurrected in the second and third century AD. At the end of the second century Tertullian takes care to mark out the difference for the men of Carthage: "A better philosophy has now been designed to honour thee, ever since thou hast begun to be a Christian vesture!"[60] The Christians developed the use of the sign language of poor dresses according to their own objectives: instead of propagating their ideas by provoking and scandalizing the majority like the Cynics they aimed rather to achieve some pedagogical and missionary goals, they wanted to incite commotion and conversion. Saint John Chrysostom (347-407), Archbishop of Constantin-

---

[58] 'Lucian, *The Cynic,*' in *Lucian with an English Translation,* ed. Austin Morris Harmon, Loeb Classical Library (Cambridge MA and London 1913), 1, 409; on the Cynic movement see Robert Bracht Branham and Marie-Odile Goulet-Caze, ed., *The Cynics: The Cynic Movement in Antiquity and Its Legacy* (Berkeley, 1997).

[59] Erving Goffman, *Stigma: Notes on the Management of Spoiled Identity* (Englewood Cliffs, 1963); for the use of similar categories in the analysis of contemporary subcultures, see Dick Hebdige, *Subculture, the Meaning of Style* (London, 1979).

[60] Tertullianus, *De pallio,* VI, 4, ed. Vinzenz Bulhart, CSEL 76 (Vienna, 1957); I cite the English translation of Alexander Roberts and James Donaldson, ed., *The Ante-Nicene fathers* (Buffalo, 1885), 12.

ople described the attire of Christian monastic communities with the following words:

> Those who desire public esteem, wealth and luxury, ought to be taken to the communities of these holy men – there would be no need for my words after that... They see the sons of rich and distinguished people in clothes that even the poorest among them would scorn. And they also see that these people are happy in these humble clothes. Think of the solace this gives to the poor and needy. While the rich, if they visit such places, may well feel ashamed and return home in a more modest, reformed frame of mind.[61]

The sign language of poor attire, however, could not be fully expropriated by the emergent Christian church, it was also used by various religious movements deemed heretic in late Antiquity, such as the Gnostics and the Messalians, and this increased the awareness of the fact that signs and symbols may also be used in an abusive, fraudulent manner, the external appearance can also mislead. St. Jerome cautioned one of his adepts, saying:

> Avoid men, when you see them loaded with chains and wearing their hair long like women, contrary to the apostle's precept, not to speak of beards like those of goats, black coats, and bare feet craving the cold. All these things are tokens of the devil.

The truthfulness of the symbolic message of outward appearance did also raise some suspicions among the critics of the Cynics. Lucian condemned as trickery their appearance and claimed that they had gold in their haversacks instead of black bread.[62] In the fifth century, Salvianus, a presbyter of Marseilles warned the representatives of the ascetic lifestyle: "Do not think that you can practise the lie of monastic life by wearing a habit, the lie of loyalty with a chain belt, or the lie of sanctity with your cloak (*pallium*)..."[63]

* * *

---

[61] Johannes Chrysostomus, *In Evangelium Matthaei homilia,* 69, Patrologia Graeca 58, col. 645. The quotation is translated from the Latin.

[62] Lucian, *The dead come to life or the Fisherman,* in Harmon, *Lucian* (*op. cit. supra*, n. 58), 3, 121.

[63] Salvianus, *Adversus Avaritiam Timothei ad Ecclesiam,* IV, 5, 24, ed. Franz Pauly, CSEL 8 (Vienna, 1883), 380; cf. Philip Oppenheim, *Das Mönchskleid im christlichen Altertum* (Freiburg im Breisgau, 1931).

The voluntary poverty only makes sense in those societies where conspicuous luxury is a visible and debated problem. With the early Middle Ages, this problem came off the agenda for several centuries in Latin Christianity. We encounter it again only around the turn of the first Millennium, with the new emergence of courtly society, with its prestige hierarchies, ceremonies and fashions. For its illustration, let me quote a passage from the life of Bruno, Bishop of Cologne, brother of Emperor Otto I:

> He frequently declined to wear the kinds of soft and fine clothing in which he had grown up and come to manhood, even when he visited the courts of the kings. Amidst purple garbed courtiers and knights radiant in gold, he wore simple robes and rustic sheepskins."[64]

The appearance of courtly fashions and the scandals it caused among those courtly clerics who sided with the ascetic claims of the emerging monastic reform movements can be documented from the beginning of the eleventh century. The new male fashions of shaving of the beard and wearing short tunics at the court of Queen Constance, third wife of Robert the Pious, King of France, outraged William of Volpiano, a leading spokesman of ascetic reform movements, whose invectives are reproted by Roul Glaber.[65] As fashions tend to develop, after this new kind of male attire, despite the criticism and the scandals it provoked, conquered the courts of France, Germany and England, towards the last decades of the eleventh century it precise opposite developed into a new fashion for courtly youth, and provoked a renewed and hefty reaction. As we learn from the chronicles by Eadmer[66] and Orderic Vital,[67] now the courtiers adopted long and puffy clothes, a long beard, a

[64] "Molles et delicatas vestes, in quibus nutritus et ad hominem usque perductus est, etiam in domibus regum multoties declinavit; inter purpuratos ministros et milites suos auroque nitidos vilem ipse tunicam et rusticana ovium pelles induxit," *Vita Sancti Brunonis arciepiscopi Coloniensis auctore Ruotgero,* in *Lebensbeschreibung einiger Bischöfe des 10./12. Jahrhunderts,* ed. Hatto Kallfelz (Darmstadt, 1973), 222; C. Stephen Jaeger, *The Origins of Courtliness. Civilizing Trends and the Formation of Courtly Ideals 939-1210* (Philadelphia, 1985), 154-155.

[65] Rodulphus Glaber, *Historiarum libri quinque*, ed. et trans.John France (Oxford, 1989), 164-167; Henri Platelle, 'Le problème du scandale,' *Revue belge de philologie et d'histoire* 53 (1975), 1071-1096; Patrick Geary, *Phantoms of Remembrance. Memory and Oblivion at the End of the First Millennium* (Princeton, 1997), 3-9.

[66] *Eadmer's History of Recent Events in England (Historia novorum in Anglia),* tr. Geoffrey Bosanquet (London, 1964), 47-49.

[67] *The Ecclesiastical History of Ordericus Vitalis,* ed. and tr. Marjorie Chibnall, vol. IV (Oxford, 1973), 65-67, 187-189.

shaved forehead and a long curly hair at the back. The courtly fashions provoked hefty debates, some bishops such as Ratbode of Tournai or Saint Anselm of Canterbury resorted to an even more vigorous action, cutting with scissors, with their own hand, the "superfluous" clothes and hair locks of the fashionable courtly youth to a "manly fashion."[68]

The sign language of poverty adopted by the already described apostolic itinerant preachers of the age is to be assessed as an antipode to this context of new royal and aristocratic courts throughout Europe, with their emerging fashions and conspicuous luxury. The most direct reference of the former to the latter was made by the foundation of the military order or the Templars, whose chief spokesman, Saint Bernard of Clairvaux contrasted in 1136 the two kinds of knights:

> "... a brave fighter needs three basic qualities. Circumspection, agility and quickness in dueling and moving, and bravery to wound and kill te enemy. Why then do you let your hair grow like women; the locks hanging into your eyes hinder your capacity to see. Your arms weighed down with puffy sleeves, you have difficulty in reaching out from them with your hands...

The ascetic fighter is exactly the opposite:

> his hair is cut very short..., he never combs his hair and seldom washes; he goes around with a stubble and covered in dust, his body is chastised with an iron shirt and worn out by the heat...[69]

In fact, not only the male fashions of the courtiers had to be disciplined, but even more the female attitude to fashion, which was considered to be one of the principal sources of evil by the moral preaching of the age. We have already seen that this became precisely one of the aims of the mendicant orders in the thirteenth century. The fashions and the luxury in urban society was disciplined by the introduction of sumptuary laws. A very early representative of this innovation was introduced in Toulouse shortly after the

---

[68] Platelle, 'Le problème du scandale' (*op. cit. supra*, n. 65); I discuss these fashion-scandals in a greater detail in my 'Fashionable Beards and Heretic Rags,' (*op. cit. supra*, n. 55), 60-65.

[69] "nunquam compti, raro loti, magis autem neglecto crine hispidi, pulvere foedi, lorica et caumate fusci..." *Liber ad milites Templi de laude novae militiae,* ed. Jean Leclercq and Henri Rochais, Sancti Bernardi opera 3 (1963), 217 and 220.

triumph of the Albigensian crusade.[70] These measures soon provoked a sharp counter-reaction by a Toulouse poet: "If one leads a pure life, no man becomes enemy of God by putting on beautiful clothes. Just as they [the friars] will not go to heaven, merely because they wear a white cowl and a black habit."[71] A similar effect was created by the great *Alleluia* in Italian cities in 1233, a vast popular movement for peace and religious reform under the leadership of Dominican and Franciscan preachers, and the flagellant upheaval in 1260. The leaders of these movements introduced in the urban statutes, among others, sumptuary decrees prohibiting the wearing of luxurious dresses, jewellery, or materials woven with gold thread.[72] The same impact, as we have seen could be achieved in royal and aristocratic courts, by the cooperation of saintly princesses and their mendicant confessors.

We cannot follow here the growth of sumptuary legislation in late medieval Europe,[73] and the leading role the mendicant orders have played in this

---

[70] René Nelli, *La vie quotidienne des cathares en Languedoc au XIIIe siècle* (Paris, 1969), 79-81, 183.

[71] '*Sirventès del tot vey remaner valor*,' in Jules Coulet, *Le troubadour Guilhem Montanhagol* (Toulouse, 1898), 87-89.

[72] Salimbene de Adam, *Cronica,* ed. Giuseppe Scalia (Bari, 1966), 99-101. He describes a sumptuary law in Lombardy, in the time of Pope Nicholas III, to the initiative of the Dominican Fratre Latino: p. 246.

[73] Liselotte Constanze Eisenbart, *Kleiderordnungen der deutschen Städte zwischen 1350 und 1700. Ein Beitrag zur Kulturgeschichte des deutschen Bürgertums* (Göttingen, Berlin and Frankfurt, 1962; Neithard Bulst, Zum Problem städtischer und territorialer Kleider-, Aufwands- und Luxusgesetzgebung in Deutschland (13.- Mitte 16. Jahrhundert),' in *Renaissance du pouvoir législatif et genèse de l'Etat,* ed. André Gouron and Albert Rigaudière (Montpellier, 1992), 29-57; *idem*, 'Les ordonnances somptuaires en Allemagne: expression de l'ordre social urbain (XIV-XVI. s.),' in *Académie des Inscriptions & Belles Lettres, comptes rendus…* 1993, 771-783; *idem,* 'Kleidung als sozialer Konfliktstoff. Probleme kleidergesetzlicher Normierung im sozialen Gefüge,' *Saeculum* 44 (1993), 32-47; Diane Owen Hughes, 'Le mode femminili e il loro controllo,' in Georges Duby – Michelle Perrot, *Storia delle donne in Occidente. Il Medioevo* (Rome, 1990), 166-193; *eadem*, "Sumptuary Law and Social Relations in Renaissance Italy," in John Bossy, *Disputes and Settlements: Law and Human Relations in the West* (Cambridge, 1983, 69-99); Maria Giuseppina Muzzarelli, 'La disciplina delle apparenze. Vesti e ornamenti nella legislazione suntuaria bolognese fra XIII e XV secolo,' in *Disciplina dell'anima, disciplina del corpo e disciplina della società tra Medioevo ed Età moderna,* Atti del convegno tenutosi a Bologna il 7-9 ottobre 1993, *Annali dell'Istituto storico italo-germanico* 40 (1994), 757-784; *eadem*, *Gli inganni delle apparenze: disciplina di vesti e ornamenti alla fine del medioevo* (Torino, 1996); *eadem*, ed., *La legislazione suntuaria. Secoli XIII-XVI. Emilia-Romagna* (Rome, 2002).

way of regulating the system of dresses till the end of the Middle Ages, until the "bonfires of vanities" lit by Bernardino of Siena, John Capistran, Savonarola, and other leaders of Franciscan and Dominican observance.[74] This perspective, however, makes us aware that the sign language of poverty, emerging as a symbol of compassion and protest, and growing into a complex symbolic language expressing an entire religious worldview based on voluntary poverty, could become, in a third phase, when imposed to urban and courtly society by moral preaching and sumptuary legislation, a coercive tool to discipline society and wipe out alternative sign languages of traditional clothing system or newly emerging fashions.

[74] Thomas M. Izbicki, 'Pyres of Vanities: Mendicant Preaching on Vanity of Women and Its Lay Audience,' in *De Ore Domini: Preacher and Word in the Middle Ages*, ed. Thomas L. Amos, Eugene A. Green and Beverly Mayne Kienzle (Kalamazoo, 1989), 211-235; Gábor Klaniczay, 'The "Bonfires of the Vanities" and the Mendicants,' in *Material Culture and Emotions in the Middle Ages*, ed. Gerhard Jaritz (Vienna, 2003), 31-60.

MELITTA WEISS ADAMSON

Poverty on the Menu: Towards a Culinary Vocabulary of Poverty in Medieval Europe

Clothing and food together with housing were the most prominent social markers in the Middle Ages. The *Nibelungenlied* with its endless stream of dressmaking strophes, and descriptions of banquets is just one example of many illustrating the medieval preoccupation with appearance and dining. To what extent the food eaten by the parent generation was thought to determine the social status of the children becomes evident in the *RígsÞula* of the *Poetic Edda*, a saga, presumably going back to the tenth century, and originating in a mixed Norse-Irish milieu.[1] It discusses the three classes of peasants, craftsmen, and nobles by paying special attention to their physical attributes, housing, dress, and food. A peasant woman living on "a gross loaf, weighty and thick, wedged with grains[2] ... Broth was in the bowl," even though she may be impregnated by a god, Rígr, only gives birth to hard laborers.[3] Her son Thrall, wrapped in rough linen, is black-skinned, and has heavy eyes. He grows into a man whose hands have wrinkled skin, gnarled knuckles, scabbed nails, and thick fingers. He has an unlovely face bent back, and long heels. The male progeny he and Thrallwoman beget are given

---

[1] For the text see Ursula Dronke, ed. and tr., *The Poetic Edda*, vol. II, *Mythological Poems* (Oxford, 1997), 162-173. As for the dating, see Russell Poole: "Although a few scholars (e.g., Klaus von See, of Frankfurt) date it to the twelfth century and link it to general discussion of estates in high medieval Europe, the more likely assessment is that it belongs to the tenth century, originates in a mixed Norse-Irish milieu, and legitimates the pattern of governance (distribution between kings and earls) that obtained in late-Iron-Age-through-medieval Norway." (Personal communication, 25 August 2005). See also Frederic Amory, 'The Historical Worth of *Rígsþula*', *Alvíssmál* 10 (2001), 3-20.

[2] Also translated as "and swollen with husk," see Henry Adams Bellows, tr., *The Poetic Edda* (New York, 1969), 204.

[3] Dronke, *The Poetic Edda* (*op. cit. supra*, n. 1), 163.

such significant names as Bawler (*Hreimr*), Byreboy (*Fiósner*), Clump (*Klúrr*), Clegg (*Kleggi*), Bedmate (*Kefser*), Stinker (*Fúlner*), Stump (*Drumbr*), Stout (*Digraldi*), Sluggish (*Dröttr*), Grizzled (*Hösver*), Stooper (*Lútr*), and Longleg (*Leggialdi*), and the female progeny Stumpy (*Drumba*), Dumpy (*Kumba*), Bulgingcalves (*Økkvinkálfa*), Eaglenose (*Arinnefia*), Shouter (*Ysia*), Servingmaid (*Ambátt*), Greatgossip (*Eikintiasna*), Tattered-coat (*Tötrughypia*), and Craneshanks (*Trönubeina*).[4]

The craftsman and his wife are substantially better groomed and dressed, they are weavers, and their food is described as "a yeasty loaf, high-risen and brown, of barley meal".[5] The son born to them nine months after Rígr's visit is called Carl. He is a red-haired and rosy boy, wrapped in fine linen, who grows into a competent freehold tenant. His marriage is a more elaborate affair, featuring a bridal veil and the dispensation of rings. The names of their sons are again very telling, many of them pointing to their roles in society: Goodman (*Halr*), Gallant (*Drengr*), Franklin (*Höldr*), Liegeman (*Þegn*), Craftsman (*Smiđr*), Broad Fellow (*Breiđr*), Farmer (*Bóndi*), Boundbeard (*Bundinskeggi*), Husbandman (*Búi*), Householder (*Boddi*), Steepboard (*Brattskeggr*), and Squire (*Seggr*), while the girls are called Lass (*Snót*), Bride (*Brúđr*), Finedame (*Svanni*), Damsel (*Svarri*), Dainty (*Sprakki*), Mistress (*Flióđ*), Madam (*Sprund*), Matron (*Víf*), Shymiss (*Feima*), and Sharpmiss (*Ristill*).[6] From the hovel and the hall, Rígr's path finally leads to a wealthy manor in which the man of the house is engaged in knightly pursuit, tending to his bowstring and arrows, and his wife to her fine linen and dress. The description of her appearance is the standard description found in countless examples of courtly literature: "High curved her head-dress, / a coin-brooch was at her bosom, / a trailing robe she wore, / a bodice blue-dyed – / her eyebrow brighter, / breast fairer, / throat whiter / than pure driven snow".[7] Needless to say, the table culture shows a lot more class as well: a patterned tablecloth made of thick, white linen, tableware of silver, filled to the brim, slim loaves of white bread, fresh game, pig's flesh, and roasted fowl, and wine in a flagon, drunk from ornamented goblets. Their son,

---

[4] *Ibid.*, 164f., strophes 12 and 13.

[5] *Ibid.*, 166. The line "Boiled veal there was, / best of dainties" concludes strophe 18 in Dronke and describes the craftsman's diet, whereas in Bellows, *The Poetic Edda* (*op. cit. supra*, n. 2), 204, it concludes strophe 4 and describes the diet of the peasants. Both translators regard the line as spurious.

[6] Dronke, *The Poetic Edda* (*op. cit. supra*, n. 1), 167f., strophes 24 and 25.

[7] *Ibid.*, 168, strophe 29.

wrapped in silk, and named Jarl, has blond hair, brilliant cheeks, and baleful eyes. Naturally he is drawn like his father to knightly pursuit, to shields, bows, and arrows, spears, lances, to riding stallions, hunting, and swimming. Rígr even gives him his own name, and teaches him runes. Rígr Jarl marries a sophisticated woman of equal station, and their progeny bear names such as Boychild (*Burr*), Bairn (*Barn*), Offspring (*Ióđ*), High Kind (*Ađal*), Heir (*Arfi*), Scion (*Mögr*), Kin (*Niđr*), Kinsman (*Niđiungr*), Nearkin (*Kundr*), and Noblekin (*Konr*).[8]

From this saga it would appear that the medieval concept of what determines social status was not dissimilar from what goes on in a beehive: the fertilized egg when deposited in a regular cell and nourished with regular pollen, results in a worker bee. The same egg in a roomier cell and nourished with royal jelly results in a queen bee. Far be it from me to insinuate that the medieval world took its cues from the beehive, but, as my recent work on the concept of baby-food has shown, in the question of nature versus nurture both the medieval medical community and the medieval church came down firmly on the side of nurture.[9] As forests gradually gave way to grain fields in the early Middle Ages, and the meat of wild and domesticated animals became the prerogative of the upper class, the diet of the poor became more and more plant-based. Like the skin of the protagonists in the *Rígsþula* saga, their bread became progressively lighter and finer the higher their station in life was, and not just in Scandinavia but throughout Europe in the high and late Middle Ages. Given the popularity of dietetic treatises that expounded the qualities of a wide variety of foodstuffs and dishes, one might assume that the diet of the aristocracy was the healthy one and that of the peasants unhealthy, but this was not always perceived that way. When it comes to bread, Konrad von Eichstätt's *Regimen sanitatis* in the general guidelines on food and drink appears to sing the praises of bran bread, describing it as "more easily digested than fine and pure bread such as white bread. Therefore, the rustics (*rustici*) have coarser farts than those using white bread."[10]

---

[8] *Ibid*., 171f., strophe 42.

[9] Melitta Weiss Adamson, 'Baby-Food in the Middle Ages', in *Nurture: Proceedings of the Oxford Symposium on Food and Cookery 2003* (Bristol, 2004), 1-11; and *eadem*, 'Infants and Wine: Medieval Medical Views on the Controversial Issue of Wine as Baby-Food,' *Medium Aevum Quotidianum* 50 (2004), 13-21.

[10] Munich, Bayerische Staatsbibliothek, Clm. 12389, fol. 259ra. See the edition in Christa Hagenmeyer, *Das Regimen Sanitatis Konrads von Eichstätt. Quellen – Texte – Wirkungsgeschichte*, Sudhoffs Archiv Beih. 35 (Stuttgart, 1995), 72. See also Melitta Weis Adam-

A later German version of this passage contained in Pseudo-Ortolf's *Regimen vite* goes even further and proclaims, "You should know that bread with its bran is more easily digested than fine or wheat bread. Hence the peasant is healthier than the lord and cleans his stomach more thoroughly than the lord."[11] However, this value judgement is deceptive. It has only little in common with Konrad's more elaborate passage in his chapter on bread in which he points out that white bread provides superior nourishment, although digesting it is harder and takes longer. Bran bread, though more easily digested, is of little nourishment, and the blood generated from it retains too little of the melancholic humor.[12] This comment paints a much less flattering picture of the benefits of dark bread than Pseudo-Ortolf's version, and shows the extent to which medical literature could be spun. When it comes to digestion, dark bread may have had a cleansing effect, but was this really desirable to the nobility, a class engaged in a civilizing process that sought to control all bodily functions, farts and belches included? One thing becomes clear when looking through the lists of foodstuffs described in the *Regimen sanitatis* literature: those foods with the lowest prestige and eaten by the peasants and the poor in general were frequently those that had carminative or laxative effects, such as lentils, beans, onions, leeks, cabbage, or turnips. Not only did many of them produce gas, but gas had since antiquity been associated with inciting lust and clouding the mind. Gas was perceived as the medium that caused an erection in men, and gas traveling through the body to the brain supposedly made people act in strange ways.[13] Hence the food of the poor also made them lose their judgement and behave like animals, a

---

son, '*Unus theutonicus plus bibit quam duo latini*: Food and Drink in Late-Medieval Germany', *Medium Aevum Quotidianum* 33 (1995), 8-20, esp. 12f.

[11] Pseudo-Ortolf, *Regimen vite*, fol. 59v. See Hagenmeyer, *Das Regimen Sanitatis Konrads von Eichstätt* (*op. cit. supra*, n. 10), 198.

[12] *Scias etiam, quod panis, qui fit de simula, maioris ets nutrimenti, et eius nutrimentum est melius, sed est tardioris penetrationis et tardioris descensus. Panis autem, quid fit de communi farina, qui multum habet de furfure, velocioris ets penetrationis et descensus et cicius digeritur, sed est pauci nutrimenti. Sanguis enim ex eo generatus melanconie parum attinet*. (*Ibid*., 94).

[13] See Melitta Weiss Adamson, 'Das Image(problem) der Bohne in der Antike und im Mittelalter: Einige Überlegungen zu Walthers Bohnenspruch,' in *Der 800jährige Pelzrock: Walther von der Vogelweide – Wolfger von Erla – Zeiselmauer. Vorträge gehalten am Walther-Symposion der Österreichischen Akademie der Wissenschaften vom 24. bis 27. September 2003 in Zeiselmauer (Niederösterreich)*, ed. Helmut Birkhan (Vienna, 2005), 545-559.

theme that lies at the heart of Heinrich Wittenwiler's fifteenth-century peasant satire called the *Ring*, to which I will return later.

The theory, often just implied in the medieval regimens addressed to the rich, that people engaged in hard physical labor have a different digestive system and different dietary needs, is discussed in detail in the sixteenth century by a Frenchman who was one of the first to turn his attention to the health care and nutrition of the poor. According to Jacques Dubois, also known as Sylvius, coarse food is ideal for day laborers, peasants, artisans, and journeymen, and delicate, easily digestible food for the rich, for bureaucrats, and scholars, all those subscribing to a sedentary lifestyle.[14] The latter group should live on white bread, the meat of birds, fried veal, pork, fresh eggs, and tangy fruits such as oranges, lemons, cherries, quinces, and black currants, and wine rather than beer. Particularly bad for their dainty stomachs are leeks, onions, garlic, chives, mustard, salt, smoked meat, dry vegetables, lentils, peas, and beans, all of which were, of course, the staples of the poor then. In a German regimen from 1549, asparagus, venison, chickpeas, pigeons, saffron, cranes, hares, peacocks, and pheasants are listed as upperclass food, garlic, oats, cabbage, chestnuts, beans, millet, and turnips as lower-class food. Targeting a middle-class audience, its author, Walther Ryff, is critical of items on both lists: deer meat, peacock, crane, and pheasant on one end of the spectrum, and oats, millet, cabbage, chestnuts, beans, and turnips, on the other.[15] A food hierarchy did not only exist between meat and plant food, but also within the category of meat, with wild and domestic birds at the top, and beef at the bottom. And so when in post-plague Europe the general population began to partake on a large scale in meat, it was often

---

[14] Jean Dupebe, 'La diététique et l'alimentation des pauvres selon Sylvius,' in *Pratiques et Discours Alimentaires à la Renaissance: Actes du colloque de Tours de mars 1979, Centre d'études supérieures de la Renaissance*, ed. Jean-Claude Margolin and Robert Sauzet (Paris, 1982), 40-56; see also Melitta Weiss Adamson, *Food in Medieval Times* (Westport, Connecticut, and London, 2004), 227-229.

[15] Guualterus H. Rivius [Walther Ryff], *Kurtze aber vast eigentliche nutzliche vnd in pflegung der gesundheyt notwendige beschreibung der natur / eigenschafft / Krafft / Tugent / Wirckung / rechten Bereyttung vnd gebrauch / inn speyß vnd drancks von noeten / vnd bey vns Teutschen inn teglichem Gebrauch sind / etc.* (Würzburg: Johan Myller, 1549). The text does not give page numbers, but lists the foodstuffs in alphabetical order with their Latin names. See also Adamson, '*Unus theutonicus plus bibit quam duo latini*', (*op. cit. supra*, n. 10) 15f.

beef, described by Ryff as coarse, hard to digest, and generating a melancholic humor.[16]

Poverty and food deprivation were presented in a positive light by the medieval church, not as something unhealthy, but as something to strive for. However, early ascetics aside who were engaged in extreme fasting, the church did eventually opt for periodic fasts to be observed by its believers, fasts that had the effect of fueling the appetite for meat in the general public even more. And as always, a food hierarchy was in place during these fasts. Exquisite plant food, fish, and seafood for the rich, more of the same lowly grains, legumes, vegetables, and the occasional herring or cod, dried or salted, for the poor. Medieval artists who tried to capture in an image the upper or lower-class status of a food, faced a dilemma. Much of the highly processed food would not have been instantly recognizable as upperclass, after all *blanc manger*, the famous white dish, was not dissimilar in appearance to porridge or gruel. The iconographic shorthand artists frequently reverted to, was to portray animals or animal parts being served on platters (birds, boar's head and the like), and to convey a sense of luxury in the table setting, interior decoration, and the appearance of the dinner guests.

Shorthand was also at work in the courtly and didactic literature of the high and late Middle Ages. In a fourteen-liner commonly referred to as the "Bohnenspruch" (Bean Song), Walther von der Vogelweide turns a lowly lenten food, the broad bean, into a lady whose attributes he subsequently compares with those of the wheat stalk. The verses, full of sexual innuendo, make the bean look so bad that in the end the poem calls for a ban of the legume.[17] Around the same time an old folktale was put to parchment in Latin bearing the name *Rapularius*, or turnip.[18] It is the story of a rich knight and his poor brother who grows a giant turnip which he gives to his lord and gets rewarded royally for the generous present, whereupon the rich brother gives his wealth to the lord banking on equally high returns for his gift. Concluding that the rich knight has everything, the lord presents him with the turnip as a one-of-a-kind gift. In this rags to riches (and riches to rags) tale, the turnip is representative of a whole class, that of the poor peasants.

---

[16] Ryff, *Bvbula caro* (*op. cit. supra*, n. 15).

[17] L 17,25; see Christoph Cormeau, *Walther von der Vogelweide. Leich, Lieder, Sangsprüche*, 14th revised ed. Of Karl Lachmann's edition (Berlin and New York, 1996). See also the study by Adamson, 'Das Image(problem) der Bohne' (*op. cit. supra*, n. 13), 545-559.

[18] 'Rapularius' in *Waltharius, Ruodlieb, Märchenepen*, ed. and tr. Karl Langosch (Berlin, n. d.), 307-331.

Walther's "Bohnenspruch" and this charming story of greed aside, poor man's food does not figure prominently in the courtly literature of the twelfth and early thirteenth century.

In Hartmann von Aue's *Erec* we learn of red deer, wild boars, bears, and hares being hunted by the nobility. The food offered at Penefrec castle is described as fish, game, white bread, and wine.[19] More pointed even is the list of upperclass foods in Hartmann von Aue's *Iwein*: meat and fish.[20] Ulrich von Zatzikhoven's *Lanzelet* also zooms in on the meat, but differentiates between the meat of domesticated and wild animals, as does Freidank in his *Bescheidenheit* from about the same period.[21] In his *Willehalm,* Wolfram von Eschenbach speaks of the preparation of the meat first, roasted and boiled, and then defines it as fish and meat, of wild and domesticated animals.[22] Heinrich von Neustadt in his *Apollonius von Tyrus* written a century later adds chicken to game and fish as the food eaten at the round table.[23] *Seifried Helbling* is familiar with this shorthand for upperclass food, but uses it mainly in the negative, as something that is rarely seen or completely absent from the tables of the personalities he is describing. Hence we read, for example, "one rarely sees white bread on his table and clear wine, he may well be without game" (*man sihet selten semeln wîz / ûf sînem tisch und klâren wîn, / er mac wol âne wiltprœt sin*), "without game they were said to be, [...], fish and eels they let the lords eat, that was the custom" (*ân wiltprœt solden sie sîn, / [...] / visch und öl sie liezen schôn / die herren ezzen, daz was sit*), or "had I neither game nor fish" (*het ich niht wiltbrœt noch vische*).[24] How enduring this list of stereotypical upperclass fare was, can be seen from the

---

[19] Hartmann von Aue, *Erec*, ed. Albert Leitzmann, Altdeutsche Textbibliothek 39, 3rd ed. (Tübingen, 1963), v. 7191f. For a collection of stock phrases regarding upper-class and lower-class food in medieval German literature see also George Fenwick Jones, 'The Function of Food in Medieval German Literature', *Speculum* 35 (1960), 78-86.

[20] Hartmann von Aue, *Iwein*, ed. Georg Friedrich Benecke and Karl Lachmann, revised by Ludwig Wolff, 7th edition, vol. 1: Text (Berlin, 1968), v. 6217.

[21] Ulrich von Zatzikhoven, *Lanzelet*: *Eine Erzählung*, ed. K. A. Hahn (Berlin, 1965), v. 7134; *Freidankes Bescheidenheit*, ed. Heinrich Ernst Bezzenberger, reprint of the 1872 edition (Aalen, 1962), 76, v. 7.

[22] Wolfram von Eschenbach, *Willehalm*, ed. Karl Lachmann, 6th ed. (Berlin and Leipzig, 1926), str. 133, vv. 12-15.

[23] Heinrich von Neustadt, *Leben und Abenteuer des großen Königs Apollonius von Tyrus zu Land und zur See*, tr. Helmut Birkhan (Bern, 2001), 298.

[24] *Seifried Helbling*, ed. Joseph Seemüller (Halle a. S., 1886), I, vv. 48-50; VIII, vv. 882, 884f; II, v. 4.

fact that as late as the sixteenth century Sebastian Brant still uses it in his *Narrenschiff*. Under the heading "Von unnützem Reichtum" (Of unnecessary wealth) he remarks "The rich you invite to dinner, and bring them game, birds, fish" (*Die Reichen lädt man ein zu Tisch / Und bringt ihnen Wildbret, Vögel, Fisch*).[25]

Among the German authors around 1200 Hartmann von Aue stands out as one of the few who allows his upperclass protagonists to experience first-hand or at least be confronted with the lifestyle of the lower classes. In *Der arme Heinrich*, the protagonist, once courtly society's brightest star, is stricken with leprosy. As an outcast he decides to live with a peasant family on his estate that eventually provides him with a cure and marital bliss in the form of the peasant girl. Iwein, in the romance with the same name, upon losing both his wife and his honor in one strike goes temporarily mad. Stealing himself away from court, he rips off his clothes and flees into the wilderness.[26] There, his dark skin and his diet of raw meat, later grilled and complemented with bread and water received from a hermit, attest to the primitive state in which he has chosen to live. As he rebuilds his new identity that ultimately allows him to be reintegrated into courtly society, his diet progresses from raw to cooked to spiced food, in other words he retraces the steps of human civilization from a hunter-gatherer to a barter to a money economy. His dark skin is not just the result of being exposed to the elements, but also of the preponderance of *cholé melaina* or black bile that is responsible for his melancholy. Once cured of his illness with an ointment concocted by Feimorgan, Iwein receives a makeover in the Lady of Narison's castle in the form of beautiful clothes, a splendid horse, exquisite food, and a bath. With Iwein no longer living like a wild animal, unkempt, and suffering from melancholy, it is only a matter of time, one can assume, until his skin returns to its aristocratic whiteness. And if it did not, medieval medicine had a wide range of recipes in store, especially for women, that were designed to whiten the skin, such as the following:

---

[25] Sebastian Brant, *Das Narrenschiff*, ed. Hermann A. Junghans and Hans-Joachim Mähl (Stuttgart., 1980), 68.

[26] Hartmann von Aue, *Iwein*, vv. 3221-3702. See also Melitta Weiss Adamson, 'Illness and Cure in Hartmann von Aue's *Der Arme Heinrich* and *Iwein*' in *A Companion to the Works of Hartmann von Aue*, ed. Francis G. Gentry (Rochester, NY, 2005), 134-137.

For Whitening the Face

> *[236] An ointment for whitening the face. Take two ounces of the very best white lead, let them be ground; afterward let them be sifted through a cloth, and that which remains in the cloth, let it be thrown out. Let it be mixed in with rainwater and let it cook until the consumption of the water, which can be recognized when we will see it almost completely dried out. Then let it be cooled. And when it is dried out and cooled, let rose water be added, and again boil it until it becomes hard and thick, so that from it very small pills can be formed. And when you wish to be anointed, take one pill and liquefy it in the hand with water and then rub it well on the face, so that the face will be dried. Then let it be washed with pure water, and this [whitened look] will last for eight days.[27]

In Hartmann von Aue's *Gregorius*, the fisherman's wife offers Gregorius the rind of oat bread and water for a meal. A look at Gregorius's noble body tells the fisherman, however, that oat bread and water are not the guest's usual fare. Reminiscent of the connection between food and outward appearance in the *Rígsþula* saga and *Iwein*, the fisherman observes that the visitor did not get his plump and rosy cheeks from oat bread and water, that he is well fed, has straight thighs, arched feet, long toes close together, and clean and white nails, his hair is straight and well-groomed, his body that of a well-fed glutton, his arms and hands are white and well-formed, in other words that there is a discrepancy between appearance and diet.[28] Slightly richer than oat bread and water is the food mentioned in *Der guote Gêrhart* from ca. 1300 as alms for the poor: sour beer and rye bread.[29] This handful of examples aside, it is not until the didactic literature of the late thirteenth to fifteenth centuries that food for the poor becomes a central theme, juxtaposed to that of the rich, or merged with the latter to make the social criticism even more biting.

---

[27] Monica Green, ed. and trans., *The Trotula: A Medieval Compendium of Women's Medicine* (Philadelphia, 2001), 162-163. See also the long list of recipes for whitening the face in *ibid.*, 178-185.

[28] Hartmann von Aue, *Gregorius, der gute Sünder* (Stuttgart, 1959), vv. 2892-94, and vv. 2906-34. Trotula also has a recipe for whitening the hands: "*[241] For whitening and smoothing the hands, let some ramsons be cooked in water until the water has been consumed. And stirring well, add tartar and afterwards two eggs, and with this you will rub the hands." See Green, *The Trotula* (*op. cit. supra*, n. 27), 164-165.

[29] Rudolf von Ems, *Der guote Gêrhart*, ed. John A. Asher, 2nd rev. ed. (Tübingen, 1971), v. 946.

Dress and food are of central importance in Wernher der Gärtner's *Helmbrecht*, a moral tale in which a peasant son refuses to accept his god-given role in society and opts instead for becoming a robber knight. Focusing first on young Helmbrecht's luxurious dress, the narrator soon turns to the topic of food and the question as to what constitutes appropriate peasant and noble fare. Presented in a pointed dialogue between the old and young Helmbrecht, wine and *clamirre*, an Austrian dish whose exact composition is unknown, but which has been translated as "meat filled pies," furthermore chicken traded for stolen cattle, a goose for a stolen horse, and expensive fish are the foods singled out as examples of the upperclass diet young Helmbrecht aspires to, when he should be content with water, oat and rye as befits his peasant background, according to his father.[30] The parallels between the diet of old Helmbrecht, the hermit in *Iwein*, and the fisherman and his wife in *Gregorius* are striking. To old Helmbrecht's warnings the son retorts that his father is welcome to his diet of water and gruel, but that he intends to live on wine, roast chicken, and white bread. The father's more extensive list of upperclass foods is in the son's rebuttal condensed to the standard threesome of bread, meat, and drink, so pervasive in courtly literature. On the occasion of young Helmbrecht's first and triumphant return after having become a robber knight, the family prepares a festive meal for him, as festive as their peasant status would allow on rare occasions. It consists of finely cut cabbage, sidemeat, fatty and brittle cheese, a roasted goose, and a fried and cooked chicken. While on the meat front the peasant family can meet the standards of the upperclass, the two other elements, white bread and wine, they are sorely lacking. Bread is not mentioned at all, and of wine the father can only speak in the subjunctive, as something he would drink on an occasion such as this. Instead he is forced to offer his son the finest spring water.[31] When the father learns how his son has chosen to make a living, he wants to know the names of his comrades. What the reader gets is a list of significant names many of which point to a lack of table manners, and to wild animals, notably the wolf: "lamb devourer" (*Lemberslint*), who will eventually marry Helmbrecht's sister, "ram swallower" (*Slickenwider*), "hell sack" (*Hellesac*), "rattle the box" (*Rütelschrîn)*, "cow devourer" (*Küfrâz*), "jug smasher" (*Müschenkelh*), "wolf jaws" (*Wolvesgoume*), "wolf snout" (*Wolvesdrüzzel*), and "wolf belly" (*Wolvesdarm*). Helmbrecht senior then

[30] Wernher der Gärtner, *Helmbrecht. Mittelhochdeutsch – Neuhochdeutsch*, tr. Fritz Tschirch (Stuttgart, 2002), vv. 443-479.

[31] *Ibid.*, vv. 867-897.

asks the interesting question what his comrades call him to which he proudly answers, "land devourer" (*Slintezgeu*), which seems to suggest that he is the worst of them all.[32] Later in the text the narrator repeats this list of significant names and ascribes an office at court to each bearer: "land devourer" becomes the master of ceremonies, "ram swallower" the butler, "hell sack" the steward, "rattle the box" the chamberlain, "cow devourer" the master cook, and "jug smasher" the pantler.[33] As befits their names, "wolf jaws," "wolf belly," and "wolf snout" literally wolf down their food so fast, there is not even a bone left for the dogs. As the downward spiral of young Helmbrecht's life picks up speed with his sister now caught up in it, too, it is she who realizes that an honorable if modest life as a peasant would have been preferable to a dishonorable life in luxury. In the juxtaposition of upper and lower-class diet the foods are now poignantly reduced to one single food item each: fish versus cabbage.[34] Eventually punished for his crime by losing his eyesight, a hand and a foot, Helmbrecht returns home a second time, but is locked out of the house by his father. Only his mother has mercy on him and gives him what beggars received in those days: a piece of bread.[35]

Only a few years after *Helmbrecht*, fifteen satirical poems were written known today by the name of *Seifried Helbling*. The work, briefly mentioned before, is a treasure trove of information on daily life in Lower Austria at the time when the Habsburgs began their rule over the region. The stock phrases outlining upperclass food are contrasted with a much more diverse and varied repertoire of lower class food items. To the dishes eaten by peasants on meat days, [cheap] meat and cabbage, as well as barley porridge, are now added such fast-day variants as hemp, lentils, and beans.[36] Dietary transgressions, normally committed by peasants such as Helmbrecht junior, or the upwardly mobile urban middle class of the late Middle Ages that was the subject of many a sumptuary law, is in the first of the *Seifried Helbling* poems committed by a wife against her husband. While Rüegêr is out in the fields working, with only a piece of bread crust for lunch, his wife Matz secretly indulges in the quintessential upperclass food, a roasted chicken,

---

[32] *Ibid.*, vv. 1185-1237.

[33] *Ibid.*, vv. 1535-1550; see also Trude Ehlert, '*Doch so fülle dich nicht satt !* Gesundheitslehre und Hochzeitsmahl in Wittenwilers "Ring"', *Zeitschrift für deutsche Philologie* 109 (1990), 72.

[34] Wernher der Gärtner, *Helmbrecht* (*op. cit. supra*, n. 30), vv. 1603-1606.

[35] *Ibid.*, vv. 1712-1813.

[36] *Seifried Helbling* (*op. cit. supra*, n. 24), VIII, v. 881, 883.

good wine, and white bread.[37] Upon his return in the evening she serves him barley bread and a big bowl of beans. Believed since antiquity and beyond to incite lust, the beans do their trick on the peasant who later in bed starts fondling his wife, only to notice, like the fisherman in *Gregorius*, that a plump and round body like hers does not come from modest peasant food.[38]

In *Seifried Helbling* significant names are also used, and sometimes to great effect. Among them we find the "wolf belly" (*Wolvesdarm*) encountered earlier in *Helmbrecht*, as well as "vulture goitre" (*Gîrskropf*), and "master turnipwind" *(meister Rübentunst)*, pointing yet again to a peasant body that resists the civilizing process.[39] Other examples for names referring to plants and animals are "viper sweat" (*Nâternsweiz*), "weed" (*Unkrût*), and "goat foot" (*Geizfuoz*).[40] The activities of the lower classes are expressed in such names as "scrape nail" (*Scharnagel*), "hard digger" (*Grebelhart*), "smash the beam" (*Müschenrigel*), "plundersac" (*Struttensac*), and "full of holes guzzler" (*Durkelswelch*).[41] Social conflict and death are thematized in the names "break the peace" (*Brichenfrid*), "peasant hatred" (*Gebûrenhaz*), "hurry to the grave" (*Îlinsgrap*), "stand by the sword blade" (*Stantbîderfletschen*), "end without regret" (*Endânriu*), and "ban of the soul" (*Æhtersêl*).[42]

The practice of using significant names is turned into an art-form in Heinrich Wittenwiler's *Ring* where a myriad of names literally identify the bearers with their food, bodily function, sexual practice, and social behavior, but also with animals, and even worse, their excrements.[43] The examples from the animal world range from "great titmouse" (*Spiegelmais*), "fluffed-up little bird" (*Fesafögili*),[44] "snail" (*Snegg*), "wolf" (*Eisengrein*),[45] "stork

---

[37] *Ibid.*, I, vv. 969-980.

[38] *Ibid.*, I, vv. 1220-1276.

[39] *Ibid.*, I, v. 372, v. 394; II, v. 1296.

[40] *Ibid.*, II, v. 1382; XIII, v. 144, v. 171

[41] *Ibid.*, II, v. 1382; XIII, v. 163, v. 166f.

[42] *Ibid.*, I, v. 372, v. 394; II, v. 1296, v. 1382; XIII, v. 144, v. 171; II, v. 1382; XIII, v. 163, v. 166, v. 167, v. 145, v. 154, v. 160. *Fletschen* can also mean "barn-floor.'

[43] *Heinrich Wittenwilers Ring. Nach der Meininger Handschrift*, ed. Edmund Wiessner (Darmstadt, 1973); for a modern German prose translation see Helmut Birkhan, *Heinrich Wittenwiler. Der Ring*, Fabulae Mediaevales 3 (Vienna, 1983); for a bilingual edition see *Der Ring von Heinrich Wittenwiler. Frühneuhochdeutsch – Neuhochdeutsch*, tr. and ed. Horst Brunner (Ditzingen, 1991).

[44] If, as Helmut Birkhan suggests, the first part of the term is the Middle-High-German word *vese*, meaning "penis,"and not the verb *vesen*, meaning "untangle," then the name "penis birdie" would have a strong sexual connotation. See Birkhan, *Heinrich Wittenwiler. Der Ring* (*op. cit. supra*, n. 43), 295, note 60.

leg" (*Storchenpain*), "beak" (*Zingg*), and "ox goiter" (*Ochsenchroph*), to "fly shit" (*Fleugenschaiss*), chicken fart (*Giggenfist*), and "cow dung" (*Rindtaisch*).[46] Food and table manners are reflected in the names "flat cake rind" (*Fladenranft*), "ox cheese" (*Ochsenchäs*), "pepper hot" (*Pfefferräss*), "cabbage" (*Gumpost*), "ham meat" (*Pachenflaisch*), "stir the must" (*Rüerenmost*), "bad smell" (*Übelgsmak*), "guzzle" (*Trinkavil*), "improper" (*Ungemäss*), "pot nibbler" (*Hafenschlek*), "lick the spit" (*Lechspiss*), and "devour the bacon" (*Schlinddenspek*). Digestion is the theme of the names "shit into the flowers" (*Scheissindpluomen*), "vomit into the bucket" (*Spötzinnkübel*), and "piss into the jug" (*Saichinchruog*). Human body parts used for naming are "rotten tooth" (*Fülizan*), "limp leg" (*Gnepferin*), "empty head" (*Lärenchoph*), "molar tooth" (*Paggenzan*), "squint a little" (*Schielawingg*), "drip nose" (*Triefnas*), "shock-headed" (*Straub*), and "bouncing Adam's apple (*Snellagödili*). Sexual practices are alluded to with names such as "reach into the cow" (*Varindkuo*), "navel rubber" (*Nabelreiber*),"dig into the chamber" (*Grabinsgaden*), "peak into the nest" (*Gugginsnest*), "little whore" (*Hüdel*), "tickle bowel" (*Kützeldarm*), "scrape the hole" (*Schabenloch*), "stir the penis" (*Rüerenzumph*), "stump" (*Stumph*), and "fall into the straw" (*Vallinsstro*). The name "lick the spit" (*Lechspiss*) has the dual function of food and sexual metaphor. That the work and living conditions of the peasants in the *Ring* are less than ideal becomes evident from significant names such as "nowhere at home" (*Nienderthaim*), "blow into the ashes" (*Blasindäschen*), "stoke the flames" (*Schürenprand*), and "water carrier" (*Wasserschepferin*). The disregard for laws, social mores, and the inability to control one's emotions find expression in names such as "loiter" (*Chnotz*), "chatterbox" (*Snattereina*), "thief bone" (*Deupenpain*), "slide into the sack" (*Scheubinsak*), "burn the land" (*Siertdazland*), "honor curse" (*Erenfluoch*), "gallow hoax" (*Galgenswanch*), "bang into the wall" (*Varindwand*), and maniac (*Wüetreich*). Damnation is the only possible consequence of such an uncivilized life, as the names "hell ghost" (*Hellegaist*), "roar into hell" (*Reuschindhell*), "devil's chamber" (*Teufalsgaden*), and "sack of vices" (*Lastersak*), another word for the devil, make unmistakeably clear to the audience. The names in

---

45 Wittenwiler here uses the German fable name for the "wolf."

46 An alphabetical list of names in the *Ring* together with modern German translation is found in Birkhan, *Heinrich Wittenwiler. Der Ring* (*op. cit. supra*, n. 43), 288f. Names as well as source references are contained in the alphabetical vocabulary list of the *Ring* by Edmund Wiessner, *Der Wortschatz von Heinrich Wittenwilers Ring*, ed. Bruno Boesch (Bern, 1970).

the *Ring* situate the peasants on both sides of the human and animal divide. They describe them as ugly, physically and mentally deficient, driven by unbridled lust for food and sex, wallowing in the anal sphere, disregarding all social norms, and destined for hell. They conjure up an almost Bakhtinian world of the Grotesque and Carnevalesque, and yet, the plot of the work obviously takes its cues from the courtly epic: a poem singing the praises of a young maiden, followed by a tournament, the courting of the maiden by the male protagonist, her temporary confinement, advisers discussing the pros and cons of marriage, the eventual nuptuals, a lavish banquet, and a war resulting in near-complete annihilation are as much elements of the *Ring* as they are of the *Nibelungenlied.* But the peasant girl Mätzli Rüerenzumph is no Kriemhild. Of degenerate "nobility," she is portrayed as lame and crooked, with teeth and hands as black as coal, a mouth as red as the sand in the sea, a braid like a mouse tail, a goiter hanging down to her belly, a back so bent one could cast a bell over it, feet so thick and wide no wind could knock her over, cheeks as rosy as ashes, breasts as delicate as fat pouches, eyes shining like fog, breath of sulphur, a frumpy dress, and the behavior of a three-year-old.[47] The tournament held in her honor is a perfect fusion of upperclass ritual and lower-class symbolism. The escutcheon of Bertschi Triefnas, her future husband, depicts two forks on a dung-heap. Another peasant dons a dead rabbit in a green field on his shield, a third two wooden cherry hooks, a fourth a rake, a fifth three nuts on a vine, a sixth three flies in a glass, a seventh nine spoons in a bowl, an eighth two roasted turnips, a ninth cattle pulling a plow, a tenth four cheeses on a rack, an eleventh eggs, and the last one, Master Neidhart himself, a fox tail. Mätzli's token for which these "knights" compete, is a calf in a stork's nest. They ride on a sundry collection of donkeys and farm horses, and wear armor and weapons originally designed for farmwork.[48] Perhaps in keeping with Mätzli's childish behavior, or perhaps an allusion to her unbridled sexuality, is her response to Bertschi serenading her: She sticks her naked behind out the window.[49] Locked away in a granary and out of reach of her suitor, Mätzli is shown talking not to her mother about the pains of love, as is typical of courtly literature, but to her genitalia in what may be the earliest literary

[47] *Heinrich Wittenwilers Ring* (*op. cit. supra*, n. 43), vv. 76-96; see also vv. 3426-3438 where her lack of shame and her poverty are added to the description. For the male beauty ideal given in lieu of Bertschi's actual looks, see vv. 3650-3676.

[48] *Ibid.*, vv. 103-182.

[49] *Ibid.*, vv. 1564-1627.

example of *The Vagina Monologues*.[50] With actual communication impossible, the illiterate lovers resort to sending love letters written on their behalf by members of the educated class, namely the clerk and the doctor. The latter robs Mätzli of her virginity but also provides her with the recipe for restoring it, which is similar in nature to the ones found in the medical collection ascribed to Trotula of Salerno.[51]

In addition to sex and combat, food and table manners play a central role in the *Ring*.[52] As the plot moves inexorably towards the wedding of Mätzli and Bertschi to be celebrated with a banquet, the appropriate food for peasants and lords is well established: wine, pepper, and fish for the lords, turnips, barley, cheese, bread, eggs, and nuts for the peasants.[53] The didactic passages marked in the only extant manuscript from Meiningen with a red line, also increase in frequency and length, culminating in detailed guidelines for students, a catalogue of Christian virtues, a regimen of health, a catalogue of worldly virtues, and advice for householders.[54] All of them extol the virtues of moderation, control over oneself, and learning. The target group for this message is not the peasantry who will always behave like fools, nor the aristocracy who is expected to already live according to these rules, but the upwardly mobile urban middle class engaged in a civilizing process that promises as a reward a rise in status and wealth.[55]

---

[50] *The Vagina Monologues* is an award-winning episodic play written by Eve Ensler that was first performed Off-Broadway in 1996, and has since been translated into over 24 languages, and performed in 76 countries.

[51] *Heinrich Wittenwilers Ring* (*op. cit. supra*, n. 43), vv. 1643-2000, vv. 2001-2562. The recipes for restoring a woman's virginity are found in Green, *The Trotula* (*op. cit. supra*, n. 27), 145-147.

[52] How inseparably linked food and sex are in the peasant imagination as portrayed in the *Ring*, is illustrated by "lick the spit" who pulls a chair from under his wife as she cuts herself a piece of ham. She falls and lands on her back whereupon he lifts her skirt and kisses her three times on the belly. See *Heinrich Wittenwilers Ring* (*op. cit. supra*, n. 43), vv. 750-759.

[53] *Ibid.*, vv. 2906-2908 (*pfeffer* could be both the spice or the pepper broth in which venison was traditionally prepared), v. 1990, vv. 1522-1524, v. 1057f., v. 1128, vv. 3373-3379. A well-stocked larder is described as containing wine, grain, millet, cabbage, beans, peas, barley, lard, lentils, meat for drying, salt, cheese, fruit, and other things when in season. See vv. 5025-5031.

[54] *Ibid.*, vv. 3836-3925, vv. 3926-4187, vv.4188-4401, vv. 4402-4962, vv. 4963-5200.

[55] Helmut Birkhan, *Das Historische im 'Ring' des Heinrich Wittenwiler* (Vienna, 1973); Eckart Conrad Lutz, *Spiritualis fornicatio: Heinrich Wittenwiler, seine Welt und sein*

The recommendation to watch the peasants and always do the opposite if one wants to become a courtier,[56] sets the stage for a wedding banquet in which the protagonists break every rule in the book.[57] Acting like pigs at the trough, they spill the soup, but continue eating it off the ground, they consume big quantities of barley and rye bread, drink from jugs and buckets rather than goblets, peel apples and pears the wrong way, and eat these fruit together with nuts and cheese at the beginning rather than the end of the meal, as advised by the dietetic literature, indulge in large quantities of must and cider, followed by perry, sloe water, sour milk, and eventually water. The main course is an odd combination of upper and lower-class food: cabbage, bacon, and greaves, together with fish. Not surprisingly, the fight for the pieces of fish is so fierce, it leaves one diner dead. As supplies run out, even a nutshell of must and four fried eggs make the peasants behave "like wild boars." The last course of cherries, grapes, figs, and plums is again a peculiar combination of expensive imported and local produce. As in the case of the tournament, where the peasants adopt the attributes of the nobility, escutcheons portraying such unlikely motifs as two roasted turnips or four cheeses on a rack, noble food is "desecrated" at the wedding banquet by being combined with peasant food, thereby creating a concoction that can only lead to vomiting. The vocabulary of lower-class food in the *Ring* is certainly the most varied of all the works mentioned here, and yet, by forcing a fusion with upperclass food, a cuisine is created so socially explosive, it heralds the beginning of the end of the villagers and their way of life.

'Ring' (Sigmaringen, 1990); Ehlert, '*Doch so fülle dich nicht satt!*' (*op. cit. supra*, n. 33), 78.

56 *Heinrich Wittenwilers Ring* (*op. cit. supra*, n. 43), vv. 4862-4866.

57 *Ibid.*, vv. 5532-6186.

Addresses of the Contributors

ADAMSON, MELITTA WEISS, Department of Modern Languages and Literatures, University of Western Ontario, London, Ontario N6A 3K7, Canada

AUSTIN, DAVID, Department of Archaeology, St. David's College, University of Wales, Lampeter, Dyfed, Wales, SA48 7ED, U.K.

BLACK, NANCY B., English Department, Brooklyn College, 2900 Bedford Avenue, Brooklyn, New York 11210, USA

BOLVIG, AXEL, Lavendelstraede 9, 2. th., 1462 Copenhagen K, Denmark

DOBOZY, MARIA, Department of Languages, University of Utah, 225 S. Central Campus Drive, Salt Lake City, UT 84112, USA

GAUVARD, CLAUDE, Centre de Recherches sur l'Histoire de l'Occident Médiéval, Université de Paris I, Panthéon Sorbonne, 17, rue de la Sorbonne, 75231 Paris Cedex 05, France

JARITZ, GERHARD, Institut für Realienkunde des Mittelalters und der frühen Neuzeit, Österreichische Akademie der Wissenschaften, Körnermarkt 13, 3500 Krems, Austria

KLANICZAY, GÁBOR, Department of Medieval Studies, Central European University, Nádor utca 9, 1051 Budapest, Hungary

PREDELLI, MARIA BENDINELLI, Department of Italian Studies, McGill University, 688 Sherbrooke Street West, Suite 425, Montreal, Quebec H3A 3R1, Canada

SIMON-MUSCHEID, KATHARINA, Historisches Institut, Universität Bern, Länggassstraße 49, 3000 Bern 9, Switzerland

SKINNER, PATRICIA, School of Humanities, University of Southampton, Highfield, Southampton, S017 1BJ, U.K.

STEINER, EPHRAIM SHOHAM, Abram-Curiel Department of History, Ben Gurion University of the Negev, P. O. Box 653, Beer Sheva, Israel

VERÖFFENTLICHUNGEN DES INSTITUTS FÜR REALIENKUNDE DES MITTELALTERS UND DER FRÜHEN NEUZEIT

Nr. 1: Die Funktion der schriftlichen Quelle in der Sachkulturforschung (Sbph 304/4/1976) 272 Seiten, 5 Abbildungen, 8°, brosch.

Nr. 2: Das Leben in der Stadt des Spätmittelalters (SBph 325/1977, 3. Aufl. 1997) 274 Seiten, 160 Abbildungen, 8°, brosch.

Nr. 3: Klösterliche Sachkultur des Spätmittelalters (SBph 367/1980, 2. Aufl. 1997) 380 Seiten, 57 Abbildungen, 8°, brosch.

Nr. 4: Europäische Sachkultur. Gedenkschrift aus Anlaß des 10jährigen Bestandes des Instituts für mittelalterliche Realienkunde (SBph 374/1980) 232 Seiten, 39 Abbildungen, 8°, brosch.

Nr. 5: Adelige Sachkultur des Spätmittelalters (SBph 400/1982) 386 Sei ten, 71 Abbildungen, 8°, brosch.

Nr. 6: Die Erforschung von Alltag und Sachkultur des Mittelalters. Metho- de – Ziel –Verwirklichung (SBph 433/1984) 230 Seiten, 18 Abbil dungen, 8°, brosch.

Nr. 7: Bäuerliche Sachkultur des Spätmittelalters (SBph 439/1984, 2. Aufl. 1997) 328 Seiten, 61 Abbildungen, 8°, brosch.

Nr. 8: Alltag und Fortschritt im Mittelalter (SBph 470/1986) 240 Seiten, 18 Abbildungen, 8°, brosch.

Nr. 9: Frau und spätmittelalterlicher Alltag (SBph 473/1986) 615 Seiten, 53 Abbildungen, 8°, brosch.

Nr. 10: Terminologie und Typologie mittelalterlicher Sachgüter: Das Bei spiel der Kleidung (SBph 511/1988) 206 Seiten, 40 Abbildungen, 8° brosch.

Nr. 11: Handwerk und Sachkultur im Spätmittelalter (SBph 513/1988) 263 Seiten, 39 Abbildungen, 8°, brosch.

Nr. 12: Materielle Kultur und religiöse Stiftung im Spätmittelalter (SBph 554/1990, 2. Aufl. 1997) 272 Seiten, 31 Abbildungen, 8°, brosch.

Nr. 13: Mensch und Objekt im Mittelalter und in der frühen Neuzeit: Leben – Alltag – Kultur (SBph 568/1990) 456 Seiten, 35 Abbildungen, 8°, brosch.

Nr. 14: Wallfahrt und Alltag in Mittelalter und früher Neuzeit (SBph 592/1992) 352 Seiten, 3 Abbildungen, 8°, brosch.

Nr. 15: Kommunikation und Alltag in Spätmittelalter und früher Neuzeit (SBph 596/1992) 460 Seiten, 61 Abbildungen, 8°, brosch.

Nr. 16: Kommunikation zwischen Orient und Okzident. Alltag und Sachkul tur (SBph 619/1994) 448 Seiten, 79 Abbildungen, 8°, brosch.

Nr. 17: Disziplinierung im Alltag des Mittelalters und der frühen Neuzeit (SBph 669/1999) 300 Seiten, 28 Abbildungen, 8°, brosch.

Nr. 18: Text als Realie (SBph 704/2003) 422 Seiten, 73 Abbildungen, 8°, brosch.

Nr. 19: Imaginäre Räume (SBph 758/2007) 234 Seiten, 33 Abbildungen, 22,5x15cm, brosch.

FORSCHUNGEN DES INSTITUTS FÜR REALIENKUNDE DES MITTELALTERS UND DER FRÜHEN NEUZEIT. DISKUSSIONEN UND MATERIALIEN

Nr. 1: Pictura quasi fictura. Die Rolle des Bildes in der Erforschung von Alltag und Sachkultur des Mittelalters und der frühen Neuzeit. Wien 1996, 208 Seiten, 48 Abbildungen, 8°, brosch.

Nr. 2: Norm und Praxis im Alltag des Mittelalters und der frühen Neuzeit. Wien 1997, 126 Seiten, 8°, brosch.

Nr. 3: Die Vielfalt der Dinge. Neue Wege zur Analyse mittelalterlicher Sachkultur. Wien 1998, 440 Seiten, 8°, brosch.

Nr. 4: History of Medieval Life and the Sciences. Wien 2000, 156 Seiten, 8°, brosch.

Nr. 5: Kontraste im Alltag des Mittelalters. Wien 2000, 245 Seiten, 8°, brosch.

Nr. 6: Die Straße. Zur Funktion und Perzeption öffentlichen Raums im späten Mittelalter. Wien 2001, 212 Seiten, 8°, brosch.

Nr. 7: Emotions and Material Culture. Wien 2003, 174 Seiten, 10 Abbildungen, 8°, brosch.